Business Leadership and Law

Anurag K. Agarwal

Business Leadership and Law

Springer

Anurag K. Agarwal
Indian Institute of Management
Ahmedabad
India

ISBN 978-81-322-3680-1   ISBN 978-81-322-3682-5   (eBook)
DOI 10.1007/978-81-322-3682-5

Library of Congress Control Number: 2016955923

Printed on acid-free paper

This Springer imprint is published by Springer Nature
The registered company is Springer (India) Pvt. Ltd.
The registered company address is: 7th Floor, Vijaya Building, 17 Barakhamba Road, New Delhi 110 001, India

To

My mother,
Late Mrs. Bimla Devi Agarwal,
An absolute positive thinker

Preface

This book is meant for business leaders who wish to remain on the right side of the law. It is essential in any jurisdiction, and much more in international business, to understand the role of law in business. A business leader can neglect law only at his and his company's peril. It is foolhardy for any business leader to think that 'law is for lawyers' and as a business person 'why should I bother about law?' Law in most evolved jurisdictions is highly dynamic and it is expected of a business leader to anticipate the changes which may take place and also to pro-actively make the best efforts to mitigate the loss which may occur due to such changes. Better, he can try to play a role in the law making—directly or indirectly—so that the changes are in tune with the requirements of his business.

The book is written to understand, appreciate and make the best use of the legal environment in which business is done. There are several questions which come to the mind of a business leader vis-à-vis law. The book tries to answer these questions. The first question is 'as a business person, do I need to know law?' and ends with the understanding that 'law is my friend, philosopher and guide'. In between, the business leaders realises the value of contracts, intellectual property, dispute resolution, role of government, etc.

I have tried my best that the book is not daunting. To make it interesting and easy to read, it has numerous case studies—often related to court decisions—and current examples. The language is lucid and devoid of legal jargon as far as possible. Primarily, the book focuses on court cases and several other business stories. The book, hopefully, will connect well and touch upon—if not answer all—a lot many issues, concerns, and queries, which often trouble a business leader. The book is meant chiefly for senior and top management, and also for business persons at any level who aspire to reach such a position. This is not industry or sector specific. This is useful for all businesses. I envisage the book to be a useful companion to global business leaders, though a tilt towards India may obviously be visible. Some of the cases are India specific but they bring out issues pertinent to any global business.

The book starts with an introduction, which talks about certain essential thoughts—certainty, anticipation and creating options—a business leader cannot escape from, and emphasises on the importance of being on the right side of the law while working to make profits.

The book covers the following topics in different chapters—knowledge of law, role of the government, law making and lobbying, using contracts to achieve the business goals, aligning business and legal strategy, significance of intellectual property in businesses, resolving and avoiding disputes, engaging a lawyer and how the judges make a difference in the legal environment, being ethical, and making law your friend, philosopher and guide. Each chapter is not a watertight compartment. Issues flow from one chapter to another. Thus, the approach to understand the subject is not modular. It has to be integrated learning. While trying to understand a particular topic the entire attention should be on that topic and thereafter the business leader must develop the ability to assimilate it and integrate it with the overall understanding.

There are many other issues related to managing a business successfully which a business leader may be concerned with. Most of them are beyond the scope of this work as it is not expected to be daunting and unwieldy. I have selected the ones which have been repeatedly emphasised in class discussions with the students and executives over the past 12 years. The book, hopefully, will connect well and touch upon—if not answer all—a lot many issues, concerns and queries, which often trouble a business leader. I envisage the book to be a useful companion to the business leaders.

I would like to sincerely thank all the students and executives with whom I had such wonderful and rich discussions in class. Deliberating about the practical problems the executives face helped me sharpen the subject and explore further. Thanks to Springer and its entire team, particularly to Ms. Sagarika Ghosh, whose persistence made this possible.

This book would have not seen the light of the day without the persistent efforts of my family in motivating and encouraging me despite getting bored at times with my untimely narration of various business cases and stories. I cannot thank my wife Manjari and sons Anant and Akshat adequately for showing tremendous understanding, patience and love as I worked for long hours in preparing the manuscript; most of these hours righty belonged to them. This book has an indelible impression of my mother—a diehard possibility thinker—in steering thoughts towards positivity at all times. I had started working on this book when she was with us, with her inspiration and blessings.

Ahmedabad, India   Anurag K. Agarwal
September 2016

Contents

About the Author

(Advocate), B.E. (Mech, NIT Allahabad), LL.B. (Lucknow), LL.M. (Gold Medalist, Lucknow), LL.M. (Harvard), LL.D. (Lucknow)

Dr. Anurag K. Agarwal is a Mechanical Engineer from MNREC, Allahabad (now know as MNNIT). After working for less than a year with Bharat Petroleum, he decided to study law. He has completed Bachelor, Master (Gold Medalist) and Doctor of Laws from the Lucknow University and a second Master of Laws from the Harvard Law School. He practised as an advocate at Lucknow for about 7 years and for about a year and a half at Delhi. He switched over to full-time teaching in 2004, with a brief stint at MDI Gurgaon. Professor Agarwal has been with Indian Institute of Management Ahmedabad (IIMA) since then in the business policy area. He has been the Chairperson of the One Year Post-Graduate Programme in Management for Executives PGPX, Business Policy Area, and the Post Graduate Programmme in Public Management and Policy PGP-PMP. He is recipient of the 'First Marti Mannariah Gurunath Outstanding Teacher Award 2013' at IIMA. He has been visiting faculty at National Judicial Academy Bhopal, Gujarat State Judicial Academy Ahmedabad and ESSEC Paris. His teaching, consulting and research interests include contracts and arbitration, infrastructure and PPPs. He conducts executive education for the government, public sector and private companies. He is the Faculty Chair for the executive education programme 'Legal and Regulatory Issues in Infrastructure'. He writes 'Lawfully Yours', a weekly column published in DNA Ahmedabad. He has authored two books: 'Contracts and Arbitration for Managers' Sage 2016 and 'Business and Intellectual Property' Random House 2010.

Introduction

'I care not today what the morrow may bring…', so starts a hymn, as there is unimpeachable faith in the Almighty.

Still, human beings are expected to use their intelligence and conduct themselves in a reasonable and prudent manner. And, there lies the importance of doing one's duty. At times, it becomes difficult to identify one's duty. As morrow is uncertain, there is confusion galore. That is why everyone prefers *certainty*. To use the clichéd statement—as it depicts it so well—'certainty is so uncertain', that it is not possible to move towards total certainty. However, with better understanding of the world we live in, one can always try to *anticipate* what the morrow may be. And, once it has been anticipated, *creating options* is the most obvious step to be taken.

Taking the business from a zone of uncertainty to a zone of certainty is the bounden duty of a business leader, and as we understand it can be done only to a certain limit, which is never 100 %. It may be 99.9999 recurring but still there is that infinitely small delta x, the uncertainty, which has the capability of destroying all the plans previously made like a house of cards. The better informed a business leader, the better is his ability to anticipate and the better the anticipation, the better the ability to create options. It is not only internal thinking, but a lot depends on external factors, most of them are usually beyond the control of the business leader. Making profits by being *ethical* and by being on *the right side of the law* is of utmost importance.

Many a time, the going may be good. The mood is upbeat and sentiments are buoyant—may be reflected or not accurately reflected at the stock exchanges—and the business leaders are extremely positive about the growth and development of business. But even at such a time, the canny business leader thinks about the uncertain times and prepares for those times.

As the former American President John F. Kennedy had said, 'the time to repair the roof is when the sun is shining', and, hence, it is particularly significant for the corporate leaders to put their house in order at a time when positive vibes are making the business environment look bright and sunny. It is good that the journey towards prosperity has begun with a step in the right direction, but a lot depends on slow and steady progress with positive thought process translated into effective action.

Political willpower and the intention to do something good always depend on the legal environment for business. It is extremely important for business leaders to be making their best efforts to remain on the right side of the law. Caution is the keyword for certain business leaders, who believe in making incremental changes and taking small steps.

However, there are definitely business leaders belonging to a second school of thought—which believes that it is far better to do it once and do it final, rather than doing anything incrementally—and, therefore, it depends on the individual leader's courage of conviction and integrity of character to take the boardroom with him, and prove to the world, later, that he was right. But such an approach requires a tremendous appetite for taking risks. Taking a calculated risk may be fine, however, knee-jerk reactions blended with obstinacy and megalomania may do no good, neither to the business leader, nor to the business, which, in wider terms means not only the shareholders, but also all the stakeholders in the business.

Business leaders cannot afford to be biased—either positive or negative—which may influence their neutral decision making ability. Though it is well known that most of the business leaders would have a definite affinity for certain type of policies, norms, legal and political environment, which makes them work easily in their zone of comfort, yet there is hardly any certainty and permanency about that sort of comfort; which makes it prudent for the business leader to be nimble, dexterous, agile, adaptable to the constantly changing—an oxymoron so widely used to explain the nature of business environment—political thinking process in a democratic form of government.

The true test of a business leader is to have a balanced view; not to be overly pessimistic during dark days, and not to be unrealistically optimistic when the going is good. A fine blend of realism with optimism usually is the best. How to achieve it? There is no sure-shot formula for it. But there is something which every business leader is supposed to do—anticipation. And, the better informed a business leader is, the better he may anticipate.

Times of great optimism provide excellent opportunities to anticipate and align the goals of the business with the policies any country may witness in the days to come. For anticipating successfully and then acting on it, experience comes handy. Experienced individuals, who have seen good and bad times, can vouch that an ounce of action is better than a tonne of abstraction.

In sum, for making profits ethically and by being on the right of the law, a business leader should endeavour to move towards *certainty*, keep antennae sharp to *anticipate* properly and thereafter *create options* to achieve the desired goal.

We will keep these thoughts in mind while going through various cases in the book. Towards the end of each chapter, there are takeaways for business leaders, which blend these ideas with the cases discussed. Those takeaways are not universal and natural laws; they are mere observations and understandings based on my experience with which one may agree or not. However, they do provide some food for thought. That is precisely the purpose of the book—to make the readers think more, understand the legal environment for business and appreciate the value of law in doing business and becoming a better, effective and more successful business leader, at whatever stage of the professional career one may be.

Chapter 1
I am a Businessperson. Do I Need to Know the Law?

As a business leader one may ask a question to oneself about the need to know the law. What is the need for me as a business leader to know the law? The answer to this question can be both yes and no.

'Yes' because knowing the law is not an option, it is mandatory to survive and thrive. A popular maxim, which provides explanation to the answer 'yes', is as follows: '*Ignorantia facti excusat, ignorantia juris non excusat*'. It means, ignorance of fact is an excuse, but ignorance of law is not an excuse. The legal systems all over the world work on this basic premise. For a moment let us imagine a person, who has been held for stealing, argues that as he did not know that stealing is illegal, he ought not to be punished. Another person may take the plea of ignorance of law for not paying taxes. Yet another person may say that he did not know that killing anyone is illegal. Should the legal system allow these people to go unpunished as they are ignorant about the law? The answer is a clear 'no'. If such an excuse is accepted by the courts, it will result in chaos and anarchy. The purpose of the law—order, peace, predictability and certainty shall be defeated. Hence, it is important to know the law. It applies to every person. The scope of the law is from womb to tomb, and cradle to grave. No one can escape from the long arm of law.

'No' because one can ignore and not know the law at one's peril. Any business person can suffer huge losses and even put the entire business to risk by not knowing the law. It is his choice. However, it is not expected from any sane person to make such a choice until and unless he has decided to move forward on the path of self-destruction—his own destruction as well as the destruction of the business.

The Law: How Much?

The entire body of different laws is collectively known as 'the law'. It is not possible for any person to know all the laws, or collectively the law. It becomes even more difficult due to the dynamic nature of law—it may change from time to

© The Author(s) 2017
A.K. Agarwal, *Business Leadership and Law*, DOI 10.1007/978-81-322-3682-5_1

time and place to place. In most of the evolved jurisdictions, law is not static: it changes as per the aspirations of the people of the country. As new situations arise, the lawmakers deliberate on the possible solutions for the problem and try to fix it either with an amendment in the existing law or by enacting a new law. This process keeps the law relevant for the society. The interpretation to an existing law is provided by the courts and it is quite possible that for the same law, courts may give different interpretations at different points of time. Anson—an authority on contract law—gave a very interesting definition of law: 'Law is the last interpretation given by the last judge'. Hence, it is extremely difficult, if not impossible, for any person to keep himself updated with all the latest interpretations and also all the latest enactments, which shall include all the ordinances promulgated.

So how much law a businessperson needs to know? Ideally—the complete law. As it is not possible for anyone to keep himself abreast of each and every development, we need to think about this question in a realistic manner. Then, the answer will be—it depends, and it depends on the context.

It depends on the nature of one's business and shall vary with an individual's keenness to know the law, and also on the geographical location in which the business is carried out. For instance, a businessperson engaged in the software business must be aware of the information technology laws, copyright law and special laws related to Internet applicable in the countries in which he is doing business. The same shall apply *mutatis mutandis* for a businessperson in the automobile industry, civil aviation, steel, cement, pharmaceuticals, hotel and hospitality, telecommunication, media and entertainment, films and television, publishing and printing, etc.

Yet, there are certain aspects of law which each and every businessperson is supposed to know, irrespective of his keenness to know the law, nature of business and the geographical location. The most important of them are: salient features of the Constitution of the country, basic principles of natural justice, company law, criminal law, tax law, tort law, international law, environmental law, contract law, competition law, dispute resolution, intellectual property rights, consumer law, etc. It is dangerous for a businessperson not to be aware of the basic principles of the above-mentioned laws, besides the specific laws applicable to his business.

Key Aspects of Study and Practise of the Law

It is imperative for a businessperson to understand a little bit about each of them.

Constitutional Law

Starting with the Constitution, it may be unwritten or written. The British constitution is unwritten, whereas that of the United States is written. The Constitution of India is also written. The Constitution may be said to be laws and principles according to which a State is governed. Some of the salient features of the Constitution of India are: provides for fundamental rights—freedom of speech and expression, religion, profession, equality, legal remedies, life and liberty, etc.; declares India to be a sovereign, socialist, secular, democratic republic. Thus, the Constitution of India cherishes equality and liberty for the people of India. For a businessperson doing business in any other country, it is a prerequisite to understand the basic principles of the Constitution of the country fairly well.

Principles of Natural Justice

There are two basic principles of natural justice. The first one is based on the Latin maxim, *Audi alteram partem*, which means 'hear the other side', or no person should be condemned unheard. This principle ensures that both the parties are given equal treatment and there is fairness on the part of the judge. The second principle is based on the maxim, *Nemo debet esse judex in propria causa*, which means 'no one shall be a judge in his own cause', or the judge must be impartial, unbiased and neutral. This is also known as the rule against bias. A third principle has also evolved, with says that all decisions must be 'reasoned'. It ensures that the orders are 'speaking orders' and not 'bald'.

Company Law

The company law is based on the basic premise that a company is a distinct legal entity—distinct from its promoters and directors, is an artificial legal person, has a perpetual existence, can sue and be sued in its own name, generally liability of members is limited to the nominal value of shares, and shares are transferable. The most important aspects for business leaders are that the company being an artificial person cannot act on its own; human beings need to make decisions for the company. Typically, they are the directors of the company and they have a fiduciary duty towards the company—duty of loyalty and duty to take care. The legal net is being widened in most of the jurisdictions to ensure better corporate governance. These individuals are expected to work in the interest of the company and ideally they should not be any conflict of interest—company and self.

Criminal Law

The essential ingredient of criminal law is 'intention' and the doctrine of *mens rea* finds special mention. According to the basic principles of criminal law, a crime is not committed if the mind of the person doing the act in question is innocent. The maxim says: *actus non facit reum, nisi mens sit rea*, which means the intent and act must both concur to constitute the crime. As a general rule the mind must be at fault before there can be a crime, however statutory law may say otherwise. It is assumed that while enacting the law, the legislative body must have thought about the intention and incorporated it in the language of the law itself. Hence, the maxim has no application to the offences which are under the penal code or other statues in India or in other countries, until and unless it is mentioned specifically. If in a particular provision of law, the penal provisions have omitted to prescribe any particular mental condition, the presumption is that the omission by legislature is intentional and, therefore, *mens rea* cannot be applied in such instances.

It is extremely important for the business leaders to keep this basic principle in mind as they are the ones to be targeted for most of the white collar crimes. Criminal action cannot be taken against them without proving intention.

Taxation Law

Benjamin Franklin said that there are only two things certain in life—death and taxes, one needs to be extra careful about the taxation law. It may not be highly desirable or a virtue to use all the loopholes traceable in the extant law, but it is legal to do so. Tax avoidance—not evasion—is permitted by law. Taxation is a very important subject and business leaders must pay full attention towards compliance. Taxation laws are interpreted strictly and often courts impose heavy penalties in case of non-compliance. In India there have been frequent amendments to taxation laws which make it difficult for any business person to keep track of the changes, however, one cannot afford to ignore them.

Law of Torts

The law of Torts is expanding globally and the same is true for India. Tort is a civil wrong as opposed to a criminal wrong and does not arise due to a breach of contract or breach of trust. This wrong finds a remedy in a legal action for 'unliquidated damages'—compensation which has not been predetermined. Any person can bring an action under tort law against the company. Business leaders have to be extremely careful as in a good number of cases the courts have held that the companies have 'strict and absolute liability'—even if they had done their best and taken all the precautions—particularly in cases of leakage of poisonous gases, radioactive material, etc. Different torts for which a company may be hauled up are: negligence, nuisance, trespassing, etc.

International Law

International law is typically governed by geopolitical issues and is, therefore, considered to be a weak law. There is no 'global sovereign' in the world, and this fact makes international law so very interesting. Holland, a jurist, remarked, 'International law is the vanishing point of jurisprudence'. To many legal thinkers, it is simply a gentleman's promise. Different countries respect international law only due to their self-interest. As sovereign nations they are not bound by the diktats of any other country. Of late, it has been experienced that a large number of nations have come together and entered into global treaties for mutual benefit of trade and commerce, giving international business law a little bit of respect. Yet, powerful nations do have their clout in political and business decisions. The bargaining power of different countries determines how international law is made and implemented.

Environmental Law

Regarding environmental law, there is generally a tension between development and environment, and businesspersons often see rules and regulations regarding protection of environment as a hurdle in their plans of development and numerous schemes for making profit. The idea of protection of environment along with development is not new and law has evolved to handle the subject with dexterity.

Two basic principles—precautionary principle and polluter pays principle—guide the judges to exercise their discretion in a manner which can be helpful to the society, resulting in balanced and sustainable development along with protection of environment. Environmental issues are becoming more and more contentious, and business leaders have no choice but to pay special attention to these issues as different countries are making their environment laws stricter and imposing very heavy penalties in case of breach.

Contract Law

The contract law is the fundamental law for most of the businesses and is based on the basic principle of voluntary action. Two or more parties enter into a contract on their own sweet will. Their consent must be 'free consent'. Contracts are absolutely voluntary and define the relationship between the parties to the contract. Parties bind themselves by agreeing to the terms and conditions of contract. A contract must be within the legal framework. There has to be a consideration—something in return, typically but not limited to, money—for a contract, however, law does not bother about the adequacy or inadequacy of the consideration. Business leaders need to be very careful that rely only on 'concluded contracts'. Any party to a contract which does not keep its promise, must either ensure 'specific performance' or pay damages, which may be liquidated—predetermined—or unliquidated. 'Contract adherence' is expected, though a lot depends on the legal environment of the country.

Competition Law (Antitrust)

Business is all about competition. It is extremely important that businesses get a level-playing field and the legal environment ensures healthy and fair competition. In India it is called the competition law, whereas in the United States, for historical reasons though being a misnomer, it is called antitrust law and is also known as the Sherman Act. The competition law in all the jurisdictions aims to crack down on monopolies and cartels. It is becoming increasingly important as businesses try to expand to new countries and have to deal with the competition law regime in these jurisdictions, which might be varying from the home jurisdiction law. The law has its application even to mergers and acquisitions to prevent creation of humongous companies which may have monopolistic tendencies. Microsoft has often been at the receiving end of the competition law, both in the United States and elsewhere. Competitors would always like to use the competition law as a strategic tool and it has the capability and potency to damage a business substantially, if not fully.

Law of Dispute Resolution

Business and disputes go together, however, it is undesirable to live with a dispute, which in most of the cases has a negative connotation—wastage of time, energy, resources and loss of opportunity. Business leaders need to cultivate the art of avoiding disputes, and also in certain cases learning how to resolve them effectively, inexpensively and timely. Disputes must be nipped in the bud. Smart business leaders develop the ability to anticipate a dispute much in advance and take necessary measures to either avoid it or resolve it. It is not at all advisable to litigate and live in uncertainty. However, there may be certain situations when a company has to fight it out in a quasi-judicial or judicial forum—a tribunal, an appellate authority, arbitral tribunal, a national court, court in a foreign country, and higher courts including the Supreme Court of the country. It is daunting but business leaders have to learn to keep themselves as cool as a cucumber, remember that patience is a great virtue, and that there is nothing certain in life. Even with one of the finest and the strong cases, one can never be sure when and what shall be decided in a judicial forum.

Intellectual Property Rights

Intellectual property rights (IPRs) are a creation of the intellect and hard work. Most of the businesses today are making their money due to the strong IPRs and their protection in secured legal environments. The United States is one of the finest examples and it is often said that the history of economic development of the US is nothing but the history of the development of patent law in the US. Intellectual property is intangible and it is possible to copy it without much difficulty. That makes these rights the most vulnerable and easy to exploit commercially. With the expansion of Internet and extensive use of computers, it has now become a child's play to copy anything. Deluge of data and information are available online and at times it becomes so tempting to 'select all', copy and paste. Piracy in music, software and publishing is rampant. Business leaders need to be aware of the threats of infringement of IPRs—patents, copyright, trademark, designs, trade secrets, confidential information, etc.

Consumer Protection Law

It is often said that consumer is king. In most of the evolved jurisdictions, consumer law protects the rights of the consumer—one who buys certain goods or avails of certain services. In India the consumer law was enacted in 1986 and since then the scope and ambit of this law has been expanded, primarily due to the wider inter-pretation given by the Supreme Court to the word consumer itself. In the beginning the idea was to give a narrow interpretation, however, with the passage of time the courts have included most of the perceivable things—goods as well as services—in this definition. Business leaders have to be very cautious vis-à-vis the consumer law as it can result in an unwanted and long litigation as well as avoidable negative publicity. Media often highlights interesting stories of consumers being cheated by companies and most of the courts are more than willing to decide in favour of the hapless consumer. A legal fight between the consumer and a big company is often seen as a fight between David and Goliath. In a good number of cases it is advisable for a company not to go ahead with the legal battle in the consumer court as the valuation of the suit may be very low but the risk of damaging the company's reputation is quite high.

Other Laws

There may be many other laws which a business person must be aware of, depending on the business he is doing, where he is doing, and also his keenness to know the law. But, the above-mentioned are truly a must. To do any business, anywhere, smart business persons make it a point to know the fundamental aspects of laws applicable in most of the places to most of the businesses. He will probably cut a sorry figure in the absence of the knowledge of these principles.

The Law: Knowledge and Its Application

The knowledge of the above-mentioned subjects will certainly help a business leader in conducting the business in a better manner. As this much knowledge is mandatory, one should not expect dramatic changes in the results, however, as 'forewarned is forearmed', a business person may be ready with several options vis-à-vis the ever-dynamic law. It needs to be appreciated that *ipso facto* the knowledge of law may not be of great help, but, it can do wonders if applied properly. How can this knowledge be applied to practical situations is a matter of individual choice and depends on decision-making capacity and the business acumen of the particular business person. Smart business persons keep their antennas very sharp and try to gather as much information as possible from varied sources, and, thereafter they apply this information to their business to their advantage.

Anticipate
A business leader is expected to anticipate, and anticipate better than others. The more the information gathering and the more the application of that information, the better and more precise shall be the capability to anticipate. Besides the basic knowledge about the legal scenario in the country as well as in different jurisdictions where the company is doing business, the business leader is expected to know much more and keep a tab on the changes happening in the business, as well as, the legal environment. Some of the business leaders may simply watch the happenings as they unfold from the fence and comment concisely and precisely, whereas other business leaders may like to play a role in how the events unfold.

Playing a Bigger Role
Law and politics go hand-in-hand, and so the evolved jurisdictions, including India, most of the lawmaking is done by elected representatives of the people, and later interpreted by the judges. It is interesting to observe that canny business persons typically like to play a bigger role in the lawmaking process so that their companies can benefit either by the enactment of new laws or amendments to the existing laws.

It would be juvenile to even expect a business person to try to do something like this if he does not know even the basic laws. It would be akin to participating in Formula One racing without even knowing how to drive a car. It does not, however, mean that anyone who knows how to drive a car can participate in Formula One racing. Similarly, simply by acquiring the basic understanding of the legal provisions, one should not think himself fit to play the game of getting the laws amended or made to further his business interests. Playing such a game requires high level of dexterity to handle a number of things—people, situations, issues, etc.—and the same level of dexterity as shown by a highly skilled surgeon in holding and using a scalpel.

Navigate the Legal Landscape

To use the law to your advantage, it, thus, becomes essential to know it, and to know it like the back of your hand. The better you know, the more confident you will be in using it in your favour and also using it against your competitor. If a person knows the streets of a city very well, he can walk or drive with ease without even the slightest of doubt or fear of being lost anywhere in the city. In case he does not know the streets very well, he can take the help of a map or a person to help him navigate, but in both the cases he would not be as confident as he shall be if he knows the city himself. The same applies to the business leader who is trying his best to navigate through the legal landscape while doing business. And, just imagine if there is no map or the map is not accurate or the map is not detailed; and if there is no navigator or the navigator does not have the full information or the navigator himself is confused and is not sure where to go; the map as well as the navigator will be of very little help. The legal landscape is not so easy to be mapped and it is also not so easy to find a good navigator who can help a business person to find the best way in the legal maze.

Business Leaders and the Law

It would be a bit difficult to give examples of business leaders who failed as they did not know the law, for the simple reason that failure is rarely documented in detail, and it is not very common for anyone to talk about his failures, however, the list of business leaders who cared to know law and succeeded in their business is quite long. The fact of the matter is that it can be said with little doubt that almost all the successful business leaders at some point of time in their business careers had a brush with the law. It might have been due to the actions of an aggressive competitor, or moving the court to push the frontier of law in order to get a favourable interpretation of any particular word in the statute. It could have also been due to actions taken by the government, law enforcement agencies, regulatory bodies, etc.

Thomas Alva Edison in the nineteenth century fought a long legal battle for the protection of the patent for his electric bulb. **Henry Ford** would not have succeeded in selling Ford cars had he not troubled himself to know the law of the land and challenge the might of an existing patent, interestingly, owned by an attorney in the United States.

Of late, Indian companies and business leaders have been proactively protecting their intellectual property and the dispute between **Bajaj and TVS** arose with respect to sale of their motorcycles. Top business leaders from both the companies entered into negotiations and later initiated litigation, which is still pending, however, having tasted a mix of victory and defeat, though not finally, they have decided to live in peace and keep doing business.

Bill Gates, much later, also had challenged the might of a big company, which did not make the best efforts to sell the software made by Microsoft. Gates won the case due to his sharp legal understanding, which is also evident in the initialisation of end users' licence agreement for software.

During the present times, **Steve jobs**, and later Tim Cook of Apple, took the intellectual property rights very seriously and challenged Samsung and other competitors in a number of jurisdictions all over the globe. **Coca-Cola** had challenged **Pepsi** Cola, as it was known then, for the use of the word Cola. It is a different story that Coca-Cola lost that case in the Privy Council in England and settled the matter with Pepsi in 1942. Much later, when Coca-Cola and Pepsi were busy in cut-throat competition in India in 1990s, Pepsi challenged Coca-Cola in an Indian court primarily alleging poaching of key personnel. Pepsi lost the case, but the legal fight, and determination of the outer periphery of law, facilitated the market in achieving maturity.

Knowing the law and at times trying to get the law modified to suit your business interests has been at the top priority of highly successful business leaders. Top business leaders at the big car and oil companies in the United States knew the law in great detail and lobbied hard with the lawmakers, so that gasoline taxes were not increased.

In India, **Ambani brothers**—Mukesh and Anil—of Reliance group of companies used the finer aspects of law regarding the oil and gas dispute, citing a family settlement, which according to them could not be made public. It is only the law, which can provide any protection of confidentiality or whatsoever to such a family settlement, even if the entire country was held to ransom. The **Adani group** tried to use the law regarding special economic zone to its immense advantage. Mature groups like **Tata and Birla** did not waste their time, effort and money on dispute resolution clauses which did not help them. It could not have been possible without proper understanding of the legal issues involved and anticipation by top business leaders in both the companies.

Some of the business leaders like **J.R.D Tata** knew the law, but went a step ahead and made ethical conduct as their reference point rather than be guided only by the periphery of legal framework. On the other hand, some business leaders tried to test the outer periphery of law, without bothering a bit about decency, fairness and ethical behaviour, and finally had to pay heavily. Henry Ford, Jr had been one such business leader.

A few years back **Ratan Tata**, heading the Tata Group, had a tough time with the political leaders in the State of West Bengal, particularly Mamata Banerjee, with respect to the manufacturing plant for the small car Nano. Though his company had entered into a contract with the state of West Bengal, the events turned nasty and unruly, and the company decided to shift its operations to the State of Gujarat. Thus, simply entering into a contract may not be sufficient, conducive legal environment is necessary for the enforcement of any contract. And, business leaders must anticipate its presence or absence.

The **Sahara group** in India has been ordered by the Supreme Court to pay a huge sum of money to investors, but the company, ironically, using the best legal minds, had tried its best to wriggle out of the situation. The same can be said to be true about Kingfisher airlines in India. Business leaders, who know too much of the law, can put their knowledge, either positive use or negative use. A number of failures on the part of business leaders may be chiefly due to heavy reliance on the technical aspects of law without giving adequate attention to the spirit of law.

Starbucks and a number of other companies have been doing business in several countries, and of late, there have been strong protests in the UK as even after making huge profits, these companies had not been paying their due as taxes using certain loopholes in the law. This is purely a matter for any business leader to make up his mind as to using the law to make unfair gains, or follow the strategy of being on the right side of law, not only in letter, but in the spirit also. **Vodafone** faced a similar problem in India.

Rupert Murdoch and his association with the British government and media was the talk of the town sometime back, and as a business leader, who was regarded very highly, there was considerable erosion in his reputation, and also that of the British police, government, and bureaucrats as he had a finger in every pie. He used to take the law for granted, would be an understatement.

The last few years have been quite tumultuous for the Wall Street, with the Occupy Wall Street movement and the American prosecutors bent upon cleansing the entire system. Business leaders like **Rajat Gupta**, who have been held at a very high pedestal in the business fraternity, faced the wrath of the team of American prosecutors, including the notable **lawyer Preet Bharara**. Lawyers can make or mar any business. Business leaders who had the advantage of prudent advice of experienced lawyers, an exceptional example can be **Nani A. Palkhivala**, made fantastic strides in their business. On the other hand, business leaders, who did not pay attention to good lawyers, or paid too much attention to inefficient and lousy lawyers suffered immensely.

There have been many business leaders who either made the best use of law by knowing it and using it, and also a number of business leaders who did not bother to know the law, or even if they knew it, did not make reasonable efforts to use the law to the advantage of their business; on the contrary, they either allowed competitors to make use of the law against them, or used the provisions of law in a manner which finally hurt them and their business.

In nutshell, every business leader has to realise that it is his business and it is in his best interest to be on the right side of law, know the law, and let the law be its friend, philosopher and guide.

In the chapters that follow, we shall be going through some of the cases mentioned above in detail, however, let us go through a few cases which highlight the importance of the maxim, *ignorantia facti excusat, ignorantia juris non excusat.*

Heien Versus North Carolina (US Supreme Court, 2014)[1]

On 29 April 2009, Nicholas Brady Heien was driving a car on Interstate 77 in North Carolina with one of the two brake lights broken. Sergeant Matt Darisse stopped Nicholas and issued him a warning ticket. However, actions and replies of Heien and the other occupant of the car were not normal and because of this reason Darisse got suspicious. He searched the car and found cocaine. Heien was arrested.

Interestingly, the North Carolina law stated that a car must be 'equipped with a stop lamp'. It nowhere mentioned that a car should have two stop lamps. Also it did not say that if a car had more than one stop lamp, usually two in number, all—or both—should function. Hence, according to strict interpretation, a car with only a single brake light or stop lamp was complying with the law and there was no justification to stop a car with only one brake light broken.

Obviously, Darisse stopped the car without knowing the law on the subject fully and hence can be termed to be ignorant about it. However, his ignorance helped the police nab a person involved in drug trafficking.

The Fourth Amendment to the United States Constitution—adopted in 1792—prohibits unreasonable searches and seizures. It has been interpreted that any action based on a reasonable factual mistake is permissible. However, the question is about a reasonable mistake of law. Whether it is permitted or not?

Heien relied on the Fourth Amendment protection in the trial court and averred that as Darisse was ignorant about the law, he could not have stopped the car and thus his action was not in accordance with the Constitutional provisions. The trial court did not agree and decided in favour of Darisse on the basis that there was reasonable mistake of law, which is permitted by the Fourth Amendment. The North Carolina Court of Appeals reversed the decision on the ground that the law on the subject required only a stop lamp, and even one stop lamp was sufficient. Thus, the action of stopping the car by Darisse was in violation of the Constitutional protection provided to the people. The Supreme Court of North Carolina reversed the Court of Appeals decision and upheld the decision of the trial court giving the reason that the mistaken understanding of Darisse was reasonable and hence the action of stopping the car was well within the Constitutional framework.

In an appeal in the US Supreme Court, the decision of the North Carolina Supreme Court was upheld by the US Supreme Court, 8-1, in December 2014 on the same reasoning. It further added that the Fourth Amendment required government officials to act reasonably and not perfectly. The Amendment gives fair leeway for enforcing the law. However, mistakes of fact or law must be those of a reasonable person.

Thus, reasonable mistake of law has been accepted by the US Supreme Court in this landmark decision.

---

[1]Heien v. North Carolina, United States Supreme Court, (2014), No. 13-604, Argued: October 6, 2014, Decided: December 15, 2014; 574 US ___ (2014).

It is an interesting case which targets the very basic assumption on which the application of principles of jurisprudence is based. It is expected that a policeman must know the law, particularly those laws which are directly applicable to his field of work, though each and every person is assumed to know the law and the entire body of law fully updated. The tension develops when it becomes humanly impossible in a realistic manner to know the entire body of the law while carrying on one's duties in the field. It may be possible for legal experts who keep on updating their legal knowledge day in and day out, however, even for them it can never be said with hundred percent certainty that each of the members of the legal fraternity knows the law fully and completely.

For public servants, it often becomes a matter of concern to act upon a set of known facts while applying the rules as there are two genuine concerns: first, the facts may not be completely known or all relevant facts may not be known, and, second, full knowledge of applicable rules is questionable as the number of rules being added to the rule book every year is huge. Another serious problem is the issue of interpretation of the rules in different sets of circumstances. Also, interpretation of seemingly contradictory rules is another issue which hinders the working and decision-making of public servants. Thus, it results in less than perfect final decisions being made.

There are two choices: first, wait for things to become perfect and thereafter make any decision, or, second, try to be reasonable and make the best possible decisions. As the society wishes to move with time, rather than be static and frozen in a time warp, the second option is practical and chosen in all evolved jurisdictions. Hence, it is quite possible that even the best of the police officers may not know the complete law, with all the interpretations made by several courts, however, it is useful to work with the best of the knowledge and by making best efforts not to decide anything wrong deliberately.

The judgment is a landmark one because it makes it crystal clear that we live in a less than perfect world and simply assuming that everyone knows the law fully may not work in making the society a better place to live in. There are situations where the individual judges would have to exercise judicial discretion and decide according to the circumstances by giving leeway to the basic premise of complete knowledge of the law.

Douglas Versus Hello! (House of Lords, 2007)[2]

Famous film actors Michael Douglas and Catherine Zeta-Jones had planned to get married on 18 November 2000 at the Plaza Hotel, New York. To retain exclusivity of their wedding photographs, they had signed a contract with the celebrity magazine

---

[2]OBG Ltd and another v Allan and others; Douglas and others v Hello! Ltd and others; Mainstream Properties Ltd v Young; House of Lords, 2 May 2007; [2007] UKHL 21; [2008] 1 A. C. 1.

'OK!' for £1 million. One of the clauses of the contract mentioned that it was the duty of the bride and bridegroom to ensure by making the best efforts that no photograph was taken at the function by anyone except by the approved photographer.

Despite the best efforts, Rupert Thorpe, son of former British politician Jeremy Thorpe, managed to click some photographs clandestinely without any authority or approval. Thorpe sold the photographs to OK!'s competitor 'Hello!'.

Both OK! and Hello! published the photograph and later the former sued latter for breach of confidence and for the tort of causing loss by lawful means. The couple had also sued the magazine and the court had awarded a small amount as compensation, however, in the fight between the two magazines, the court finally awarded a compensation of more than £ 1 million primarily on the reasoning that the competitor magazine Hello! very well knew that there was a contract between the film actors and OK!, and, therefore, when Hello! paid handsomely for photographs to Thorpe, it was an action which leaves no choice for the court, but to draw the inference of necessary intention, assuming the knowledge of the existence of the contract.

The court relied on the accepted maxim of the law, *ignorantia juris non excusat*, and made the observation that the principle was not only applicable in the criminal law, but also to the civil law. Actions of Thorpe and Hello! magazine were not accidental, they were well thought out and deliberate. In such a scenario, there was no difficulty in establishing intention, which could even be inferred from reckless conduct in another set of facts and circumstances. Knowing the existence of a contract, if any person interferes without any justification, he should be liable for the consequences. If the liability cannot be extended reasonably to all the consequences, it can surely be extended to the necessary and inevitable consequences of the actions of interference in a contractual relationship entered by two parties to which he is not privy. For determining liability, it is not necessary that the intention must be to cause injury. The main intention to interfere in the contract deliberately is enough to make the interferer liable.

There were a number of other issues related to this dispute, and the most important being that of privacy rights and the intellectual property rights. According to the European Convention on Human Rights, privacy of individuals is an integral aspect of these rights. In the present case, it was the privacy of the couple, which was being protected by the Convention, however, when the couple itself granted certain rights as per the contract to the magazine OK!, it was a commercial transaction, which had to be honoured. Also, the photographs of the event were protected by the copyright law, with the owner being the couple. Those matters, however, have not been the subject matter of the dispute, and thus, the court did not dwell on them.

The most important aspect of the entire dispute has been the knowledge of the contract between the couple and magazine OK! to all and sundry and most importantly to the competitors of the magazine OK! and other paparazzi who were looking for an opportunity to get a glimpse and capture it, and thereafter sell it to anyone who was willing to pay the price. Thorpe due to his connections in the higher echelons of society could manage to enter the venue and also click photographs. At no point of time, he took the plea that he was ignorant about the deal, and, therefore, it was too obvious that he had done that for commercial gains and the magazine Hello! also paid handsomely to him to get those photographs for commercial benefit.

A question arises regarding the issue of privacy and confidentiality of personal events in any celebrity's life. It is a double-edged sword, as a celebrity is not a celebrity without his or her fans, whereas he or she also needs certain privacy. The question is where to draw the line. In highly evolved jurisdictions like the United States and the United Kingdom, where the rule of law has evolved and developed in the last so many centuries along with the presence of the legal machinery to make such contracts work, it is possible to enforce a contract which requires tremendous physical security and inspection despite technological advancements and easy accessibility to cutting-edge spy cameras and other sophisticated gadgets as has been clearly demonstrated and vindicated in the present case, however, such contracts are of little or almost no value in jurisdictions with weaker legal environment and lenient security arrangements.

Ashok Kumar Sharma Versus State of Rajasthan (Supreme Court of India, 2013)[3]

On 25 February 2001 in the city of Jaipur in India, a senior police officer— Additional Superintendent of Police (Crimes)—stopped Ashok Kumar Sharma on the suspicion that he was carrying narcotics with him. He was informed that if he wished, he could be searched before a Magistrate or a Gazetted Officer. He gave his consent in writing that he had full confidence in the police officer and agreed for search. Narcotics were found, he was jailed and trial started. The court found him guilty, convicted and sentenced him. His appeal in the High Court was rejected, and thereafter, he appealed in the Supreme Court on the ground that a false case was foisted against him.

The law on the subject matter was and is the *Narcotic Drugs and Psychotropic Substances Act, 1985* (NDPS Act) which provided that any accused had the right under Section 50 to get himself searched either before a Magistrate or a Gazetted officer. Such a provision had been incorporated in the law to prevent misuse of the NDPS Act by the police.

Further, the law has been interpreted by the Supreme Court in earlier cases that it was obligatory on the part of the police officer to inform the accused that he had such a right. In case the accused had not been informed about his right, it would

---

[3]Ashok Kumar Sharma versus State of Rajasthan, Supreme Court of India, Bench: K.S. Radhakrishnan, Dipak Misra, JJ.; 9 January 2013; Cr.A. No. 817 of 2008; Reported in 2013 Indlaw SC 14; (2013) 2 SCC 67; 2013 (1) MLJ(Crl) 622; 2013 (2) RCR(Criminal) 1; 2013 (1) RLW 676; 2013(1) SCALE 193; [2013] 1 S.C.R. 236.

have amounted to non-compliance of the legal provisions resulting in vitiating the trial.

In the instant case, according to witnesses, it was amply clear that the accused had been only informed that he could be searched before a Magistrate or a Gazetted Officer if he so wished, however, he was not told categorically that he had such a right under the law. The Supreme Court held that the police officer failed in communicating the right to the accused, and thus the entire proceedings were vitiated. The Supreme Court, consequently, had set aside the conviction and sentencing, and released the accused from jail.

The Supreme Court commented on the argument that according to the maxim, *ignorantia juris non excusat*, the accused was expected to know the law and the police officer was not bound by law to communicate the same to the accused in the following words:

> We may, in this connection, also examine the general maxim "ignorantia juris non excusat" and whether in such a situation the accused could take a defence that he was unaware of the procedure laid down in S. 50 of the NDPS Act. Ignorance does not normally afford any defence under the criminal law, since a person is presumed to know the law. Indisputedly ignorance of law often in reality exists, though as a general proposition, it is true, that knowledge of law must be imputed to every person. But it must be too much to impute knowledge in certain situations, for example, we cannot expect a rustic villager, totally illiterate, a poor man on the street, to be aware of the various law laid down in this country i.e. leave aside the NDPS Act.[4]

This case raises interesting questions, particularly in the light of the Heien case discussed earlier. Interestingly, in both the cases, the accused were carrying narcotics. The role of the police officer in communicating the rights of the accused in the present case has been questioned by the Supreme Court, whereas, in the Heien case, it was the reasonable ignorance of law, which was upheld by the United States Supreme Court. Both the cases, though, based on the basic principle, *ignorantia juris non excusat*, have been dealt with differently by the courts, and one of the important reasons has been the social milieu in which the law has to be applied.

In both the cases, police officers would have been expected to know the law in a better manner, if not fully, as compared to the accused. Even then the United States Supreme Court tilted in favour of the police officer by granting him the benefit of reasonable ignorance, whereas, the Supreme Court of India did not show any leniency as far as the police officer was concerned, despite the fact that the trial court had found the accused guilty of carrying narcotics.

There are two views. The first one would favour the practical and real aspects of applying law to a particular set of circumstances and the second view would treat the matter in a strict and far more theoretical manner. The legal provision in the Indian law has been made to prevent misuse, given the widespread illiteracy, poverty and unemployment in the country. The social situation in the United States is different and the level of illiteracy, poverty and unemployment is undoubtedly

---

[4]Paragraph 9, Ashok Kumar Sharma case; Reported in 2013 Indlaw SC 14.

much lower than that in India. Because of this reason, there can be a reasonable expectation that people in general in the United States are more aware of the legal provisions and have better protection against the occasional abuse of law by the police. In India, the situation is very different and people in general hardly have any practical protection against the abuse of law by the police. Hence, the Supreme Court of India rightly preferred to follow the strict interpretation of law and did not leave any avenue open for its misuse.

The burden may appear to be too heavy on the police in India, but no one can deny that there are, unfortunately, several instances of abuse and misuse of law by the police against the common people as reported in the media and also on record in several Supreme Court and High Court judgements. The police officer dealing with such a serious matter should have been much more cautious in complying with all the provisions of law. In comparison, the United States Supreme Court appreciated the fact that the meaning of a stoplight could have different interpretations, and, moreover, the only question before the court was regarding the Fourth Amendment.

Takeaway for Business Leaders

1. Ignorance versus Reasonable Mistake of Law
   Heien raises the question as to where to draw the line. If a highly educated person with all the resources—time, expertise, money, etc.—available to him takes shelter behind the shield of ignorance, should he be given the benefit of not knowing the law? To most of us, the answer is clear 'no', whereas, in the instant case, with different interpretation and confusion regarding the applicable law, it was rather the duty of the policeman to stop the accused and question him. Thus, the door for the exercise of judicial discretion has been left open. Business Leaders must be wary of situations whose outcome depends on the exercise of discretion. One cannot be fully certain of the result whenever discretionary power is to be exercised.
2. Ignorance of a Contract
   Douglas tells us that simply feigning ignorance about the existence of a contract between one's competitors may not help as the courts in evolved and evolving jurisdictions would equate such ignorance with ignorance of law. Such ignorance cannot be excused in most of the cases where competing parties are involved and it is highly improbable that they did not have knowledge about the existence of a contract. Interference with any such contract should not be tolerated on the ground of ignorance. All these are interesting and very useful extensions and corollaries of the basic principle *ignorantia juris non excusat*, but their effectiveness depends on the legal environment in which they are being tested.
3. The Government and the law
   Business leaders often fear getting tangled up with lawyers, lobbyists, and bureaucrats, so they keep their distance from the government and legal matters.

This aversion leads many to neglect law as a competitive tool. Business leaders should play by the rules. The question is who should make the rules. Do these leaders have a role in making the rules? Is it the job of the legislature only to make rules? The government surely has a much bigger role in rule-making by getting the power of delegated legislation from the legislature. It is often the government which makes the rules for the businesses. Ironically, it is the same government which is responsible for executing these rules. Thus, the government becomes a leviathan to deal with. Add to it the quasi-judicial power of different tribunals and it is simply a nightmare for any business leader.

Astute business leaders know that they should not neglect the law and the government. The law is an integral part of their business strategy. How the leader deals with the government and the counsel may make all the important difference in the end result. Facing competition with a sound business strategy is essential, however, aligning legal strategy with the business strategy or vice versa is mandatory for winning legally.

4. Certainty, Anticipate and Creating Options

Better knowledge of the law undoubtedly helps in moving towards certainty with tremendous confidence. Any law which has not been changed or amended almost gets perpetual existence, however, it may be changed anytime with a stroke of the pen. Knowing the changing scenario in a better manner will help a business leader to anticipate the chances of any well-established law to be changed and he can with a much higher possibility create options to handle any change. He will be much better prepared for the change. Also, he may plan to have a say in the change of the law. That itself is one of the options. Another option may be to sit pretty and wait for the changes to take place, but keep oneself prepared to act nimbly. Many other options may be created by the agile and informed business leader.

Chapter 2
How Can the Government Affect My Business?

All businesses are subject to legal and regulatory framework, and it is the job of the government to ensure that businesses are conducted within that framework. We are talking of only those businesses which would like to be on the right side of law. There are a number of businesses—smuggling, drugs, arms, etc.—which do not care to be on the right side of the law. These businesses are conducted brazenly and with impunity by being on the wrong side of law.

Before proceeding further with this discussion, it is important to understand what the government is. To govern a country means to control or direct public affairs of a country. Collectively, the group of people responsible to do so it can be called the government. Interestingly, it is said that in Great Britain the sovereign reigns but does not govern. As we normally understand and experience in our day-to-day life, the government in any country, to say loosely, makes the rules for proper conduct of everyday life, which includes businesses, and is supposed to take care of most of the things for the people.

Three Arms of the Government

There are three main powers of the government: legislative, executive and judicial. In most of the modern and evolved jurisdictions there has been an effort not to converge all the three powers into one department or organ of government or individual or group of individuals. It is based on the doctrine of 'separation of powers', which was propounded by Montesquieu, a French gentleman. The basic idea of this doctrine is that in case all the powers are combined together, there is a tendency of misuse and abuse of such power. Hence, the three powers should be vested in three different organs of the state with no overlapping functions and persons.

Lord Acton had said, 'Power tends to corrupt, and absolute power corrupts absolutely'. Thus, it is important that the three powers are separated. It serves the dual purpose: first, the powers are separated, and second, powers with different organs provide the necessary checks and balances in the system.

© The Author(s) 2017
A.K. Agarwal, *Business Leadership and Law*, DOI 10.1007/978-81-322-3682-5_2

India

The Constitution of India provides for separation of powers. Legislature is vested with legislative powers and its job is to 'make' the law. The Executive is vested with the power to 'implement' the law made by the Legislature. The role of the judiciary is to 'interpret' the law, and also uphold the rule of law.

The Constitution of India exhibits certain characteristics of federalism, however, it is not strictly federal. The Constitution further provides in the Seventh Schedule, the three lists: List I—Union List, List II—State List, and List III—Concurrent List. There is a distribution of powers between the Central government and the State government and certain powers are covered by the concurrent list and, hence, both the Central as well as the State governments have jurisdiction. In case the laws made by the Central government and the State government on the same subject in the concurrent list are conflicting, the Central law prevails.

At the Central level, the Legislature comprises the two houses of Parliament— *Lok Sabha* and *Rajya Sabha*—and the President of India. The Chief Executive of the country is the President of India, who works at the advice of the Council of Ministers which is headed by the Prime Minister. A smaller group of the Council of Ministers is called the Cabinet, and another still smaller group may be called, informally, as the kitchen cabinet or the coterie. The President of India is the *de jure* head, whereas the Prime Minister is supposed to be the de facto head. All major executive decisions are taken in the name of the President of India. The judiciary at the highest level is the Supreme Court of India, which comprised the Chief Justice of India and the puisne (pronounced puny) judges, who are in no way inferior or subordinate to the Chief Justice as far as judicial competence and powers are concerned. The Chief Justice is simply *primus inter peres*—first among equals.

Interestingly, the President is common in both the Legislature and the Executive, making them overlap, rather than being disjoint sets. Further, each minister of the Council of Ministers has to be a member of either of the houses; and in case he is not, he must become a member within a period of 6 months. Thus, it is very clear that there is further overlap between the Legislature and the Executive. On closer observation, we can also say that the Executive—as far as persons concerned—is a subset of the Legislature. Therefore, we can conclude that in India the doctrine of separation of powers is not followed strictly as far as the Legislature and the Executive are concerned. There is, however, no overlap between the judiciary and either the Legislature or the Executive. No judge can be a member of either of the houses, or a Minister. The same is true in the states as well, where a judge of any of the High Court cannot be a member of either of the Houses in the State Legislature or a Minister in the State Government.

The Executive comprising the *de facto* head, the Prime Minister, and the Council of Ministers is very powerful. They are the persons who are responsible for execution of all the laws made by the Legislature. Interestingly, they are persons who initiate the process of law-making as they are the driving force of any government. Rarely a bill initiated by a private member has become a law. The same is true in different states where the ministers in the government are the most powerful persons.

Executature

It has been said by Lord Hailsham for the Westminster model, that the most powerful people are the 'Executature'—an amalgam of the Executive and the Legislature. As India follows very closely the Westminster model, the same applies to the Indian polity and the most powerful body is the Executature—the overlap of the executive and the legislature. In other words, we can say that the most powerful individuals are the members of the Council of Ministers. Still powerful are members of the Cabinet; and the ultimate power lies with the individuals who belong to the inner circle called the coterie or the kitchen cabinet. These are the individuals who initiate most of the lawmaking processes, formulate government policies, manoeuvre the entire government machinery and are the real driving force of the entire country. They are the people who can get almost anything done—making a new law, amending an existing law, getting the rules and bylaws made under the power of delegated legislation, etc.

Let us discuss a few cases from different countries.

Chinese Government Made Mattel to Eat Crow (2007)

In 2007, Mattel—one of the largest toys makers in the world—had to apologise to the manufacturers in China and the people of China, due to enormous bargaining power of the Chinese government, and its ability to exercise it. It so happened that Mattel used to get, and still gets, a large number of its toys manufactured in China, which were later sold in the United States and several other countries in the world. There were complaints in the US that Mattel toys contained lead in paint, which was and is not permitted in the US and many other countries, and also used very small magnets.

As we all know, magnets have two poles—north and south—and similar poles repel each other, whereas opposite poles attract each other. While a child was playing with the toys, she mistakenly, and which is quite possible for a small child, swallowed two tiny magnets and later, as per doctors' diagnosis, opposite poles attracted each other inside the intestine, resulting in her death. Mattel, in all probability anticipated expensive and damaging legal claims, recalled a large number of similar toys from the market and at the same time shifted the entire blame on the Chinese manufacturers.

Within a short period of time the Chinese manufacturers, backed by the Chinese Government, reacted sharply and counter-alleged that they had manufactured the toys as per the designs provided by Mattel, and hence, it was not their fault if lead paint or small magnets were used in the toys. They shifted the entire responsibility on the toys company.

Mattel had not expected that there would be such a serious counterattack. Realizing that it would not be prudent for Mattel to snap ties with Chinese manufacturers—as there were and are huge benefits of getting toys manufactured in

China, not wrongly named as 'factory of the world'—Mattel made a quick decision of withdrawing its earlier statement. Mattel was made to eat crow.

A senior official, Mattel's executive vice president for worldwide operations, Thomas Debrowski flew to Beijing, met the Chinese product safety chief Li Changjiang, apologised for his company's own weak safety controls in the presence of the global media—widely reported by BBC, Reuters, Time, etc.—and said:

> Our reputation has been damaged lately by these recalls ... And Mattel takes full responsibility for these recalls and apologizes personally to you, the Chinese people, and all of our customers who received the toys. ...The vast majority of those products that were recalled were the result of a design flaw in Mattel's design, not through a manufacturing flaw in China's manufacturers. ... We understand and appreciate deeply the issues that this has caused for the reputation of Chinese manufacturers.[1]

Governments can have immense influence on the business. In a global economy it is not only the government of one's own country but also the governments of other countries with whom one has a business connection, can have an impact on one's business.

In this case, it is quite obvious that had Mattel decided to pursue the matter either legally or diplomatically or both, it would have been a very uncertain situation as no one would have been able to provide any tentative time frame for the resolution of such a dispute. Was Mattel on weak ground due to the bargaining power of manufacturers? Not exactly. Mattel could have managed the manufacturers but managing the Chinese government was not possible. Hence, there was no option left for Mattel but to own up and apologise.

It is next to impossible to continue to fight a battle in which a party is backed by the government, and, that is true, without even the slightest doubt, about Chinese government in this matter. But, that may not be true for all business parties and all governments. The symbiotic relationship between the business and government, and the influence the government has on the business will determine the backing given by the government to any business. Moreover, higher the volume of business and monetary value, higher the interest of the government in supporting any domestic company or business.

Iraq and Exxonmobil (2011)

In December 2011, the Iraqi Government refused to pay $50 m to ExxonMobil, one of the largest oil companies in the world, headquartered in Irving, Texas in the US. Officially, it was said only to be a bureaucratic delay in making the payment, however, it was well known that the Iraqi Government in Baghdad was flexing its muscles and arm twisting ExxonMobil for engaging in south-eastern part of Iraq

---

[1]Why Mattel Apologized to China, Time, Friday, Sep. 21, 2007, by Jyoti Thottam, http://www.time.com/time/printout/0,8816,1664428,00.html, last accessed September 14, 2016.

with the leaders of the semi-autonomous Kurdistan region, which was considered to be illegal by Baghdad.

Earlier, Iraq had entered into a contract with ExxonMobil and it simply refused to honour the contract for certain unconnected reasons. It was under dictatorship for a very long time and its conversion into a democratic system starting sometime in the recent past could not be instantaneous. For a democratic system to function—which includes a proper judicial system—nurturing democratic principles, tolerance, maturity, free speech, and being responsible for decisions made are necessary. And, all these did not necessarily visibly exist in Iraq.

Oddly just at that time, President Obama in a meeting with Iraqi Prime Minister Maliki had praised the Government in Iraq and said that Iraq as a country had become,

...sovereign, self-reliant and democratic.[2]

But, sovereign governments can be whimsical and arbitrary, as has been in the case of the Iraqi Government. The role of government in honouring a contract, and that too, an international contract, is extremely important and must be exemplary. In only extreme cases of violation of certain clauses of contract or situations of violation of public policy, principles or anything against public interest, any sovereign should exercise the power not to honour a contract. And, this needs to be done only in exceptional circumstances. The Government of Iraq did not make a payment of $50 m, a small amount both for Iraq and ExxonMobil. Ironically, it was not based on any legal provisions in the contract. One has to accept that this is how the governments of certain countries work when it comes to their business and political interests.

Two questions arise: first, the issue of sovereignty and how international businesses should deal with sovereign nations, and, second, how risky is it in doing business with nascent and unstable democratic countries?

International businesses, with strong hold on their domestic governments, as is the case with Texan Oil companies, are in a much better position as far as dealing with governments of other countries is concerned, however, sovereign nations, theoretically, are not commanded by anyone, and until and unless they are cornered for any reason—most common being financial, military, natural resources like oil and gas, etc.—there is every possibility of them not paying any heed to the foreign firm's grievances, howsoever genuine and legitimate they may be. Thus, dealing with a sovereign is always tricky. And, if the entire decision-making is in the hands on one individual, the business, realistically, depends on the whims and fancies of that individual. There can be no escape from the mood swings of the leader, who may be a dictator, autocrat, or benevolent ruler at different points of time.

---

[2]Exxon Spars With Iraq Over Lack of Payment, NYT, December 22, 2011, http://www.nytimes. com/2011/12/23/business/energy-environment/exxon-mobil-and-iraq-clash-over-payment.html?_ r=1&ref=business, last accessed September 14, 2016.

Sovereignty of the nation, in such a situation, means the sovereignty of that individual only.

It may be better in a democratic set-up, with decision-making in the hands of elected representative(s). However, in nascent democracies, which mostly are unstable in the beginning and gain stability with the passage of time with tolerance and free speech practised regularly, expecting instant shift in the mind set from personal welfare to public welfare is like asking for the moon. It does not happen overnight and the biggest hindrance is being overzealous in exhibiting patriotism and working towards public welfare by ignoring international contractual obligations. Keeping the masses happy and playing to the galleries cast a shadow on rational decision-making, which often is myopic and detrimental in the long run.

It is, therefore, quite risky doing business in nascent democracies. Businesses must factor it in while formulating the strategy for entry any such market and if already there, how to continue to get superior return on investment. Exit option must be thought about to mitigate the pain of leaving a well-established profitable business.

India: Lavasa and HCC (2010)[3]

Lavasa is a serene hill station near Pune, in the state of Maharashtra, India. One of the biggest construction companies in India—Hindustan Construction Company (HCC)—was building a private city in Lavasa and it was well reported in the media that several of its plans were sanctioned by the Maharashtra Government without much objection or delay. It had also been reported that a senior politician—Sharad Pawar, former Maharashtra Chief Minister and who at one point of time was a Prime Ministerial aspirant, a fact which helps us to gauge his position in the political pecking order—had an interest in the project, and that was why it had been smooth sailing for HCC as far as government permissions were concerned.

His closeness was reported in the media:

> The former Maharashtra chief minister, who has also held the defence portfolio in the early 1990s, has not hidden his proximity to the Lavasa project. In an interview to a newspaper in early November, the agriculture minister said he had selected the site for the project and introduced the site to his friend Ajit Gulabchand, the chairman of Hindustan Construction Company, Lavasa's parent.[4]

---

[3]Lavasa gets Jairam Ramesh blow: All work in lake city illegal; DNA; Nov 27, 2010; by Harish Gupta; http://www.dnaindia.com/india/report-lavasa-gets-jairam-ramesh-blow-all-work-in-lake-city-illegal-1472750, last accessed September 14, 2016.

[4]Pawar, Jairam face off on Lavasa showcause notice; The Economic Times; Dec 1, 2010; http://articles.economictimes.indiatimes.com/2010-12-01/news/27569811_1_lavasa-corporation-lavasa-project-ajit-gulabchand, last accessed September 14, 2016.

The role of the government can never be underestimated, and it can never be certain, as HCC experienced. In 2009, when the United Progressive Alliance (UPA) government, with Dr. Manmohan Singh as the Prime Minister started its second term, Jairam Ramesh was made Minister of State in the central government and was given independent charge of the Environment Ministry. For certain reasons, he made up his mind to scrutinise the Lavasa project in great detail. There were a number of lapses found and it was estimated that the city project would be clearly detrimental to environment. All of a sudden the Environment Ministry took a tough stand and ordered to stop work in Lavasa. HCC was hurt badly. The company had planned an Initial Public Offering (IPO) to raise about Rs. 2000 crores (almost equivalent to $400 m at that time), but could not go ahead due to the orders passed by the Ministry against the company resulting in enormous negative publicity. There couldn't have been a worse time for the IPO. Political intervention even by Pawar did not yield the desired result for HCC.

The charges were serious; mostly for irreparable damage to environment. The decision on any such project needs the exercise of discretion in a judicious manner, and it typically depends on the individual who is making such a decision. Ramesh, in his wisdom, made a decision—and which was the decision of the Ministry, and of the government—to get the work stopped at Lavasa. According to HCC, it was suffering a loss of more than Rs. 2 crore (almost equivalent to $400,000 at that time) per day. It was a very serious matter and a business leader like Ajit Gulabchand, Chairman and Managing Director of HCC, faced this dilemma—to try to get the matter resolved through negotiation, or to take the matter to the court.

Later on the matter was resolved through a combination of both—a petition filed in the court and political negotiations. There was pressure from the Prime Minister's Office (PMO) on Ramesh to clear the project. With certain ifs and buts, the project was cleared. A fine of Rs. 100 crores (almost equivalent to $20 m at that time) was imposed on the company. Perceiving Ramesh as a potential threat to any such project, there was strong lobbying to get him shifted from the Environment Ministry. And, he was indeed shifted to an insignificant Ministry—as compared to Ministry of environment—Ministry of rural development, drinking water and sanitation.

But in the process, HCC also suffered—the project got delayed and had to be shrunk and HCC could not come up with its IPO at the scheduled time.

Who suffered?

May be both, but the loss for HCC has been much more as compared to that of the minister, who was shifted to an insignificant ministry. Moreover, ministers are always there till the time of the confidence of the Prime Minister and even the government continues till the time of next elections, and in case it is re-elected, the same person may or may not be given a ministerial berth, and even if given, any particular ministry is also a matter of chance. Hence, for the minister Ramesh, there was very little to lose. HCC, however, lost significant time, reputation, earnings in the form of new investments and the steam to go ahead with everything rosy. Any business leader detests such a situation. Whether it was the personal rivalry between two political giants, can merely be a subject of speculation. Exercise of discretion by the minister wreaked havoc for the business. It was not something which could not have been anticipated by a top business leader.

There has always been a debate between protection of environment and the need for growth and development. With burgeoning population, it was and is becoming difficult to protect the environment fully, and hence, it has been left to the discretion of the government—particularly the Ministry of Environment and Forests—to see that minimum damage is caused to environment while any project is planned and later executed. One of the most important principles to be followed in the decision-making process is: 'polluter pays', which means that it is the duty of the person or the company—which has to carry out the unavoidable development work resulting in certain amount of damage to environment—must pay for restoration, in the form of tree plantation, relocation, rehabilitation, using technology to lessen the impact of degradation of environment, etc. A very fine balance has to be achieved between environment on the one hand and development on the other.

For a business leader, one question is very obvious and needs to be answered. Were the environmental clearance requirements so vague that multiple interpretations could be made? It can easily be inferred from the events that the difference in the interpretation of the ministry and the company was so much that it was not possible to converge and reconcile. Now, another question: how could the company continue the project for so long with the impression that it had complied with all the environment clearance norms? There are many such questions which need to be answered before taking up any such project. One must understand that even if clearance has been granted by the government, it can possibly be withdrawn with a new person in command, or change in circumstances.

Google in Germany; Privacy Issues (2013)

In April 2013, Google—a large company by any standards—was fined by the German privacy regulator, responsible for supervising data protection, a sum of €145,000 for collecting personal data without approval. Earlier, Google had collected data for its Street View around the world with the help of its fleet of automobiles by covering almost 8 million km in about 50 countries. While doing this exercise, Google had collected from Wi-Fi routers in Germany and elsewhere personal details of emails, photographs and other unencrypted data, which obviously was a breach of privacy of any person owning the data.

The Telegraph had reported:

> The data protection office in the northern city of Hamburg said it had imposed a 145,000-euro ($189,000) penalty on Google for privacy violations on what it called a nearly unprecedented scale.... 'In my opinion this case constitutes one of the biggest known data protection violations in history', said the office's chief, Johannes Caspar. The company, which cooperated with the probe, was also ordered to delete the data

immediately. Caspar complained that under German law his office was not able to impose a more painful penalty on a major multinational company, noting that the maximum fine for an accidental violation was 150,000 euros. Hamburg prosecutors had abandoned a criminal case against Google in November, when the data protection office picked it up as an administrative offence. It found that the company had inadvertently assembled the data, but noted this constituted 'a significant lapse of Google's internal control mechanisms'. ... Authorities in Germany, where privacy concerns are particularly sharp due to gross violations under the Nazi and communist dictatorships, had already imposed restrictions on Google after a protracted dispute over Street View.[5]

Google had taken the stand that the collection of entire personal data was inadvertently done and the company had no intention of using that data, or even having a look at that data. This was not the first time Google had faced the problem of breaching privacy and collecting data of personal kind. Last month, Google had settled a lawsuit filed by 38 US states and agreed to monitor its own employees in a strict manner so that the data collected from and about any person was given due respect, and was not used without proper authorisation and approval.

The company had also faced problems in France. In 2011, the French National Commission on Computing and Liberty had fined Google a sum of €100,000, which at best can be called to be a token sum. Ireland and Britain had been more magnanimous and did not impose any fine after Google apologised and undertook to delete the data collected illegally.

Such is the reach and impact of cutting-edge technology that in today's world it could be easily said that there is nothing like 'privacy'. The word 'privacy' can only be found in dictionaries, as law enforcing agencies watch helplessly companies violating the data protection laws with impunity.

For companies like Google, small sums of money like €100,000, or €145,000 are tiny droplets in a large ocean. Forget about global standards, even with Indian norms—with much lower per capita income as compared to the United States or European countries—the sum of €145,000, equivalent to less than $200,000, is about Rs. 1 crore (Indian Rupees 10 million), which may just let one buy an entry-level German luxury car in India.

The economic analysis of law very clearly states the purpose of imposition of any fine: there should be necessary deterrent effect with the quantum of fine imposed reaching to the threshold so that it really makes a dent in the account books and reputation of the company; or a token amount as a fine must produce the required impact in the form of remorse and an overwhelming sense of wrongdoing, accompanied by an unsaid statement—or at times stated clearly—that the act for which the fine has been imposed would never be repeated. In the case of Google, nothing of the two is evident.

The regulator has expressed in clear terms that the quantum of fine levied is insufficient and woefully inadequate to stop any of the large companies, or for that

---

[5]Germany fines Google for "unprecedented" privacy violations; The Telegraph; April 22, 2013; http://www.telegraph.co.uk/technology/google/10010228/Germany-fines-Google-for-unprecedented-privacy-violations.html, last accessed September 14, 2016.

matter, even small companies, to take the law regarding data protection seriously. It has been argued by regulators all over the world that the fines must increase, so that the companies at fault really feel the pinch, and it has been suggested that the fines can go up to 2 % of a company's annual sales, which in the case of Google would be about $1 billion, based on its last year's revenue.

There has not been much unanimity in the European Union as the British government is in favour of a light touch regulatory regime—following the well-known principle that 'the least governed is the best governed' and the Thatcherite policy on regulation that 'every regulation is a restriction of liberty'— whereas Germany and France, along with other continental governments, favour strict regulatory control. It would be extremely difficult, as is being foreseen, that members of the European Parliament may not see eye to eye on this issue and any enhancement in the fines to be imposed, which is in fact a national law and can be done by the national legislatures, however, for that to be done at the national level, agreement in principle is necessary at the EU level.

Google has also been in trouble regarding privacy issues in the Netherlands and Spain. In December 2014, the Dutch watchdog had threatened with a fine of €15 million, if it did not stop violating privacy of internet users.

A question arises about the efficacy of different policies being followed by different countries in the EU. Broad understanding and unanimity will surely help in achieving the goal of protecting privacy of the people of each country as well as foreigners visiting these countries. The role of government vis-à-vis humongous companies like Google is being tested.

What should the top leadership in Google do—meekly agree and comply; fight it out till the last drop of blood; try to circumvent the law; lobby with the lawmakers to mould the law to its own interest; use its deep pockets to achieve the desired result; take the moral high ground, etc.? There are many options. It depends on the top management to find a way out keeping the bigger picture in mind.

Australia: Adani and Coal Mines (2015)

In August 2015, the Federal Court in Australia had cancelled the permission granted by the Federal Government to Adani, an Indian company, for the biggest coal project Carmichael in Australia citing possibility of extinction of two species of reptile and snake.

Court's action could not be termed as shocking or unprecedented as Australia follows the same 'Common Law' which India does and judicial review is very well accepted as the norm. Though England believed in the supremacy of the parliament and judicial review of legislative actions was unheard of earlier, yet of late there has been acceptance to the review of even legislative actions on the grounds of public interest and welfare of the people. Judicial review of executive and administrative decisions has never been debated and with the same legacy, Australia, as well as India, lives with the supremacy of judiciary, though there are checks and balances between the three organs of State—legislature, executive and judiciary.

Thus, legally speaking, the courts were well within their rights to decide in this manner. It is, according to the constitution, not only a right, but a duty, to safeguard the interests of the people of the country as the *sentinel on the qui vive*. Hence, for even the uninitiated in the legal fraternity, the court's decision did not come as a surprise.

However, what was surprising was the reaction of the then Australian Prime Minster, Tony Abbott. He had termed the decision as 'sabotaging' and expressed his feelings of being 'frustrated'. The Guardian reported:

> Tony Abbott has reaffirmed his support for the huge Adani coalmine in central Queensland, arguing Australia has "a problem as a nation" if the courts could "be turned into a means of sabotaging" such projects. The prime minister warned against becoming "a nation of naysayers"...[6]

He had mentioned that the delay in the coal project would have meant loss of lots of jobs to Australians in Australia and a large number of people in India would have to continue living without electricity. He had even made an emotional statement of asking the Australian people and judges as to how did it feel in today's modern world to live without electricity? A lot of Indians would have been denied of the right to get clean and cheap power because of this court decision.

As luck would have it, in a month's time, Abbott was voted out of power and a new government under the leadership of Malcolm Turnbull came to power. The Environment Minister Greg Hunt gave new permission to the coal mine to proceed with the 'the strictest conditions in Australian history'.[7] It was again challenged by environment groups in the court, but this time the court dismissed it and allowed the project to go on but with highly tightened environmental conditions.[8] This has been a big victory for the Indian company along with the Australian government. The success in courts has, however, been bitter-sweet for Adani, as it has to comply with some of the toughest environmental protection norms. The balance between the judiciary—government—business has been restored with changing times and needs of the society.

---

[6]Abbott warns against courts "sabotaging" projects such as Carmichael coalmine; The Guardian; August 7, 2015; http://www.theguardian.com/environment/2015/aug/07/abbott-warns-against-courts-sabotaging-projects-such-as-carmichael-coalmine, last accessed September 14, 2016.

[7]Adani Carmichael: Australia's largest coal mine free to proceed after Greg Hunt gives approval; The Sydney Morning Herald; October 16, 2015; http://www.smh.com.au/federal-politics/political-news/adani-carmichael-australias-largest-coal-mine-to-proceed-after-greg-hunt-gives-approval-20151015-gk9wof.html, last accessed September 14, 2016.

[8]Queensland court dismisses green group's challenge to Adani coalmine; The Guardian; December 15, 2015; http://www.theguardian.com/environment/2015/dec/15/queensland-court-dismisses-green-groups-challenge-to-adani-coalmine, last accessed September 14, 2016.

The Economic Times in India had reported:

> The project has been in the centre of controversies since the start with environmentalists warning of severe damage to the Great Barrier Reef but in August it faced its biggest jolt after a federal court in Sydney revoked the environmental clearance given to the project citing that the project threatened the Yakka skink, Australia's native lizard and a species of ornamental snake found in the area. This decision was later reversed by the Australian government which gave it a green nod but imposed more conditions relating to community issues and environmental standards. Adani Group has suspended work at the mining project due to delay in approvals amid local protests.[9]

A few questions deserve honest answers:

How far did the Australian PM's commitment to the project go? Why was he going out of the way to express his frustration? Why was he so much concerned about the people in India? What should have been paramount for the Australian courts—interest of Australia or India? There were several other questions which asked about the relationship of the business and political interests, both in India and Australia.

This can easily be said to be over-reaction of the Prime Minister and an effort to tilt the power balance in favour of the executive. It cannot be accepted in any country committed to the rule of law with powers of judicial review vested in courts, whether it's India or Australia. The coal project was in trouble as neither the Australian government nor the company had gone to the court with 'clean hands'. Legal remedies were available for both. Irresponsible utterances by anyone in the government and the business organisations speak a lot about the business environment in any jurisdiction.

The relationship between the Australian government and the company appear to be too cosy for the comfort of the Australian people and that's why the judiciary had to intervene. The Australian PM need not have used the situation of people in India without electricity to his advantage. It was a lame excuse and surely would not have cut any ice with a seasoned judge.

The best route which could have been taken by the company was to comply with the legal requirements and honour the decision of the court. And, of course, the Australian government also should have thought more about honouring the decision of its own courts rather than providing electricity to the people in India.

It is interesting to note that environment requirements are being taken very seriously by the governments in the first world countries and if the government shows any slackness, courts in countries with highly evolved judicial systems put the things back on track. The doctrine of judicial review ensures that governments do not work in favour of businesses unbridled.

---

[9]Australia clears Adani's Abbot Point coal terminal expansion plan; The Economic Times; December 23, 2015; http://articles.economictimes.indiatimes.com/2015-12-23/news/69261351_1_gautam-adani-adani-group-queensland-government, last accessed September 14, 2016.

Royal Dutch Shell in Russia (2006)

The famous petroleum company Royal Dutch Shell, along with its Japanese partners, Mitsui and Mitsubishi, had invested a lot of money in Russia's Sakhalin Island for oil and gas exploration. The company had faced a number of problems including environmental issues and government intervention. The company's projected cost had doubled to $20 million. In 1990s, when Russia had invited the foreign oil companies to invest in its oil and gas exploration, the country had been extremely generous and needed the cutting-edge technology in its oil-rich but frozen seas.

The company had signed in 1990s a production sharing agreement (PSA) with conditions perceived as unfairly generous by Russians. State-owned Gazprom had already started negotiations for controlling a stake, however, delay in the completion of project was not taken kindly, both by the Russian government and the people. With the passage of time Royal Dutch Shell, along with its partners, and other companies had brought in the latest in technology by putting in a lot of time, effort and money to make the entire exercise financially viable. Finally, in 2006, it was time to reap the fruit of its labour. At that moment, when the company was just looking forward to profits, the Russian government, led by Vladimir Putin as president, told the company in unambiguous terms that it would not be possible for Shell to continue in that manner, and majority stake would be taken over by Gazprom. It was a big blow for Shell and its Japanese partners. But, there was hardly anything they could do.

As per an old KGB adage, ,give me the man, and I'll find you the crime,, the Russian government was able to find minor environment lapses on the part of Shell. The sea around Sakhalin Island is frozen for half the year. A rare whale is found in this frozen sea. Offshore drilling rigs would have disturbed the environmental position as the pipelines delivering oil and gas would have to cross more than 1000 rivers and streams. The environmental regulators in Russia complained about this and took the unprecedented step of cancelling the environmental license of Royal Dutch Shell. The consortium, including the Japanese companies, faced the prospect of criminal action. This was a bit too much for Royal Dutch Shell and it felt that it was better for the company to succumb to the wishes of Vladimir Putin and sell its stake to Gazprom, rather than fight for it in a legal forum.

It was not for the first time that Russia had flexed its muscles. It had done the same earlier with its neighbours and tried to establish itself in the role of indispensable and not-to-be-taken-for-granted Big Brother. Royal Dutch Shell nursed its wounds for some time, but such is the allurement for the profits to be made by abundant oil and gas that it was back in Russia to do business in a short period of time, despite Putin being in true control of the country, whether as the President or the Prime Minister.

France: Arcelormittal Steel (2012)

ArcelorMittal Steel, with Lakshmi Niwas Mittal as the CEO, is the largest steel-making company in the world. Mittal had humble beginnings in India and rose to such position of eminence by following a model of business where he would buy sick steel mills and using his business acumen and expertise make them take a U-turn and start making profits. He followed this model in a number of countries in the world and in the process became one of the wealthiest persons in the world. He likes good living and in 2004 bought one of the mansions in London, which at that time was the most expensive house in the world. He owns several other mansions in different parts of the world.

He has business interests in France also and faced serious trouble in November–December 2012. The French government, under the new leadership of Francois Hollande, was wary of unions and protests by workers. As the going has not been good for Mittal's steel company in France, the company had decided not to operate certain blast furnaces and also reduce its workforce. Earlier, interestingly, Mittal had made a promise of investing several hundred million dollars over a period of time, however, for certain reasons, he did not keep his promise. Regarding the closure of blast furnaces and trimming workforces, there was tremendous upheaval among the workforces which, later on, turned political in nature.

French ecology Minister Delphine Batho expressed that the government had no confidence in what Mittal had said and that the government would have left no stone unturned to arm twist Mittal to make him honour his words. Arnaud Montebourg, the industrial renewal Minister, had threatened the company with nationalisation. This is quite natural as political stability depends on the sentiments of the people and in France workers' unions are quite strong. The union leaders had expressed their fears and apprehensions of Mittal closing down certain businesses that would have led to a large number of people being thrown out of the jobs. The government had no option left but to force Mittal not to take this drastic step, which otherwise might have been important for his company for long-term business and strategic reasons.

Within a few days the meeting was arranged between Mittal and the French government, and the government's view prevailed. Such is the power of the government of the day in any country that it becomes next to impossible to do business by antagonising the government. And, in a democratic country, it is imperative for the government to keep the people happy, as any government would always like to be re-elected. It is quite obvious that no government could dream of coming back to power again by displeasing the voters. The French government is no exception, and, Mittal is no novice. He, as a true business leader, must have anticipated the opposition by the workers and the government to company's plans.

Immediately thereafter, union leaders and certain political leaders voiced their concern that the government did nothing precious to safeguard workers' interests, and Mittal would have done very much the same even if the agreement had not been reached between Mittal and the government.

'Kill Mittal' Computer Game

Despite the reconciliatory moves by Mittal, such was the anger among the people at the receiving end that a computer game 'Kill Mittal' was made.

It is good to vent out anger, otherwise, it can cause a lot of psychological damage to an individual and, if the grouse is common to a large number of people, to the entire group, resulting in a perceptible adverse impact on society. But, there are a number of ways and means of doing that, and, obviously, all are not acceptable as per societal norms. These norms vary from society to society, and primarily depend on the limits of tolerance of the individuals, and are also undeniably regulated and controlled by the law of the land.

In 2013 summer, a new computer game—Kill Mittal—developed by an independent French video game maker, living at that time in Belgium, became available online and it could be downloaded for free. Mittal in this game was the steel magnate Lakshmi Mittal, the Chairman of the steel giant ArcelorMittal. Anyone playing this computer game was supposed to kill Mittal, a giant robot, to keep the steel mill open. The context of this game came from the decision made by Mittal to restructure his steel mill business in France.

Disgruntled French steelworkers had protested for several months against the closure of steel blast furnaces in Florange, France. Despite the intervention of the government and strong stand taken by the workers' union, Mittal went ahead. Earlier, he had promised that restructuring and modernisation of steel mills in France for ArcelorMittal would not result in job losses, however, it was not at all possible to do both the things at the same time—modernise and restructure, and also keep all the workers with their jobs intact and all the employment benefits coming along with that.

Often this is a very difficult decision for any top management in a company to be made and implemented, and, in some of the popular democratic societies, the decision-making requires a lot of courage to deal not only with the workers' union, a loosely formed informal association of persons not permanently employed, but on a contractual basis. The company might have to negotiate in one of the toughest manners with the local government and at times with the federal government also. As most of the politicians are looking for re-election, and would never like to displease the large number of voters, and that too in a manner which may exhibit apathy and indifference to loss of jobs, most of the politicians in these positions are compelled to oppose any such restructuring and modernisation, if that results in job losses. There is a direct correlation between job losses and the number of votes lost, and therefore, Mittal also faced a very tough French government. But, Mittal stood firm.

As it is obvious, the growth and development, and at times even sustainability and survival, of a company depend on changing with the times, it becomes incumbent on the top leadership to foresee and anticipate, and make the decisions so that the company remains fit for the future. It is extremely difficult for companies to guarantee the continuity of a job in difficult times; such times when global demand is extremely low and the world economy has been hit by recession; no company—except the public sector and the government—can continue to conduct itself in the manner as it has been being doing earlier, without responding to the changed business environment, until and unless it's on a suicidal mission. Mittal, clearly, was not on any such mission.

It was a matter of serious concern that an extremely revolting, sickening and distasteful computer game had been prepared and made available online. Free speech and expression, natural corollaries of it, and extrapolation and development of any such idea, are important for evolution of mankind and development of any society, however, there are limits, which need not be transgressed, and until and unless, there is a clear cut limit defined by law, it depends on each and every individual to draw the line.

It was also vital for companies to understand that whenever any such restructuring and modernisation process has to be undertaken, all the stakeholders, particularly the workers, have to be taken into confidence, so that the entire process can be done in a smooth manner. It might not be possible to do such an exercise flawlessly and without ruffling any feathers, but efforts have to be made. Even in routine operations, it is desirable that the top and senior management creates a good understanding and rapport with the workers, so that the work is completed in a perfect manner, as envisaged. The slightest of dispute may lead to discontentment and disruption of the work as Honda, the Japanese company, learnt it the hard way in Gurgaon, and Maruti in Manesar, around the same time.

It requires tremendous negotiation skills to persuade the other party to agree to. Whatever may be the scenario, being frank helps, and communicating the true and the real picture, howsoever disturbing and unpleasant it may be, very often makes the other party look at the entire scenario in a much more realistic and acceptable manner. The sequence of events in Florange, France, leading to the development of Kill Mittal computer game, tells us that the top management in the company failed to anticipate such developments, and even if it had anticipated them, it did not take adequate measures to arrest the fast spreading discontentment and feeling of hatred. But, that did not give any credibility and acceptance to the computer game. It was heavily condemned.

Takeaway for Business Leaders

Dealing with the government in any country is not a child's play. One of the critical issues is of the certainty of the government decisions and the certainty of the continuity of government policies. These are most uncertain. A business leader cannot take a government's stand as perpetual and should not formulate business strategy with that assumption. With change in governments in democratic countries, there is often a change in the policy. Also, in monarchies, the thought process of the monarch may change anytime. Hence, how the government is going to function can at best be anticipated.

For a business leader doing business in a democratic country, keeping the ear to the ground to know the mood of the people of the country is of utmost importance. That way he can gauge the feelings and be able to anticipate the future of the government in the next elections. Also, if there a possibility of a mid-term election can best be answered by being close to the masses and powerful and well-connected persons. In a monarchy, the business leader may remain somehow close to the palace intrigues and keep himself well informed. But, closeness to the palace in any kingdom is a double-edged sword. He needs to be cautious enough not to be so close that he catches the attention of the mighty and powerful and is seen as a players in the machinations himself. Such moves need deftness and extreme caution. Along with these qualities, he must be ready to change the course of business in a jiffy, as the monarchs and dictators do change the legal environment for doing business faster than the eye blinks.

Creating practical, realistic and doable options is the key. For this, a business leader may have to develop relationships with a number of persons he may not be comfortable with, but for the sake of the business he has to do it. Everything cannot be in writing and he must understand the importance of the unwritten communication, specially in monarchies. The business leader must have absolute clarity about the outermost periphery to which he may go to save the business and himself. With tact, he should be able to communicate the same—whether orally or in writing —to the government of the day.

Chapter 3
How Do I Align Legal and Business Strategy?

Long ago in 1946, an article was published in the Harvard Business Review which emphasised on the relationship between law and business. In this article titled 'The Supreme Court and Business Planning',[1] the author, Arthur Ballantine, wrote very clearly about the relationship of the US Supreme Court and business at that time. The article mentioned that business leaders have to be prudent and wise enough to anticipate the manner in which the Supreme Court was functioning and the way it might change its course. Thus it was important for business leaders to anticipate the trends in the US Supreme Court particularly related to business decisions, so that they could formulate their business strategy in tune with the likely trend. The same is true today.

As forewarned is forearmed, business leaders have to be smart enough to think in a proper manner about the way the legal environment is projected to change. That helps them to make the most of such change. Not only this, these business leaders could even play a role in preparing the right legal environment for their business. This is so common by way of lobbying for favourable laws and government policies. It means being very close to the people who matter—both legislature as well as the executive. It is also important to have a favourable impact on the judiciary by being on the right side of the law and in case one has to be tested by the courts, one must go with 'clean hands', a metaphor for going with clear conscience and without guilt.

In the American context, it has been observed that favourable laws have been made by the legislature for business, or to say in other words, the legislature has often refrained from making unfavourable laws for business. Examples are oil and gas, automobile, banking, consultancy, weapons, gambling, protectionism for local people, bailing out sick and almost dying companies, etc. The government for sure has been quite in favour of giving a lot of protection and help to domestic businesses in the US. The years of economic melt-down in 2008 and later saw a

---

[1]The Supreme Court and Business Planning, by Ballantine, Arthur A., Harvard Business Review; Winter 1946, Vol. 24 Issue 2, p151–163, 13p.

© The Author(s) 2017   37
A.K. Agarwal, *Business Leadership and Law*, DOI 10.1007/978-81-322-3682-5_3

dramatic shift from the famous American capitalism to almost socialism with the government doling out money to so many companies—insurance, banks and automobiles were just a few of those sectors which benefited from the benevolent treatment given by the government. Several matters were challenged in different courts, however, government support was usually upheld by the courts in the larger public interest.

Thus, it is not surprising that the effect has rubbed off on the judiciary. Per se, there is nothing wrong in it. The courts do not work in a vacuum. Law is dynamic and interpretation of law is according to the changing needs of a society. It is, rather, the duty of the courts to be in tune with the society and its problems. It would be impractical and undesirable that courts work in a theoretical and bookish manner without taking the ground realities into consideration. Thus it is important that business companies are given a fair and equal treatment and are also given an opportunity to make profits in a legal and proper manner. But there needs to be a balance between the business interests and the interest of the society. All over the world, the courts have often changed their stance regarding business with the passage of time and the more successful businesses have been able to either anticipate such changes or were able to align to such a change with great speed and alacrity. Even when the judicial decisions have been unfavourable, some companies have been able to turn the tide in their favour by blending legal and business strategy. The war between Coca-Cola and Pepsi for the use of the word 'Cola' is one of them.

Coca-Cola and Pepsi: Early Times and the Word 'Cola'

The two rivals—Coke and Pepsi—have often fought fiercely in the market, however, their rivalry has also resulted in long legal battles. A little bit of background and their history will come handy while appreciating it.

Coca-Cola is one of the largest and most popular global companies headquartered in Atlanta, Georgia, and sells its products in almost all the countries of the world, including India. Coca-Cola was invented by pharmacist John Pemberton in 1886 as a digestive drink. Pemberton's secretary and book keeper, Frank Robinson, gave the name Coca-Cola to the drink and also wrote the name of the product in Spencerian script, a script common with book keepers of that time. Since that time Coca-Cola written in this script has remained one of the best known trademarks in the world. A few years later, Pemberton sold the formula and brand to Asa Candler, who incorporated The Coca-Cola Company in 1892.

Like Coca-Cola, Pepsi is also one of the largest and most popular global companies and its products are sold in almost all the countries in the world, including India. Caleb Bradham started making a digestive drink in his drugstore in North Carolina in 1893 and called it Brad's Drink. A few years later, as the popularity of the drink grew, he called it Pepsi-Cola, which was a name coined after the digestive enzyme pepsin and kola nuts used in the preparation of the drink. In 1902, he created the Pepsi-Cola Co, which was first incorporated in 1919 in the state of Delaware. During the time of the Great Depression in the United States, the company entered into bankruptcy in 1931 and Roy C. Megargel bought the assets of the company, including the trademark. He was unsuccessful in conducting the business and sold it to Charles Guth, President of a leading candy company, Loft Inc. In 1941, Loft absorbed Pepsi and rebranded it as The Pepsi-Cola Company. Today the company is known as PepsiCo, with headquarters in Purchase, New York.

The rivalry between Coca-Cola and Pepsi is well known all over the world. It started primarily when Charles Guth, who used to sell Coca-Cola through his chain of soda fountain shops, ended his contract with Coca-Cola due to a dispute regarding volume discount. Instead of selling Coca-Cola, Guth decided to buy the bankrupt cola company Pepsi and give it a new life. As luck would have it the sale of this drink—Pepsi—picked up to the extent that Coca-Cola could not ignore it, and was compelled to take note of it very seriously. Guth and his people were smart enough to sell Pepsi on several occasions to the customers, even when they had specifically asked for Coca-Cola. It was made possible, to a large extent, by Guth as he had worked very hard to make Pepsi taste as close as possible to Coca-Cola. Obviously, this did not amuse the Coca-Cola Company, and the management decided to take legal action against Guth and his company. Guth was not able to take this legal onslaught, largely due to very heavy costs involved and uncertainty accompanying the cost, and offered to sell his company to Coca-Cola in 1933 for a mere $50,000—small change for Coca-Cola even in those days. Coca-Cola rejected the offer.

To survive in the market Guth started selling almost double the quantity of normal bottle, 12 oz of Pepsi instead of 6.5 oz of Coke, at the same price. It did hurt Coke's sale. With the economy in bad shape due to the Great Depression, people in the United States were conscious of every penny they spent and hence this tactical move by Pepsi paid off very well. In a period of almost five years Pepsi became a serious competitor for Coke and ironically, Charles Guth was forced to step down in a legal battle with the top management of Loft, which owned the Pepsi brand. It was a few years later, in 1941, that the company was rebranded as the Pepsi-Cola Co.

Pepsi had tried to sell the drink in the market with taste as close as possible to that of Coca-Cola and also used the word cola in its name by calling its product as Pepsi-Cola. Looking for certain legal tools to defend itself and legal weapons to attack its competitor, Coca-Cola decided to sue Pepsi-Cola and any other company doing business with the name Cola, but primarily the target was Pepsi-Cola. Coca-Cola decided to use a multipronged strategy and implemented it by suing Pepsi-Cola in different courts in several jurisdictions. A number of courts decided that the word Cola was simply used to convey to the user that certain common beans and nuts, chiefly kola nuts from Cola genus, had been used to make the drink and the word Cola was, therefore, generic to be used by anyone, and any company in particular could not make a claim to the exclusive use of the word Cola.

The going for Coca-Cola was not very smooth in terms of legal march against its competitors as the word spread out at that time that the company had used illegal means to stop smaller players from selling in the market and using the term Cola. Moreover, there was evidence that the company had forced the small players to state that the word Cola could have been used only by the Coca-Cola Co. and that they claimed no right over the use of the word Cola. Instead of helping the company, this news worked as negative publicity for Coca-Cola and as would have been very obvious to the top management at that time, winning that legal battle against Pepsi became difficult day by day. Public perception was against Coke.

In the meantime, Coke lost one of the important matters in the Privy Council in 1942.[2]

In 1933, for whatever wisdom prevailed in the Coca-Cola Company at that time, the management did not buy Pepsi and prudently or foolishly—different thoughts and perspectives are possible—allowed it to survive, though in a very bad state. As it is said, one should win one's opponents once and for all, Coca-Cola must have regretted this decision for a very long time. Had Coca-Cola bought Pepsi at that time, in all probability, there would not have been any such major competitor for the Coca-Cola Company. But, that did not happen.

Post-Privy Council decision, understanding the realistic situation, the Coca-Cola Company decided not to pursue the legal battle further and settled the matter with Pepsi to salvage its reputation and image in the public. Earlier, Coke had thought that it would be possible for it to drain Pepsi in a long legal war, and Pepsi, on its own, would surrender. But, that did not happen. Pepsi did not surrender and kept fighting, however, it was not easy for Pepsi to fight the legal war as the company had to spend precious time, effort and money, and also to live with uncertainty. So, the turn of events provided a win-win situation for both the companies if they would have decided to settle the matter. After the decision of the Privy Council, the Coca-Cola Company and Pepsi-Cola Company agreed to end the litigation and settle all the matters pending in the United States and foreign countries regarding use of trademark rights. Pepsi had agreed not to use the word Cola.

It can be said that better sense had prevailed as both the companies had decided to end litigation and not waste their precious time, effort and money in avoidable court proceedings. Simply the legal decision did not help Pepsi. Also, Coca-Cola could finally have the upper hand despite losing the legal battle. Both the parties could have done the same without going through the rigmarole of litigation, however, in most of the instances parties are never willing to amicably negotiate. It is only after being drained out by long litigation that the penny drops for most of the business leaders.

But, legal decisions do matter in certain cases, where it is only with the decision of the highest court that finality is achieved. The following case about Walmart is one of such cases.

---

[2]The Coca-Cola Company of Canada Limited vs. Pepsi-Cola Company of Canada Limited (Appeal No. 14 of 1941), with Pepsi-Cola Company of Canada Limited versus The Coca-Cola Company of Canada Limited (Consolidated Appeals) (from the Supreme Court of Canada) [1942] UKPC 6 (19 March 1942); Privy Council.

Walmart Versus Betty Dukes,[3] (US Supreme Court, 2011)

This decision of the US Supreme Court, pronounced on June 20, 2011 regarding a class action suit related to one of the biggest retail giants, Walmart, is an illustration of a decision heavily in favour of business. A class action suit is a legal action taken by a large number of people with a common grievance. The matter was filed by Betty Dukes who was joined by large number of women employees of Walmart. They had claimed that Walmart had discriminated against women, and that there was disparity in pay and promotions. At that time, there were about 1.5 million current and former women employees at Walmart. They had sought backpay, punitive damages, injunction and declaratory relief. Their claim was based on the ground that Walmart had violated Title VII of the Civil Rights Act of 1964. In brief, it is as follows:

> Title VII of the Civil Rights Act of 1964 (Title VII) makes it unlawful to discriminate against someone on the basis of race, color, national origin, sex or religion. The Act also makes it unlawful to retaliate against a person because the person complained about discrimination, filed a charge of discrimination, or participated in an employment discrimination investigation or lawsuit. Title VII prohibits not only intentional discrimination, but also practices that have the effect of discriminating against individuals because of their race, color, national origin, religion, or sex.[4]

The District Court had certified the 'class', which was affirmed by the Ninth Circuit. Challenging this decision, Walmart had appealed in the Supreme Court.

The Supreme Court found by 5-4 (5 justices in majority and 4 dissenting; total of 9 justices) that there was hardly anything in common in the litigants except their gender and the lawsuit. This was the reason that the Supreme Court did not consider it to be a class action suit.

In a democratic set up with a free, fair, independent and fearless judicial system, the courts have a definite impact on business. This is true for the United States of America as well as India, or any other country with free and independent judiciary. In the last several decades, there have been a number of decisions pronounced by the courts which had an impact on business. Sometimes the decisions are pro-business and sometimes pro-people.

Supreme Court's decision in this case was most surprising—also considering that it was by 5-4 majority—and shows very clearly that the Supreme Court was surely tilted towards the business. A couple of years ago, the US Supreme Court used to pay more attention to fundamental rights, gender issues, criminal law, law of torts, cases against well-known business companies, etc. The mood at that time was more towards political, social and personal rights rather than business issues.

---

[3]Wal-Mart Stores, Inc. v. Betty Dukes et al., (2011); US Supreme Court, No. 10-277; Argued: March 29, 2011; Decided: June 20, 2011; 564 US ___.

[4]The United States Department of Justice, Laws Enforced By The Employment Litigation Section, Title VII of the Civil Rights Act of 1964, http://www.justice.gov/crt/laws-enforced-employment-litgation-section, last accessed September 14, 2016.

There had been a dramatic change since Chief Justice Roberts took charge in 2005 at a remarkably young age of 50 and the judges had shown much more interest in taking up business cases. It is very different from the Indian system which has seen chief justices being appointed only towards the fag end of their career and they retire at an age of 65. The American Supreme Court does not prescribe any retirement age for judges. Thus, CJ Roberts is expected to be very much there for a long time.

The earlier trend was different. Millions of dollars were awarded as punitive damages against companies selling cigarettes, burgers, cars, tyres, coffee, etc. Gone are those days. There appears to be a balancing act. The companies are not heavily penalised in the name of public interest. Is it true that the U. S. Supreme Court does not seem to be bothered enough to espouse the cause of the common man? Not exactly true. But, that is the feeling a good number of lawyers and people have. At times the court does not give a very convincing reason, or gives a very convoluted and technically legal reason, which makes the general public a bit less confident about the working of judiciary. In certain cases, things move away from common sense and reasonableness.

For instance, the reasoning as mentioned above, about the commonality of gender and the issues in the law suit, is quite unconvincing. It is very difficult to understand and be convinced by the reasoning of the court that about 1.5 million women, who are either currently working or had worked in one organisation, do not form a group with common grievances. Rejection of a class action suit for about 1.5 million women workers may not be good for the society in the long run. The judicial pronouncement could have been a bit more balanced. But, for the company it is a legal victory and it used the legal strategy quite effectively. No doubt, it played the legal gamble, but it was possible for the company and its lawyers to sense the predominant mood of the court. Just swinging of one more justice from the majority side to the minority side could have made all the difference. After all, the issue at hand was not a mathematical problem with only one possible solution; any solution was possible by the application of the existing law to the facts.

At times, large businesses are at the receiving end of the changed political and legal scenario. Whenever it happens the business leaders have to use the legal tools available to fight it out. An interesting case has been the change in the law in Australia about packaging of cigarettes.

Australia: Tobacco Plain Packaging Act (2011)

There is no doubt that smoking is bad for health. Cigarette companies, in their zeal to sell more, have often used attractive packaging, with colourful patterns and designs on the cigarette packets. It would be wrong to say that all the smokers are attracted towards cigarettes because of attractive packaging, however, it is not untrue that there are a good number of people who are attracted to smoking because of such packaging.

In public interest, the Australian Government had decided not to allow cigarettes to be sold using such packaging to allow the people to have a free choice of smoking or not smoking, without the allurement of colourful packaging. The government could have, but did not ban tobacco. It, however, tried its best to make it unattractive. It was decided to pass legislation for packaging all cigarettes in a plain packet, without a logo of the company and only providing a small space for exhibiting the brand name. This law—Tobacco Plain Packaging Act 2011—was passed and according to this law cigarettes had to be sold in a dark brown packaging from December 1, 2012.

The decision was based on research, which earlier had found that one of the most unattractive colours for such a packaging was olive green. Unexpectedly, there were strong protests by farmers and traders of olives in Australia, and the government was forced to choose the colour dark brown, which, according to research, was also one of the least attractive colours.

This government action was in direct conflict with big names in cigarettes— Phillip Morris, British American Tobacco (BAT), Imperial Tobacco, etc. For many decades, these and similar other companies had invested millions of dollars in creating brands—names, logos, slogans, icons; positioning them in the highly competitive market, protecting intellectual property which included trademarks, copyright, packaging, designs, etc. Such a move by the Australian Government had clearly caused a lot of financial damage and damage to reputation of the cigarette companies.

What were the options for these companies?

The first and the simplest option was to abide by the government action without any resistance. Other options included resisting the change by defying the new law and be ready to face the music, or lobbying with the government to save as much as possible, or challenge it in the courts. The last option could only be exercised in countries which are committed to the rule of law and have a positive legal environment for business, otherwise the final result would be well known even before challenging.

These companies joined hands and challenged the new law in the Australia's highest court. After a fiercely contested legal battle, the Australian High Court[5] upheld the law in 2012 and agreed with the government that plain packaging would surely make smoking unglamorous, if not fully unattractive. It said:

> On 17-19 April this year the High Court heard challenges by several tobacco companies to the validity of the Tobacco Plain Packaging Act 2011 (Cth) ("the Act"). The plaintiffs sought to rely upon the restraint upon the legislative power of the Commonwealth Parliament found in s 51(xxxi) of the Constitution, which empowers the Parliament to make laws with respect to "the acquisition of property on just terms". The plaintiffs argued that some or all of the provisions of the Act were invalid because they were an acquisition of the

---

[5]JT International SA v Commonwealth of Australia, British American Tobacco Australasia Limited v The Commonwealth, [2012] HCA 43; Date of Order: 15 August 2012; Date of Publication of Reasons: 5 October 2012; S409/2011 & S389/2011; High Court of Australia; http://eresources.hcourt.gov.au/downloadPdf/2012/HCA/43, last accessed September 14, 2016.

plaintiffs' property otherwise than on just terms. At least a majority of the Court is of the opinion that the Act is not contrary to s 51(xxxi). Today the Court made orders accordingly. The Court will publish its reasons for decision at a later date.[6]

The cigarette companies besides public advocacy and media campaigns had taken the legal route of challenging in the Australian courts, where they had lost the case. Philip Morris International, in June 2011, used a provision in the Hong Kong—Australia Bilateral Investment Treaty (BIT) of 1993 and invoked arbitration. It sought permanent injunction on the new law and damages for loss of intellectual property valuation. In December 2015, the Arbitral Tribunal at the Permanent Court of Arbitration declined to hear the matter and held that it had no jurisdiction. However, the company insisted that it was not a defeat for the company as the tribunal decided on procedural issue and it would consider other legal options available. At that time The Guardian had reported:

> Philip Morris said it was reviewing the decision in detail to consider its next options, but sought to head off suggestions that other countries should follow suit. "There is nothing in today's outcome that addresses, let alone validates, plain packaging in Australia or anywhere else," said Marc Firestone, Philip Morris International senior vice president and general counsel. "It is regrettable that the outcome hinged entirely on a procedural issue that Australia chose to advocate instead of confronting head on the merits of whether plain packaging is legal or even works."[7]

The companies had lobbied with the governments of several countries and challenged the matter in the World Trade Organisation (WTO) Dispute Settlement Body. These countries were Ukraine, Honduras, Indonesia, Dominican Republic and Cuba. More than forty members of WTO had joined these disputes as third party. The basic argument was that by enacting the Tobacco Plain Packaging law, Australia had violated its obligations to WTO under the Agreement on Trade-Related Aspects of Intellectual Property Rights (TRIPs), the Agreement on Technical Barriers to Trade and the General Agreement on Tariffs and Trade 1994. A panel had been made to hear the five parties together according to the WTO norms.

With the contentious issue settled legally by the Australian High Court, the government also got an opportunity to use these packets for promoting its health care and cautionary messages regarding smoking. With such a law, the Australian Government had hit two birds with the same stone—made smoking unglamorous, and propagated healthcare messages—and additionally received appreciation from the World Health Organization (WHO) and several countries which were contemplating to bring a similar legislation.

---

[6]Order of the Court, August 15, 2012. Reasons published later on October 5, 2012, http://www.hcourt.gov.au/assets/publications/judgment-summaries/2012/projt-2012-08-15.pdf, last accessed September 14, 2016.

[7]Australia wins international legal battle with Philip Morris over plain packaging; The Guardian; December 18, 2015; http://www.theguardian.com/australia-news/2015/dec/18/australia-wins-international-legal-battle-with-philip-morris-over-plain-packaging, last accessed September 14, 2016.

But, the big question was—would it have helped in reducing the number of smokers? Experts had believed that expecting any dramatic results was unrealistic for the simple reason that smokers would have found it no different to buy their favourite brand. On the contrary, prior to change in the law, cigarette companies might have found it necessary to differentiate their products using colourful and attractive packaging to attract new smokers. Well-established companies, often with very deep pockets, would have found it simpler to do business as it became extremely difficult for a new company, or even an old company, to launch a new brand. Hence, the threat of a new entrant simply vanished. These companies might have, in all probability, saved some money, which they had previously been spending in differentiating their packaging.

After about four years of the law coming into force, there are contradictory claims. The Government, the WHO, nongovernment organisations (NGOs), health workers and advocates of cigarette ban have claimed huge success of the law enforcement by citing numbers of reduced smokers. On the other hand, cigarette companies have claimed that there was hardly any drop in the number of smokers and the law had totally failed.

Preponderance of laws like the plain packaging law in numerous jurisdictions often tends to serve as mere lip service to the uninitiated and hardly has any perceptible impact on the experienced. Business leaders use the enactment of such laws as incidents of being victimised in the real and brutal world full of several dangers and threats including guns, nuclear weapons, even extra sugar, fat and salt in food, etc. Business leaders need to be wary of these types of laws which usually blur the dividing line between law and ethics. Legal action along with formulation and implementation of sound business strategy is the only answer. However, it is quite certain that strict laws typically spur more creativity—in legal challenge, marketing and advertising, dealing with the government and public awareness campaigns.

Taking the legal recourse may not always result in victory, even if the courts decide in one's favour. There are interesting and implausible possibilities like the law being changed with retrospective effect. How can a business leader think and anticipate in such a business and legal environment? Vodafone faced such a situation in India.

Vodafone: Tax Issues in India

Vodafone—a British mobile company—had decided to enter the Indian telecom market in 2007. It had indirectly acquired through Vodafone International Holdings BV—a Dutch entity—the complete share capital in CGP—a company registered in the Cayman Islands, a tax haven—which controlled 67 % of an Indian company Hutchison Essar Limited, which was a joint venture between the Essar Group from India and the Hutchison group from Hong Kong. The JV, popularly and commonly called Hutch, was in the mobile telephony business for quite some time and was also doing quite well. The entire transaction between Hutchison and Vodafone was conducted in the Cayman Islands to ensure minimum tax liability on either of them. Vodafone paid about $11 billion for this deal. Not even a single penny was paid by any of the parties as capital gains tax in India. As per the taxation law of India applicable at that point of time, the parties—to the best of their understanding—had followed the law in letter, however it meant that even when the assets involved in the deal were located in India, they could have got away without paying any tax to the government of India.

The tax department in India issued a show-cause notice to Vodafone to explain as to why it did not deduct the capital gains tax while making the payment. If it did not do that, it was Vodafone's fault. And, for Vodafone's fault why should the government have suffered? In other words, Vodafone was asked to pay to the tax department. It was not a small sum of money. It was more than $1 billion and after adding penalty and interest, the sum was even more than $2.5 billion.

Finding itself cornered and left with no option, Vodafone decided to challenge this order in a proper judicial forum. It filed a petition in the Bombay High Court and to its shock the court held that as the assets were situated in India, the transaction would be deemed to be one of transfer of assets in India, and hence Vodafone was liable to pay.

Vodafone challenged the Bombay High Court order in the Supreme Court of India. The special leave petition—SLP—filed by Vodafone was admitted and the Supreme Court ordered Vodafone to deposit Rs. 2500 crores (about $500 million) and also provide a bank guarantee of Rs. 8500 crores (about $1.7 billion) before hearing the matter. The decision of the Supreme Court in this matter was pronounced on 20 January, 2012 in favour of Vodafone and *inter alia* it said:

> For the above reasons, we set aside the impugned judgment of the Bombay High Court dated 8.09.2010 in Writ Petition No. 1325 of 2010. Accordingly, the Civil Appeal stands allowed with no order as to costs. The Department is hereby directed to return the sum of Rs.2,500 crores, which came to be deposited by the appellant in terms of our interim order, with interest at the rate of 4 % per annum within two months from today. The interest shall be calculated from the date of withdrawal by the Department from the Registry of the Supreme Court up to the date of payment. The Registry is directed to return the Bank Guarantee given by the appellant within four weeks.[8]

The government of India was completely embarrassed. Though the government had lost the matter in the Supreme Court, it did not concede defeat. With all the might of a powerful government of a big, mighty and sovereign nation, the government of India made it clear in unequivocal terms that the fight had not ended. After some time, the government announced that it had decided to amend the relevant law retrospectively so as to plug any such loophole which might have provided an opportunity to Vodafone and other companies to circumvent the legal framework of tax department to avoid paying taxes. The government of India was

---

[8]Vodafone International Holdings BV versus Union of India and Another; Supreme Court of India; Bench: Chief Justice S.H. Kapadia, Justice K.S. Radhakrishnan, and Justice Swatanter Kumar; 20 January 2012; Civil Appeal No. 733 of 2012 (arising out of S.L.P. (C) No. 26529 of 2010); 2012 Indlaw SC 20.

emphasising that it was necessary to follow the law in the spirit—which would have obviously meant that the company should not intentionally avoid paying taxes—whereas the businesses, including Vodafone, were of the view that compliance of the law in letter was more than enough, and that was the only thing expected of them. The government was not convinced.

The law was amended retrospectively and thereafter a fresh demand notice was sent by the tax department to Vodafone. The company did not challenge the retrospective amendment in the court and had since been using diplomatic and political negotiations to settle the matter. It had also invoked arbitration under the Netherlands—India Bilateral Investment Promotion and Protection Agreement (BIPA), which is ongoing.

It appears to be ironical that the dispute which has already been decided by the highest court in the country—the Supreme Court—was raked up again by the Government in a blatant manner by changing the law retrospectively. Vodafone had already invoked international arbitration against the Government of India. It made legal sense. However, Vodafone might have also evaluated its business interests in India and its long-term goal of doing business in India. While formulating business strategy and making the next tactical move, Vodafone must have thought seriously about crossing swords with the government.

Even if the arbitration award in the ongoing proceedings goes in favour of Vodafone, there is no surety that the award will be executed without being dragged to a court of law. Typically, it has been observed that arbitration awards of heavy stakes are usually challenged and after meandering through the courts at different levels, the matter gets finally laid to rest at the Supreme Court. But, this case is different: it has already been to the Supreme Court and the matter has already been decided in favour of Vodafone. But, still the procedure of law has to be followed. And, that may prove to be tricky for the company.

Unsurprisingly, the Government of India while presenting the budget that year proposed to enact a law which would have allowed taxation on such mergers and acquisitions—as in the case of Vodafone and Hutch—and the application of the law was proposed to be with retrospective effect. Enactment of any law, which permits its application with retrospective effect, is not considered to be proper, though it is the prerogative of the lawmaking body and it can be done by the sovereign in the interest of the country and its people. However, the Finance Minister in 2016, Arun Jaitley, severely criticised the practise of retrospective tax laws in the context of Vodafone case and assured to the investors and businesses that India would not as far as possible resort to retrospective taxation. He said:

> Did the provisions of retrospective taxation help India or did they hurt India? My answer is very clear, they hurt India because at the end of the day we have not been able to collect those taxes and we scared investors away.[9]

---

[9]Retrospective tax law scared investors away, says Jaitley; Business Standard; January 2, 2016; http://www.business-standard.com/article/pti-stories/retrospective-tax-law-hurt-india-scared-away-investors-fm-116010200211_1.html, last accessed September 14, 2016.

The mood in the country among the political leadership and businesses was very much against retrospective taxation. Seeing the big picture and putting things in the right business perspective, it was expected that the Vodafone matter might in all probability be decided at a political and bureaucratic level. The law might have taken a back seat in this case, but this case became a hot potato and the business leaders could not get it resolved by the political masters and bureaucrats due to excessive coverage the issue had received in the media and also negative sentiments attached with it. They found the courts and other judicial forums as convenient safe harbours and stuck to the statement that their lips were sealed as the matter was *sub judice*. Vodafone, to a large extent, did not lose much as it continued doing business in India and also did not pay the tax—something akin to having your cake and eating it too.

Still, one question keeps troubling the curious watchers. Was such a turn of events beyond the comprehension of top leadership in Vodafone? A related question is: were they not able to anticipate such developments as retrospective taxation is not unique to India? Or, was this—as the events unfolded—the strategy the company had formulated? It is difficult to answer till the time the company itself admits, but one thing is sure: the legal recourse may not be helpful fully in all the situations even if one gets a decision in its favour from the highest court. There might not have been any fault on the part of the company as it planned its course of action according to the set rules of the game. Anticipating a change in the rules once the game has begun is also a part of the idea of aligning business and legal strategy.

There are business leaders who know very well, from the beginning, that their company is doing something wrong and illegal willingly. What can be the reason for formulating and implementing such a strategy? Simply answered, greed is the only reason. In such a situation, it becomes difficult, well-nigh impossible, to save the company from the long arms of law as Volkswagen had experienced in the United States because of its cheat device.

Volkswagen Emission Cheating (2015)

In September 2015, Volkswagen admitted to cheating on emission standards and using software for this purpose. The defeat device was able to lower emission during testing process to conform to the regulatory standards, whereas in real driving conditions the emission was as much as forty times more than that during testing conditions. This was for a good number of Volkswagen cars using programmed turbocharged direct injection (TDI) diesel engines. The engines emitted nitrogen oxide (NOx) in large quantities in real driving conditions, whereas during the mandatory testing, the emission was well within the set norms.

This software was used in more than 11 million cars all over the world and in more than half a million cars in the United States for almost 6 years. In September that year, the United States Environmental Protection Agency (EPA) sent a notice to Volkswagen under the Clean Air Act. EPA had acted on the findings of the

International Council on Clean Transportation (ICCT), which had researched on the discrepancies between emissions by European and US models of Volkswagen vehicles. The California Air Resources Board (CARB) was also instrumental in zeroing in on Volkswagen.

Initially Volkswagen did not admit the wrongdoing and insisted that the discrepancies resulted due to certain technical glitches. However, when the regulatory bodies confronted Volkswagen with conclusive data proving beyond doubt that it had cheated by using the diesel engine software to circumvent the US emissions tests and was also threatened with the withholding of approval for its new diesel models to be launched in 2016, the company had no choice but to admit.

Company's CEO, Prof. Dr. Martin Winterkorn made the following statement on September 20, 2015:

> ...The Board of Management at Volkswagen AG takes these findings very seriously. I personally am deeply sorry that we have broken the trust of our customers and the public. We will cooperate fully with the responsible agencies, with transparency and urgency, to clearly, openly, and completely establish all of the facts of this case. Volkswagen has ordered an external investigation of this matter...[10]

Initially, Winterkorn had refused to step down, however, with too much pressure from all quarters, he had buckled and resigned as CEO on September 23, 2015. Despite assurance of cooperating fully with the investigative agencies, Volkswagen refused to share documents related to emission scandal, citing confidentiality under the German law. Volkswagen had engaged the American law firm Jones Day for carrying out an independent external investigation. Earlier, the company had admitted that more than 11 million cars were involved and the company had earmarked more than $7 billion for taking the corrective measures after recalling the cars. It was also reported in the media that the top management in the company knew about the software and that it was illegal to use the software to comply with the regulatory norms only. But, the CEO denied it.

At the time of resigning from the CEO's position, Winterkorn made the following statement:

> I am shocked by the events of the past few days. Above all, I am stunned that misconduct on such a scale was possible in the Volkswagen Group. As CEO I accept responsibility for the irregularities that have been found in diesel engines and have therefore requested the Supervisory Board to agree on terminating my function as CEO of the Volkswagen Group. I am doing this in the interests of the company even though I am not aware of any wrong doing on my part....[11]

---

[10]Statement of Prof. Dr. Martin Winterkorn, CEO of Volkswagen AG; Wolfsburg, 2015-09-20; http://www.volkswagenag.com/content/vwcorp/info_center/en/news/2015/09/statement_ceo_of_volkswagen_ag.html; also reported in The Guardian, September 20, 2015, VW software scandal: chief apologises for breaking public trust; http://www.theguardian.com/business/2015/sep/20/vw-software-scandal-chief-apologises-for-breaking-public-trust, last accessed September 14, 2016.

[11]Statement by Prof. Dr. Winterkorn; Wolfsburg, 2015-09-23; http://www.volkswagenag.com/content/vwcorp/info_center/en/news/2015/09/Statement.html; also reported in FT, September 23,

Thereafter, Matthias Müller was appointed the CEO. At that time, he had said that winning back trust of people was his most urgent task and had also promised maximum transparency. But, during investigation in the United States, hardly any openness had been shown. Interestingly, Volkswagen as a company was known for its insular culture.

Two important questions arise: first, why did the top management at Volkswagen choose to turn a blind eye to cheating, and, second, did Winterkorn know about it?

Volkswagen is known for its marquee brands—Porsche, Audi, Bentley, Bugatti, Lamborghini, Škoda and several others. With such high end brands under its umbrella, what could have been the reason for Volkswagen to resort to cheating?

All these questions and several others can be answered by trying to understand as to how the minds of top leadership would have worked and what were the goals the company might have wished to achieve? Globally, environmental concerns had been voiced by several government and nongovernment organisations. It had been concluded that automobiles contributed to a substantial extent to global pollution, and, hence, it had been the effort of policy makers, regulators, manufacturers, users, etc. to reduce pollution. It was considered to be desirable that the top end car makers adopted stringent quality controls and pollution standards as pricing of their products was not so much an issue as compared to car companies manufacturing vehicles for use by masses.

From the perspective of *certainty*, Volkswagen top leadership had done its bit to move towards the certainty of having great sales figure, however, the only catch was that it was done in an unethical and illegal manner. For any business leader it is almost a certain route to be followed to prosecution and possibly jail. Will you like to take such a route? That is matter of individual discretion and until and unless greed is the primary guiding factor, any reasonable and prudent person will not take that path deliberately. Individuals in senior and top management positions must be extremely careful to avoid it even inadvertently.

Later in January 2016, Volkswagen stated in an American court that if it was not possible for it to fix the cars fitted with the cheat device, it would be ready to buy them back.[12] This can be said to be extremely unfortunate situation, which could have easily been *anticipated* by the business leaders in decision-making positions.

Did Volkswagen *create options* to handle any such crisis, even while planning to cheat its customers and the regulators? Surely, Volkswagen did that. The company had made conscious efforts to have the documentation complete yet secretive, and made the right moves with the help of its lawyers. Also, it had hedged its top business leaders as Winterkorn walked away with booty and no one had been even

(Footnote 11 continued)

2015; Volkswagen CEO's resignation statement in full; http://www.ft.com/fastft/2015/09/23/volkswagen-ceos-resignation-statement-full/, last accessed September 14, 2016.

[12]VW May Buy Back Cars That Can't Be Fixed; Time; Jan 29, 2016; http://time.com/4199544/volkswagen-emissions-scandal-buy-back/, last accessed September 14, 2016.

arrested. However, the company had not created any options to *manage* the prospective customers. Its sales plummeted throughout the world after the scandal and several diehard fans of Volkswagen sold their prized VW cars in anguish and anger, with a firm resolution never to own a VW model. The company fully failed in creating any options to pacify the customers.

Interestingly, the company later admitted to cheating its customers in the United States but not in Europe.[13] What could have been the reason for this admission? Could it be any different that it was caught with ample evidence in the United States and not in Europe? Was VW following and practising the 'Eleventh Commandment'—*thou shalt not get caught*—the popular novel by Jeffrey Archer? And, a natural corollary shall be that when caught, admit.

Another example of emission related matter—but this is about aircraft—was the tussle between the airlines in the US and the EU about stringent emission norms in the EU. These norms were denting the business of airlines in the US as their aircraft were not compliant with the strict EU norms.

Carbon Fees for Airlines in Europe and Crisis in America

It was decided that from 1 January, 2012 all carriers entering or leaving the airports in the European Union would have to reduce their emissions or pay a charge. The European Union had decided to implement strict environmental regulations so that companies were forced to work towards lesser gas emissions and thus could contribute positively and expressly to have a clean and green environment. It was and is known commonly that airline industry contributes a lot negatively to global warming and newer and better technology has always been required to be used for the new aircraft to reduce it. The impact of that decision was expected to be immense, particularly for all American carriers, which had not bothered much to take care of emission norms. The reason was simple: America itself used a lot of energy and it had not been in the normal psyche of Americans to be a bit more careful about using energy.

Thomas Friedman gave a good insight in his book 'Hot, Flat and Crowded', published in 2008. He wrote that in May 2001, when the then White House spokesman Ari Fleischer was asked, 'Does the President believe that, given the amount of energy Americans consume per capita—how much it exceeds any other citizens in any other country in the world—does the President believe we need to correct our lifestyles to address the energy problem?' Fleischer had responded, 'That's a big no. The President believes that it's an American way of life, and that it

---

[13]VW Admits Cheating in the US, but Not in Europe; New York Times; Jan 22, 2016, http://www.nytimes.com/2016/01/22/business/international/vw-admits-cheating-in-the-us-but-not-in-europe.html?_r=0, last accessed September 14, 2016.

should be the goal of policy makers to protect the American way of life. The American way of life is a blessed one'.

It is also widely known that Detroit—the automobile companies—and Texas— the oil industry—in the United States had consistently lobbied Congress against raising gasoline taxes, thus encouraging people to buy bigger cars—SUVs and Hummers. On the other hand, the European governments had imposed very high gasoline taxes and taxes on engine size. And, they kept on imposing these taxes, whereas Americans kept on asking for bigger and bigger cars. Friedman further wrote, 'Big Oil and Big Auto used their leverage in Washington to shape the market. So, people would ask for those cars that consume the most oil and earned their companies the most profits—and our Congress never got in the way. It was bought off'.

These were strong words indeed. But as the lifestyle of individuals can give an opportunity to others to wag their tongues, living style and preferences of a nation give other countries a golden opportunity to vent out their pent up feelings. Interestingly, when United States had reached the brink of financial collapse and debt-ceiling crisis in 2011—and was saved by a last minute legislative action of amending the law—the Russian Prime Minister at that time, Vladimir Putin could not conceal his disdain for the US and commented that America was a parasite on the global economy. He had further said 'they are living beyond their means and shifting a part of the weight of their problems to the world economy'.[14] Really, pearls of wisdom from Russia to the United States, which were not accepted and the US continued and continues to live according to the stated way of life.

Coming back to the issue of carbon fees for airlines, the battle between the United States and Europe had started, with legal options being explored. Other airlines in the world were also going to be affected a lot but the impact on American carriers was expected to be noteworthy, for the simple reason that traffic connecting the two sides of the Atlantic has always been enormous. The United States Airline industry had filed a law suit before the European Court of Justice, the European Union's highest court. The industry argued that the E.U. had no legal right to regulate the American carriers. The decision was against it.

Interestingly the Kyoto Protocol 1997 for reducing emissions was never ratified by the United States. European countries had accepted these norms as they had understood and appreciated the gravity of the situation. The emission of carbon dioxide from aircraft is one of the most serious reasons for warming the planet as these are released high in the atmosphere. This type of climate change is typically caused by human beings and can, to the possible extent, be easily corrected or controlled with a little bit of effort. Slight tightening of the belt is sure to mitigate the damage being done and give rich dividends in the near future. However, willingness is necessary. And, before willingness, acceptance of the reality is essential. There is still resistance by certain nations including the US to accept the

---

[14]Putin says US is 'parasite' on global economy, Reuters, Aug 1, 2011, http://www.reuters.com/ article/us-russia-putin-usa-idUSTRE77052R20110801, last accessed September 14, 2016.

plain facts. Political will is needed to make such hard decisions and in democratic countries where the government of the day is usually more interested and inclined to keep the population happy with a goal to get reelected, it is quite difficult to make these hard decisions.

Unsurprisingly, American companies and American government did not respond to the climate change international norms in a sincere and honest manner. Truly speaking, the companies do not give two hoots about energy conservation and innovating for better use of energy. When the Detroit leaders had gone to the then President-elect Obama for a bail out in 2008, they had used company's jets to fly, only to be told curtly that one does not travel in a jet with a begging bowl. Later the same chiefs had travelled in hybrid cars. Realising the gravity of the situation to a certain extent, American Airlines had bought more than 250 new aircraft from French company Airbus, as it found the aircraft to be better in terms of efficiency as compared to those manufactured by the American giant Boeing. It speaks volumes about the American way of life and concerns about energy conservation. Is it just lip service?

The energy crisis the world faces every now and then may be an opportunity and a blessing in disguise to introspect. These crises typically force the world leaders to channelise all their thoughts towards better use of renewable energy. Presently, with global oil prices touching the rock bottom, it may be difficult to think in that direction, however, energy situation in the world has always been very dynamic and it may change dramatically anytime.

The moral of the story with which we Indians are well-versed is: cut the coat according to the cloth. Also, stretch your arm no farther than the sleeve will reach. It is high time America and the rest of developed world appreciate it.

Takeaway for Business Leaders

1. Mastering the Art

    Mastering legal aspects of business requires leaders to dovetail the business strategy with the legal strategy. One good method to understand different legal strategic responses to a particular set of problem is to use the five forces model developed by Michael Porter.[15] It presents clearly the pressures faced by a business leader within any given industry. The model identifies five competitive forces, viz. potential entrants, substitutes, suppliers, buyers and rivals. The model helps us see competitive legal battles from the strategy perspective. At times, the forces compel the business leader to make hard decisions to survive in business or expand the business and it is at this time the competitive legal skills make the difference. Law determines the relationship of businesses with rivals,

---

[15]PORTER, MICHAEL E. 1980. Competitive Strategy: Techniques for Analyzing Industries and Competitors. The Free Press, New York.

suppliers and buyers. Also, using law, effective entry barriers can be created. Launch of substitutes can also be stopped or at least delayed by efficacious use of law.

Porter also talks about it as 'government policy' and its effect on the business environment. For small localised businesses, the provincial law is mainly the legal boundary, however, for multinational players, international business law along with domestic law of different countries where they do business creates the legal boundary. Interestingly, such a legal boundary is quite hazy and at times permeable. Big fish tend to easily move out of such boundaries and small fish get caught. It does not happen because of law favouring big fish but because of the fact that big fish know the contours of law very well and can avail the advice of the best lawyers. A business leader has to master the art of blending business strategy with legal strategy.

2. Natural law versus man-made law

   One interesting characteristic of business law, which is man-made, is that just like other man-made laws, it can also be changed, amended, modified or repealed. This unique feature provides the business leader an opportunity to strike at the law itself, instead of worrying about complying with it. Natural laws cannot be changed and businesses—leaders, engineers, researchers, etc.—have to find a way of tackling them. For instance, gravity and friction have to be overcome by scientific methods. One cannot escape from them. However, businesses can escape the clutches of law, either by arguing an interpretation of law which suits their business or by influencing the law makers to change the law. In some instances, businesses admit their mistakes, plead guilty, pay the fines and continue doing business. On other occasions, businesses may take the risk of not complying with the law. It depends on weighing the cost of non-compliance with fines and compliance. But, in all business matters, law cannot be ignored. A business leader must understand the fine distinction between the laws which have to be treated as gospel truth and the laws which can be tried to be modified. This is the least that is expected from a business leader. Any mistake in differentiating the two can pose new problems, which may be difficult or impossible to be resolved.

3. Legal Victory

   A business leader cannot afford to forget that victory in the business arena must be legal and through legal means. The ends do not justify the means. From the very beginning, businesses must comply with the law, rules, regulations, etc. both in letter and in spirit. It is a strategic decision to be made at the outset. There is nothing like almost total compliance. There is either compliance or no compliance. In jurisdictions with prevalence of 'rule of law', it becomes still more important to comply fully with the substantive and procedural law. With rising concern about corporate governance, businesses would do well to walk that extra mile to ensure compliance. A slight oversight or inadvertence may result in a lot of damage for the company both in terms of tangible—money and time—and intangible, which is reputation. Means are often more important than the ends. Thus, a business leader has to pay special attention to the means followed to achieve the desired ends. In most of the evolved jurisdictions, procedural law is equally important to substantive law, if not more.

4. The Human Element

Human beings make a company function. Though the company is a juristic person and is considered to be different from the persons who work for the company, the large number of frauds and scams has made it desirable for the courts to pierce the corporate veil and find out the real people who were behind the show. Every company should focus on the legal aspects of employer–employee relationship. Harassment of employees in any manner may prove to be very costly for a company. Social welfare legislation for the protection of employees is the norm in all progressive jurisdictions including India. This protection is generally for the blue collared workers and does not apply to leaders. However, the leaders get their protection from other general laws and the contract they sign with the company. A contract is signed by the parties voluntarily, but terms of the contract should be reasonable.

5. Certainty, Anticipate and Create Options

Strategy formulation is based on selected assumptions. The closer the assumptions to reality, the higher shall be the chances of effective implementation of the strategy. Selecting assumptions is thus the key for the success of business strategy. Usually, while formulating the strategy, the business leader and his team take the legal environment as constant. This itself is one of the most important assumptions as even a little change—for instance change in the rate of taxation—may have a cascading effect on the execution and final performance. Everything may get shattered. It may be a logical assumption in highly stable jurisdictions, both politically and legally, but in disturbed jurisdictions a business leader is expected to keep the turbulent state in mind while formulating strategy for business. For determining realistic assumptions about the legal position, a business leader must necessarily have the knowledge and good understanding of the legal environment, which includes various laws, legal institutions and key individuals involved in the entire process. With good understanding of the legal environment for doing business a business leader can with little effort anticipate what may happen in the future to a large extent quite well. He can very well come up with diverse scenarios, all of which are in the realm of possibility, and not mere hypothetical. This leads him to think about creating options for different scenarios he has anticipated. With good understanding of the entire matter, an astute business leader creates feasible and doable options. He is able to blend theory with practise and idealism with realism. That ability, primarily, makes his a successful business leader, who can command respect from various quarters.

Chapter 4
Can I Have a Role in Lawmaking?

Law, in general, makes business activities more certain. The legal system sets the rules of the game. Thus, it is essential that players follow the rules of the game otherwise there is no need to have the rules. Any reasonable and prudent business leader would like to be on the right side of the law and ensure that his business complies with the applicable laws. As law is not static, it becomes important to comply with the latest changes in law and be on the right side of the law. For instance, any change in the rate of excise duty or corporate tax has to be taken into account. The business leader is responsible for any lapse even if the taxation lawyer was negligent or lax. New judgments of different courts make new laws. Anson said, 'law is the last interpretation given by the last judge', hence, the business leader has to comply with the latest judge-made laws also. The public perception about laws also changes with time and the legislature is compelled to make new laws to fulfil public aspirations. Business leaders with sharp antennae are able to anticipate such changes and make relevant modifications in the working of the company in time so that the company is not caught unawares.

Is it possible for the businesses to have a say in rule making? Yes, it is possible. Rules of the game of business are not only made by the legislature but by the business leaders themselves. These are those rules which establish any company as the leader of the pack because of any reason—cost leadership, focus, differentiation, etc. Think about companies like Microsoft, Google, Facebook, Tesla, Apple, etc.,—many a time they all make rules for the competitors. Businesses do not operate in vacuum. There is a context which is a mix of social, cultural, economic, legal, political, and many other factors. There have been entrepreneurs like Gates, Edison, Bell, etc., who have worked with the strategy of making the rules for others. These are, in fact, business decisions with the hidden legal strategy.

For a moment, let us think about a business which is not in a position to make the rules for others because of its small size, inefficient working or use of dated technology. Market does not allow it to become the leader and call the shots. Can it still go ahead and make rules or get the rules made for others? The answer is "yes". Being on the right side of the law necessarily requires a company to do what the law

© The Author(s) 2017
A.K. Agarwal, *Business Leadership and Law*, DOI 10.1007/978-81-322-3682-5_4

says. However, if the company is in a position to get a new law made or the old law amended to suit its convenience, it is as good as setting the rules of the game which others are bound to follow. Lobbying is popular for this purpose. It is prevalent particularly in the U.S. and other western countries. It is being practised covertly in India also. For a number of businesses, lobbying is an essential part of the business plan. Any new law enacted within the four corners of the Constitution can overrule decisions of courts as well as decisions of regulatory bodies. With a stroke of the pen, the legislators can make new rules or change the existing rules. In India, after the judgment of the Supreme Court[1] making judicial review of any law made by the Parliament or State Legislative Assemblies, the ball is in judiciary's court. Still, lobbying shall remain one of the most widely used strategies to get the law made in one's favour.

Eastern Railroad and Truckers in Pennsylvania

Since the invention of the steam engine and start of Railways, long-distance transportation of heavy freight on land was preferred to be done by Railways as compared to animals. This dominance continued for a very long time till the arrival of trucks, using internal combustion engines, in the early twentieth century. Within a period of two decades businesses started preferring trucks to Railways for goods transportation.

The reasons were obvious: trucks provided the flexibility of routes, door-to-door service, and picking up a variety of consignments of different size and weight. On the other hand, railroads had to follow the rigidity of the pre-established routes, no option of door-to-door service, as the goods train would have carried the goods only up to the terminal and not to the customer's depot.

One more aspect was relevant: the capital investment for starting a railroad company was huge, as different railroad companies were competing with each other and often laying down separate rail lines with different widths, which made using some other rail track impossible, and, thereby, adding to the overall cost of the rail transport network. In comparison, the truck companies had the advantage of a smaller capital investment, and they had not to worry about constructing the road, which, in any case, could have been used by any truck company, unlike the restrictions in the rail network. Construction and maintenance of roads was simpler, as compared to laying down railway tracks. The same applied to the trucks as compared to the locomotives and rakes.

Despite the application of any and all management tools and skills prevalent at that time, and, coupled with tactical moves, railroad companies found it extremely difficult to compete with the truck companies. By the end of the Second World War,

---

[1]Supreme Court of India, 2007. I.R. Coelho (Dead) By Lrs v. State of Tamil Nadu and Others. Date of decision: January 11, 2007; 2007 (2) SCC 1: 2007 AIR(SC) 861.

controlling the long-distance transportation of heavy freight became a question of survival for the railroad companies. An association of the Presidents of a number of such railroad companies known as the 'Eastern Railroad Presidents Conference', in Pennsylvania, hired a public relations firm Carl Byoir and Associates to conduct a publicity campaign against the truckers, so as to persuade the Governor of Pennsylvania to veto a new law in the making known as 'Fair Truck Bill', which was aimed to permit truckers carry heavy loads in Pennsylvania.

The PR firm started a publicity campaign against the truck companies by focusing on the damage to the roads caused by heavy and especially overweight trucks. In addition, these trucks were held responsible as heavy and fast moving hazards on the roads, creating a sense of fear among the people, causing enormous damage to the roads, and at the same time, not paying their fair share of the cost of constructing, maintaining, and repairing the roads, as taxes. The arguments made sense with the public. To hammer the point well, the PR firm used a technique known as the third-party technique which used the so-called independent and neutral participants in a survey giving their spontaneous comments, though these were, as later accepted by the firm, well-rehearsed and properly tutored.

The truck companies, in a collective effort, moved the concerned courts under the provisions of the Sherman act, the anti-trust law in the United States, making the allegation that the railroad companies where using anti-competitive practices in restraint of trade, and hence, the courts must injunct the railroad companies from continuing with such practices. Though in the lower courts, the truck companies got what they had prayed for, yet when the matter reached the Supreme Court, it did not finally agree and reversed the lower courts' orders.

The US Supreme Court emphasised that in a representative democracy, the legislature and the executive take actions on behalf of the people, and the fundamental premise of a democratic form of government would be violated in case the people of the country are not able to make their wishes known to the representatives. The court held that the railroad companies were simply trying to convey their wishes to the representatives of the people so that there is no barrier as far as communication is concerned between them, and, hence, there was no violation of competition law.

As far as using the third-party technique was concerned, the district court had held that it was characterised by deception of the public, manufacture of bogus sources of references and distortion of public sources of information. According to the Supreme Court, indeed, it fell short of the ethical standards generally approved in the US, however, such a technique in a publicity campaign was merely designed to influence the governmental action, and it would have been legally unacceptable to hold it in violation of the Sherman Act. This law, in the United States, typically, would apply to business practices, and not political practices.

The case record showed that the truckers also had resorted to lobbying and had written to and made personal contacts with legislators in support of bills increasing the weight of trucks, and also had representatives of other industries write to and made personal contacts with legislators, without disclosing their trucker connections.

Interestingly, the court also held that in any such case of publicity campaign, particularly in which both sides are involved in mudslinging, incidental damage to the reputation and business of any one party was inevitable, though, cannot be the direct consequence of the campaign. It would be impractical and imprudent on the part of the courts not to allow, in a legal manner, any such publicity campaigns, just to prevent any incidental damage. It is a part of the business game, and both the parties understand this quite well.

Lobbying, or in simple words, putting across one's views to other persons, especially elected representatives of the people, has been provided legal safeguard in the United States, and has been upheld by the US Supreme Court, even if the parties had indulged in a little bit of deception and overstatement, and even fabricated statements expressing views of the supposedly neutral and independent persons. The case was decided by the US Supreme Court in 1961 and is cited as: Eastern Railroad Presidents Conference v. Noerr Motor Freight, 365 US 127 (1961).

Poor understanding of the government and the real lawmaking process in different countries may be tricky for multinational companies doing business in several jurisdictions; many of them may not be fully committed to the rule of law. Lack of transparency in the system and lack of clarity on the part of business leaders may make them suffer. GSK in China is an apt example.

GSK in China: Ineffective Lobbying

In September 2014, one of the courts in China imposed a penalty of roughly $500 million on the pharmaceutical British giant GlaxoSmithKline (GSK) for its alleged unhealthy business practices relating to corruption and bribery for enhancing sale of its products in China. This happened despite the best efforts made by GSK to lobby with the government and the health officials. This was not at all surprising. Almost all the major pharmaceutical companies have been fined in the United States and several other countries in Europe for indulging in corrupt practices, however, it was notable that a pharmaceutical giant had been fined to such an extent for the first time in China.

Legal experts and other consultants had been raising serious concerns, in the recent past, about the rising nationalist tendencies in China and the Chinese government being pro-protectionist to the National companies. Most of them are owned and controlled by the Chinese government. According to them, foreign companies, particularly big multinational corporations, were being targeted by raising the bar for objective and subjective legal standards to levels which hitherto were unknown and never expected, and interpreting the existing law in a manner which ensured unending problems for the foreign companies. It is a matter of serious concern for a large number of multinational companies from different countries doing business in China, and also for those companies in other countries which are looking forward to entering into the Chinese market, primarily due to the highly attractive 1.4 billion population. Even a thin slice of such market can provide such lucrative business that a good number of European companies are willing to do business in China despite all the odds in the shape of unfavourable legal and government regime, as even a thin slice of market share may be much bigger than the entire population of the home country; the same applies to good number of other companies from different countries also.

However, for this foray in China to happen successfully, it is important that the powers to be in the country be convinced in the language they understand—the language of profit making and self-gratification. Lobbying with officials in China is very different from that in the truly democratic countries where "voice of the people" matters. In China, there is hardly any voice of the people and this is understood quite late by the lobbyists who are used to the practise in the western world. In this entire process which has seen Internet giants like Google leave the country because of the issues of privacy and confidentiality, coming back after a short period of time, and also Australian mining giant Rio Tinto being penalised for bribery and corruption, and also violating the legal provisions for trade secrets and confidential information sometime around 2010 making statements that they would like to continue doing business in China despite four senior officers being awarded punishment regarded by the Australian government as extremely tough by any measure.

Such incidents speak lowly about the status of the rule of law in China. Natural justice, often, takes a back seat during investigations and prosecutions in China. The right of opportunity of being heard is typically violated by not providing adequate opportunity and time to the other party to present its case. The entire exercise of casting an allegation, investigation and finally enforcing the punishment is done in quite an opaque manner which leaves much to be desired and the speed with which the courts make the decision may appear as if the courts are competing with the fastest microprocessors. Lobbying usually takes a back seat as prudence and reasonableness are casualties in hard decision-making by the government.

Compare this with the Indian scenario. The courts may be extremely slow, however, there is hardly any comparison between the status of the rule of law in China and India. The three-tier system of the courts in India—with all its inefficiencies, noises of corruption, and of late complaints of incompetence at all levels, intellectual dishonesty and rampant nepotism—still works and delivers. There is faith in the judicial system in India, even if the reason may be the unflattering reason for the people of not having any other better option. One thing is certain: the two companies which we have talked about in China—GSK and Rio Tinto—would have never agreed meekly for a similar case in India. Moreover, there might not have been any need to even start legal proceedings as there have been is a greater possibility of the entire matter being negotiated and settled at the level of political masters and bureaucrats by lobbying effectively. Most of the companies all over the world find the vibrant Indian democratic system, with a much better mechanism of the rule of law providing greater access to judicial forums at all levels, much more comforting and transparent, however, China still is able to attract them, purely for business reasons.

The moral of the story is thus, for business leaders, business is the priority, and legal environment—whether fair or unfair—takes a back seat. The rule of law only matters to a certain extent, and beyond that business leaders are willing to take the risk and be adventurous even if they are not able to achieve the desired goals by professional lobbying in tweaking the law in their favour.

Law can be made and changed with a stroke of the pen. In countries ruled by dictators, simply a nod of the head or blinking the eyes is enough to make or change the law. How different jurisdictions make the use of the simple mechanism to change the law to tackle serious problems, which if tried to be dealt with by any other method would have been extremely difficult, if not impossible, to resolve. Change of the law regarding driving in Samoa is a good example.

Samoa: Dateline and Driving on the Left

Samoa is located in the Pacific Ocean near Australia and New Zealand, and can be said to be somewhere in between New Zealand and Hawaii. It has a small population of less than 200,000 and of late, has developed strong ties with New Zealand and Australia. Historically, Samoa had strong business links with the United States, specifically since 1892. Before that, Samoa followed the Asian date, with the time in Samoa being four hours ahead of that of in Japan. In 1892 American traders convinced Samoan king to shift to the American date, with the time in Samoa being three hours behind that of in California. By adjusting the date with Americans, Samoans got the opportunity of trading on the same date and getting the benefit of having five overlapping working days in a week. Such was the influence of American business on Samoans that they made this change by repeating the American Independence Day, 4 July, in 1892.

With the passage of time, slowly but surely, Samoan business with the US had been on the decline and its business ties with Australia and New Zealand, primarily due to close proximity, had strengthened. But, Samoa faced the problem of having only four overlapping working days in a week with Australia and New Zealand due to its alignment with American date. While it was still Friday—a working day—in Samoa, people in Australia and New Zealand had already started observing the weekend; and, while Samoans were enjoying their Sunday, it was already the start of week—Monday—in Australia and New Zealand.

Problems due to different dates in Samoa, on the one hand, and in Australia and New Zealand, on the other hand, were not limited only to business relationships; these problems spilled over to personal and family relations, particularly for Samoans with family ties in Australia and New Zealand, and vice versa. They were not able to celebrate even Christmas at the same time, what to talk of rejoicing weekends together and at the same time.

To tackle the problem, Samoa decided to shift back to the pre-1892 date system and adjust its dateline with that of Australia and New Zealand. There are certain global norms which every country is supposed to conform to regarding

International Date Line and time. The international dateline is an imaginary line, which clearly demarcates one calendar day from the other. This line is running from the North Pole to the South Pole and passes somewhere through the middle of the Pacific Ocean and is on the opposite side of the earth to the Prime Meridian, which is the benchmark for defining universal Time. All time zones in the world are calculated with the Prime Meridian as the focal point.

The International Date Line is typically the 180° longitude—a straight line on the globe—but certain territories and islands, according to their preferences to be on which side of the dateline and exercising their sovereign power, make the line zigzag at certain places. A notable example is that of Republic of Kiribati, which was bent upon to be the first nation in the world to welcome the new millennium, the year 2000, to attract tourists. Though it is on the eastern side of the International Date Line, which means that it is one of the farthest territories in the Western Hemisphere, but not as far as Samoa or Tokelau, it shifted the dateline, so that it entered the new millennium first. A couple of years later most of the globe manufacturers and publishers of Atlas ignored this change and continued with the almost straight longitude as International Date Line.

Samoa shifted its dateline in the last few days of 2011, between 29th of December and 31st of December. At midnight on 29th of December, Samoa jumped to 31st December, and missed out 30th of December completely. Thus, there shall be no 30th of December, 2011 in the history of Samoa. Earlier, in 1892 Samoa had two complete days of 4th of July. By this radical change, Samoa aligned itself with Australia and New Zealand and abandoned close ties of more than a century with the United States.

Two years ago, in 2009, Samoa had changed the law regarding the side on the road on which one must drive. As is obvious, Samoa had aligned itself with the Americans, and, therefore, was driving on the right side of the road, as Americans do. Thus, the vehicles had their steering on the left side. Most of the vehicles in Samoa where imported from the US, and as American cars, typically, are not highly fuel-efficient. Samoans were paying through the nose for the fuel bills.

To add to the problem, Samoans had been importing the vehicles from the US, which meant a long distance to be covered by ships resulting in high shipping charges. Inexpensive cars with better mileage were available nearby in Australia and New Zealand. As a number of Samoans had good relationship—personal, family, business, etc.,—with people in New Zealand and Australia, they, quite obviously, longed for used vehicles from these countries. But those vehicles had the steering fitted on the right side as these countries followed the law requiring the vehicles to be driven on the left side of the road, as is the case in the UK.

Facing this dilemma of cheaper and better cars available nearby and the restriction of the existing law requiring the vehicles to be driven on the right side of the road, Samoans, as any reasonable and prudent person would do, made the decision to change the law. At 6 o'clock in the morning on Monday 7 September 2009, Samoan drivers, by law, stopped their vehicles on the right side of the road and drove them to the left side of the road. This shift had to be done to remain on the right side of the law.

It was a unique change and required a lot of determination by the government. A two-day national holiday was declared and Samoa was kept dry—no alcohol sale—for three days. Public broadcast systems worked to make the people aware of this change and police and medical professionals were on high alert to take care of any eventuality during the transition period. Interestingly, special prayers were held a day before on Sunday 6th of September for the safety of the people, and smooth transition from right to left in the country.

No wonder, law changes with a stroke of the pen!

The law may change with a stroke of the pen, however, to make it work institutions have to be created and individuals have to be trained to man the positions and exercise discretion. All this takes time and sometimes with several forces acting in different directions, things may get delayed a lot. Competition Commission in India faced such problems, even after substantial time had elapsed after the law was enacted.

Competition Commission of India: Delayed Start

Judicial control over regulatory bodies may often tend to derail the show as had happened in the case of the Competition Commission of India (CCI), in its early days. The Competition Act, 2002 received assent of the President of India on 13 January, 2003 and provided for the establishment of a Commission to prevent practices having adverse effect on competition, to promote and sustain competition in markets, to protect the interests of consumers and to ensure freedom of trade carried on by other participants in markets, in India, and for matters connected therewith. The Commission was established in October 2003.

In exercise of the Rule making power under Section 63(2)(a) read with Section 9 of the Act, the Central Government made 'The Competition Commission of India (Selection of Chairperson and Other Members of the Commission) Rules, 2003'. A senior civil servant was appointed as the Chairman, however, a petition was filed in the Supreme Court challenging his appointment on the ground that the role of CCI was mainly adjudicatory and hence, a retired judge from the judiciary would be the best person to man it. In other words, the contention was that the Chairman of the Commission had to be a person connected with the judiciary picked for the job by the head of the judiciary and he should not be a bureaucrat or other person appointed by the executive without reference to the head of the judiciary. Matter was resolved by making suitable changes in the rules though the functioning of the CCI got delayed and could become fully functional only in May 2009. Retired bureaucrats have usually been appointed to chair the Commission.

Several members of the Commission joined private consulting firms after the end of their term at CCI. The most recent being a former bureaucrat Mr. Ashok Chawla, the former Chairman of CCI, who joined the advisory board of Cyril Amarchand Mangaldas in January 2016.

Regulatory Control

With the rise in the number of government functions, it is not always possible for the government to do everything itself. A lot of functions are delegated to the bureaucrats. For instance, even the legislative functions are delegated to the executive—called delegated legislation—which in fact are in the hands of the bureaucracy. Moreover, with complexity of issues, administrative tribunals have come into existence and are gaining more and more popularity and power. It is not necessary that all the members of these tribunals are from judiciary. Some of the members are from executive, typically bureaucracy. Thus, largely the power of lawmaking and adjudication is ultimately in the hands of the bureaucracy. It is often seen that a number of businesses prefer to play the regulatory game by forcing or persuading the regulator to do what they want to be done. It is often done in the guise of public interest or public welfare. At times, it may be easier to convince the civil servants as compared to ministers or judges. The job of the regulators, as the name suggests, is to correct market failure. Thousands of rules are made by bureaucrats every week at all levels—national, state and local. All this is done in the name of 'public welfare'. For many businesses, these regulations hinder the natural flow of business and may annoy at least half the business leaders, however smart business leaders view it as an opportunity and use it to their advantage.

Thus, the appointment of retired bureaucrats raises the critical issue of conflict of interest and lobbying. There have been serious allegations of misuse of confidential information and conflict of interest in India. The most talked about have been the Radia tapes.

Radia Tapes and Lobbying

In November 2010, transcripts drawn from more than a hundred phone conversations between Niira Radia—a lobbyist—and editors, reporters, industrialists, politicians and others were published by two magazines: *Open* and *Outlook*. These recordings had been made between May and July 2009 when the UPA-II government under Dr. Manmohan Singh was in the process of reshuffling the portfolios of ministers. Earlier, conversations made by Radia were recorded as a part of Income Tax department surveillance. The department was acting on a complaint filed in 2007, alleging that Radia had built an empire of more than Rs. 300 crores (more than $60 million at that time) in a short span of time and any reasonable and prudent person would see something fishy in her climbing the social and economic ladder at such a fast pace.

Radia had used her personal connections—which she managed due to her suave and charming persona—and was working for a number of businesses, including well-known companies like Tata and Reliance, through her public relations firm *Vaishnavi Corporate Communications*. Somehow, the recorded conversations were leaked to the media and were submitted to the Supreme Court in a Public Interest Litigation (PIL) filed by activist lawyer Prashant Bhushan. These conversations led to the exposure of 2G spectrum allocation scam during the tenure of controversial telecom minister A Raja. Interestingly, these recorded conversations brought to the notice of the nation and the world at large that India was not insular to corporate lobbying, though not recognised as a profession in India, and lobbyists of all hues were having a field day in the chaotic political, economic and legal scenario prevalent in India.

It also came before the public that lobbying was not unthinkable and taboo in India, and was rather being practised in a brazen manner to influence policy formulation at the highest levels due to the nexus between lobbyists, journalists, politicians, bureaucrats, businesspersons and anyone having the slightest of relevant and critical information about a business deal or political grapevine or anyone who could have successfully posed as being privy to such information. Radia tapes were, indeed, juicy, and, they did hurt heavyweights including well-known and highly regarded business leader Ratan Tata, editors Barkha Dutt, Vir Sanghvi and sundry other politicians, journalists, bureaucrats, etc. India witnessed lobbying at its worst. There were red faces. Heads rolled. The cyberspace was abuzz with activity and comments. One of the bloggers, commenting on the pan-India influence of Radia, nicknamed the tapes and Radia phenomenon as "All India Radia", taking a cue from the state-run radio, All India Radio, popularly known as AIR.

Petitions were filed in the courts, including the Supreme Court of India. Ratan Tata filed a petition under article 22 of the Constitution—which grants the fundamental right to constitutional remedies—in the Supreme Court for protection of his fundamental right to privacy as he claimed that most of the conversation between him and Radia was of personal nature, and, hence, there was no need for that conversation to be made public. The Supreme Court took the entire matter related to Radia tapes in its hands and passed detailed orders, to be followed precisely, regarding preparation of transcripts of those recorded conversations and submission of the transcripts into the court. On 8th January 2013, these transcripts were submitted in sealed envelopes by the Income Tax department to the Supreme Court, and the Bench considered the idea of setting up an independent team to evaluate the transcripts so that only those conversations which were in public interest were revealed, and anything personal in nature was not made public.

As a number of journalists and senior editors were involved in Radia tapes controversy, unsurprisingly, most of the media houses—both print and broadcast media—did not cover the events, and there was, evidently, concerted effort on the part of these media houses to black out the details in their news coverage. Surprisingly, Radia, unfazed by her unprecedented notoriety, in 2012 started another company—*Pegasus International Advisory*, and a charitable trust called *Nayati Trust*, with the latter managing several projects at Badrinath Shrine in Uttarakhand, and the former claiming to address most core sectors in infrastructure and offering services regarding government relations and strategic advice. It is simply old wine in a new bottle, and opening of these new businesses also confirms the adage 'old habits die hard'.

Around the same time, Walmart faced lobbying accusations in India. It never had smooth sailing in the country despite its deep pockets and sophisticated professional lobbyists.

Walmart in India

In December 2012, Walmart, in a report to the U.S. Senate, disclosed that it had paid US$25 million for the Past four years on various lobbying activities, which included issues related to enhanced market access for investment in India. As this was reported by the Press Trust of India on December 9, all hell broke loose. Entry of Walmart into India's retail markets had already been a highly contentious issue and the opposition political parties had missed no opportunity to haul the ruling coalition over the coals. This report gave a fantastic opportunity to the opposition party and it raised the issue in the Parliament demanding a discussion only on this topic. As permission was not freely granted, the opposition staged a walkout and the Parliament did not function for a number of days.

Interestingly, Walmart had spent the money on lobbying activities in the United States and not even a single penny had been spent in India. Lobbying is legal in the US and is a multi-billion dollar profession. In 2011, according to media reports, more than 12,000 lobbyists reportedly had spent more than US$3 billion in trying to influence policy formulation in Washington. Lobbying, per se, is not illegal in India, but is not recognised as a profession, however, is rampant, as became evident by Niira Radia tapes. For certain strange reasons—though India is a democratic country, and the Constitution protects freedom of speech and expression—lobbying is not held to be in high esteem. The word, in India, is understood with its negative connotation and falls into the company of words like bribery, corruption, self-interest, conflict of interest, personal interest, against public interest, ... something which is not to be done; and, people who do it are simply 'bad'.

This is strange, given the fact that a large number of Indian companies doing business in the US themselves indulge in lobbying and hire professional lobbyists to put up their case before the lawmakers. Indian companies such as Reliance, Tata, Ranbaxy, etc., and business associations for software like NASSCOM, for gems and jewellery like Gems and Jewellery Export Promotion Council, rice like All Indian Rice Export Promotion Council and for carpets, the Carpet Export Promotion Council spend considerable amount of money in the US for lobbying activities.

According to American law it is a statutory requirement for all organisations to report and file quarterly reports about their lobbying activities which spend more than US$11,500 annually and employ at least one lobbyist. The same is not applicable to India, as India does not recognise lobbying as a profession. However, one thing must be clarified that as India is a democratic country elected representatives are duty bound to hear what the electorate wants to say, which includes business organisations. This by no stretch of imagination, communication between any business organisation, or group of business organisations, can be held to be illegal. On the contrary, it is one of the fundamental and founding principles of the democratic form of government.

Lobbying happens all over the world. Till the time India was a small market, multinational companies did not bother much to make inroads in this otherwise confusing and unique market, however, with the growth and development in the Indian economy along with the burgeoning middle-class with higher disposable incomes, India appears to be a much more lucrative market, as compared to other economies with either a stagnant population and market size, or growing at a very small pace, and no big company would like to miss any such opportunity. Rather, it would leave no stone unturned to capture a large share of the Indian market, and lobbying in its home country, is one of such efforts in this direction. And, at least 15 large multinational American companies spend millions on lobbying activities regarding business in India. These companies include Dell, Morgan Stanley, HP, Pfizer, Boeing, AT&T, Starbucks, Lockheed Martin, Eli Lilly, GE, etc.

Investigation was initiated in the Walmart lobbying incident and its report was made public in June 2013. The Walmart investigation regarding bribery in India had been an exercise in futility from the very beginning. It would not be wrong to say that it had been a mockery of an investigation.

The Constitution of India guarantees freedom of speech and expression, and, lobbying, to a certain extent, can get protection under this particular freedom, however, it is not yet recognised as a profession in India. In such a scenario, whatever Walmart did in the US to get the laws tweaked to suit its business in India, does not, as the fact of the matter is, come under the purview of legal scrutiny in India. However, the law enforcing agencies in India have full authority, or rather it is the duty, to investigate conclusively whether Walmart transgressed any of the legal limits as defined by the law of the land in India.

During the past few weeks in the past year, Walmart faced a lot of problems in India, and the opposition was unyielding to create as many hurdles as possible in Walmart's journey towards the Indian oasis of more than a billion. Getting regular business from even a fraction of this huge chunk of human mass is surely a dream for any retailer, and Walmart is no exception. It would not have surely left any stone unturned to fulfil this dream. And, that is why, one need not be a Sherlock Holmes to doubt that Walmart might have greased a few, or even many, palms to get the door opened in India for doing business.

Sensing the mood of the opposition and the public in general, the government had set up a one-man committee under Justice Mukul Mudgal, retired Chief Justice of Punjab and Haryana, High Court. In June 2013, the committee in its final report could not conclude definitely and blamed the lack of investigative and summoning powers.

Two questions arise: first, why did the government not give sufficient powers to the committee, and, second, why did Justice Mudgal accept to be on the committee, knowing fully well that the committee did not have sufficient powers?

Walmart, for what it is all worth with its big-name, huge workforce, deep pockets, and, hence, tremendous bargaining power, does not have a squeaky-clean image, neither in the US, nor in other countries. It had undergone investigation in Mexico for bribery and circumventing the law, and also at times getting the law changed, to suit its business interests. Interestingly, at that time, President Obama had given a pat on the back of Walmart for doing a lot of work towards saving energy, and thus working towards providing a cleaner and greener future to the children of the United States.

Unquestionably, Walmart is at its best when dealing with governments—whether it is in the United States, in Mexico or in India. Was it intentional that the government of India had set up a committee to investigate the bribery charges without sufficient powers? It would be childish to even suggest that the government did not know whether the powers of the committee were sufficient or not to investigate the charges against Walmart, a company which has done business in so many countries and dealt with so many governments that its employees, especially in the senior and top management, are a hard nut to crack. And that was precisely what had happened—its India chief, Raj Jain, did not reveal the relevant and pertinent facts. He was made to leave the company, is an absolutely different matter, and who knows, the company may reward him—for remaining silent—in some other manner, at some other time, at some other place.

Besides the role of the government in the entire comical episode, even much more intriguing is the role of the committee. Why did Justice Mudgal, a seasoned judge with tremendous experience of being on the Bench for sufficiently long time, and also rising to the highest position in a High Court, accept to be on the committee? One may say that he might not have foreseen it. One may accept this if one has to accept due to the threat of the order of a sovereign or the threat of punishment for contempt of court, but plain common sense does not permit one to do so. A weathered judge with a lot of familiarity with the subject is expected to anticipate as to what powers are required to conduct an enquiry. So, from the very beginning the committee was ill-equipped. It might have been designed in such a manner to buy time for Walmart and befool the people of this country, including the extremely fractured opposition. The People of India do not need ineffective committees.

In democratic countries, voice of the people is paramount and reflects in mandate given to political parties to rule for a certain period of time and steer the lawmaking process in the legislative bodies. Protection of free speech is essential for the voice of the people to be heard by the right persons at the right time. Funding of elections has usually been a tricky issue. India and the United States have faced these issues very often.

Election Funding and Corporates

It is well known that a lot of money is needed to contest an election in India. The legal framework provides a limit to that spending, however, it is common knowledge that the limits are generally unrealistic and it is not possible for any political aspirant to stick to those limits in the real sense. On paper most of the contestants, or rather all, would remain within those limits but, truly speaking a lot more money is spent in elections by each contestant. The way political rallies are organised, election meetings are held, large convoys of cars are arranged, the way money is spent to woo the voters by doling out hard currency for buying sweets for the children or simply as blessings from the elders leaves little to imagination.

Ingenuity is important in election campaigning. One has to differentiate oneself from the other contestants. In an election campaign in one of the states in India, one of the political aspirants, who happened to be a minister at that time, took a fire engine—full with water—to one of the villages in his constituency. He distributed small packets containing sachets of shampoo, hair oil and comb. So, where does the fire engine fit in? The children in the village were asked to collect a packet each. These children had never enjoyed shampooing their hair so this political leader with a masterly stroke told everyone to shampoo their hair and not to worry at all about the water to wash shampoo. Fire engine came handy to wash the shampoo and the children had fun and enjoyed taking a bath with shampoo—something which they had never done. Thereafter, applying hair oil and combing the hair made them look neat and tidy. Surely, their parents were happy. Making people happy leads to the possibility of a few more votes. And democracy is all a number game. Such innovative methods are rare.

Whatever is the method followed by any contestant, money—and a lot of it—is needed for electioneering. Where does this money come from? Subhash C. Kashyap, former Secretary General, Lok Sabha wrote in 2007 that huge unaccounted funds were needed for political work, parties and elections. For a number of big industrialists and business houses, it had always been a good investment with high return on investment (RoI) to fund political parties. Such funding ensured permissions, licenses, permits, contracts from the political masters. However, economic liberalisation and opening up of economy in the early 1990s, that particular source dried up for most of the political parties. Moreover, with the advent of coalition politics, the industrial houses did not see any point in funding only one party on a regular basis. Most of the business houses had started contributing on a per job basis.

In a very interesting case in the United States, the US Supreme Court held in 2010 that the government cannot ban political spending by corporations in candidate elections. This decision was by a razor thin majority, 5-4, and vindicated the most basic free speech principle that the government had no business in regulating political speech. This was the decision in the case 'Citizens United versus Federal Election Commission'. In 2008, a documentary film was made by a non-profit organisation—Citizens United—titled 'Hillary: The Movie'. The documentary was critical of the then Senator Hillary Clinton, who was a candidate for the party's presidential nomination. The matter was taken to the Supreme Court as the non-profit organisation had received certain contributions from corporations and it was argued that the law enacted in 2002—Bipartisan Campaign Reform Act— prohibited corporations and unions from using the general treasury funds to make independent expenditures for the speech that was an electioneering communication or for a speech that expressly advocated the election or defeat of a candidate.

President Obama had criticised the decision and commented that the decision had paved the way for big oil, Wall Street banks, health insurance companies and the other powerful interests that marshal their power every day in Washington to drown out the voices of everyday Americans. However, the majority of five judges was absolutely clear that the first Amendment prohibited Congress from fining or jailing citizens, or associations of citizens, for simply engaging in political speech.

In India, freedom of speech is paramount. Freedom of speech and expression are guaranteed by the constitution. Reasonable restrictions can be imposed on the freedom of speech. Regarding political funding, industrial houses and big corporations do fund political parties and individual politicians also. It would be better if such funding is done in a transparent manner and details are in public domain. That would create a better political and legal environment for business.

Takeaway for Business Leaders

1. Overdependence on lobbying: Not a good idea
   It is true that business leaders can communicate their aspirations to the lawmakers either directly or through the professional lobbyists in jurisdictions where lobbying is practised as a profession and considered to be legal. In any case, they should not depend too much on the assurances of the lawmakers that some new changes in the law will be made. There are a number of factors in democratic countries which impact lawmaking and many of them are not in control of the lawmakers a business leader might have approached. Planning for future based on the assumption that the law may be made or amended or tweaked to suit the needs of a particular business is a step in the right direction, however, over-dependence on the lobbying power and relying fully on it is not a practical idea. A business leader may try to tinker the lawmaking process, but till the time the law, rules, by-laws, regulations—whatever one wishes to target— are not modified formally, the business leader needs to keep a check on his words and deeds. There is often a slip between the cup and the lip as Walmart learnt the hard way in India. A business leader should not be over-dependent on lobbying.
2. A tight-rope walk
   As is obvious from the Eastern Railroad case and the GSK case, lobbying is a tight rope walk. It is not a simple and straightforward work. Things may go wrong anytime depending on the context and the players involved. In democratic countries like in the US, as in Eastern Railroad case, the presence of an effective judiciary is a comforting factor, however, in countries like China, where the role of judiciary for all practical purposes is next to zilch, any business leader cannot and should not try to test the limits of freedom provided by the legal environment. It is important to understand the jurisdiction, the political and legal environment for doing business and only after making a little extra effort than what a reasonable and prudent person would ordinarily do, a

business leader should take the plunge. Failing in lobbying at a political level usually does not allow another chance and even the survival may be in danger. A business leader should be wary of this fact of the tight-rope walk. Considering lobbying as a routine activity in jurisdictions with little or no culture of lobbying may be suicidal without proper study and due diligence. Even after that it is a big gamble.

3. Local knowledge

   Doing business in a foreign land is often tricky and local knowledge is supposed to be essential. That is the reason why the coined word "glocal" and the phrase "think global, act local" have become part and parcel of business education and managerial jargon. There is merit in acting local. A foreign company, howsoever big it may be, can possibly face innumerable problems because of lack of proper understanding and inadequate appreciate of the ground realities in a foreign land. GSK might have thought that it would not be too difficult to do business in China and it would be possible for the business leaders to "manage" the political leadership and bureaucracy. But, the experience was quite different. Same has been the case of Walmart in India. Even local businesses often do not have complete understanding of the hinterland and pay dearly for their ignorance. In large continental size countries like India, major national businesses frequently face this problem. For democratic processes to work effectively and get aligned with the business goals, a business leader ought to appreciate the very local political and social forces and work accordingly. Top-down approach usually does not work, until and unless finely blended with local knowledge and necessary adaptation.

4. Certainty, Anticipate, Creating Options

   Aiming for certainty is good while lobbying to get the legal requirements in one's favour, however, it itself is one of the uncertainties which a business leader must be ready to face. A rigid and static legal periphery is an exception in evolved jurisdiction, not the norm. Hence, the legal framework may change at any time due to its dynamic nature. Lobbying or no lobbying, a business leader prudently may prefer to eschew such dynamism. It is a possibility to anticipate whether the lobbying efforts will bear fruit, based on past experience and the actors involved in the decision-making process. Whatever, one's hunch is about any such possibility, creating viable options for foreseeable scenarios is the most prudent step a smart business leader would like to take. Taking the legal recourse is a plausible option only in jurisdictions with very strong legal environment.

Chapter 5
Should I *Really* Take Contracts Seriously?

Contracts are ubiquitous in any business. Contracts define relationship between the parties and define the rights and obligations of the parties to the contract. Contracts help in moving a business company from the zone of uncertainty to the zone of certainty. All contracts are agreements but all agreements are not contracts. Only those agreements which are enforceable by law are contracts. Thus, it is like the relationship between a rectangle and square: all squares are rectangles but all rectangles are not squares. Contract for any illegal purpose is not enforceable by law and thus, it would be correct not to call it even a contract—it is simply an agreement, which is not enforceable by law and hence it cannot be called a contract.

An MOU–memorandum of understanding—is simply an understanding between two or more parties defining their rights and obligations, but lacking in one of the essential ingredients which would convert it into an agreement or contract. This essential ingredient is called the 'intention to create a contractual relationship'. Thus, in most of the cases where it is only a memorandum of understanding between two or more parties, for breach of the terms mentioned therein, a party will not be able to take other parties to a court of law successfully. Often it is seen that a MoU is the first step which results in the signing of a proper binding contract. Contracts, in simple words, convert the understanding between two and more parties into either an oral understanding, which is binding and has the force of a contract or a written document which is a contract in the eyes of law. In case the parties are very sure about the conduct of the other party and they have full faith, trust and confidence in the other party's ability to fulfil the conditions of the contract, it is not important to go into a lengthy document and write down in detail all the terms and conditions. For the sake of documentation and for the record, a simple one-page contract can be signed between the two parties even if the contract is worth billions of dollars.

However, it is important that if the parties do not have unflinching faith in each other, or would prefer to put things in writing so that there is no confusion in future, it is important that the parties must go into detailed documentation of the terms and conditions, rights and obligations, expectations and deliverables, the timeline,

© The Author(s) 2017

A.K. Agarwal, *Business Leadership and Law*, DOI 10.1007/978-81-322-3682-5_5

milestones to be reached, payment conditions, compensation to be paid in case of breach of contract, how that compensation has to be calculated, place of jurisdiction, the applicable law, interest—if any—to be paid, the rate of interest, and several other details. In case the parties have a clear understanding of what they are going to do and also have unwavering trust, faith and confidence in each other, it is important that the parties are on the same wavelength and have the same understanding about at least the most important issues in a contract, for instance the applicable law, jurisdiction of courts, obligations of the parties, etc. It is, therefore, in most of the cases, advisable that the parties enter into a written contract even if it is a short one.

One thing must be noted and followed by all the parties entering into a contract: the language of the contract should be simple and even if legal jargon is required to be written down, the parties must be able to understand the true intention of the parties. The document preferably should not have any redundant and superfluous material. It helps if the parties are honest and straightforward in writing their expectations and their obligations. Putting down a contract in writing would not serve any purpose if the parties have not expressed their expectations in unambiguous terms, clearly, concisely and completely. It is essential that the parties do not try to deceive each other by putting some words or phrases in the contract at certain places where it is most unlikely to be seen by the other party. So it is important not to bury any such thing at inconspicuous places. Therefore, it also helps to have a shorter contract but completing all the aspects of the business deal. Brevity is truly the soul of wit.

As contracts bind the parties and in case of breach, legal remedy can be sought, the effectiveness of a contract depends on the legal environment in which it is enforced. A few illustrations will highlight the relevance of contracts in business.

Monsanto and Contract Signed by Farmers

On 13 May 2013, the US Supreme Court decided a matter in favour of a large multinational company Monsanto on the basis of the patent law and its strict interpretation, along with adherence to a contract signed by the farmer. While selling the patented seeds—which are resistant to diseases and result in a good yield as compared to the routinely available non-patented seeds—Monsanto ensures that each and every farmer who buys the seeds must sign a contract. One of the most essential conditions of the contract is that the farmer would not use the yield, or any part thereof, as seeds for further sowing, and this ensures that the farmer would come back to Monsanto to buy seeds every year—a business model using the patent law to the hilt.

One of the farmers in the United States—Bowman—had signed the contract, but later on breached the contract, according to Monsanto, not by saving seeds from the resulting crop, but by buying a mix of non-patented seeds from the market, sowing them and spraying them with a particular herbicide. Interestingly, only the

Monsanto seeds survived as they were resistant to the herbicide. So, it was not difficult for Bowman to segregate Monsanto seeds and the other seeds. Now the question arises as to how he was able to buy the mixed seeds in the market. It is quite simple. These mixed seeds are sold in the market not for sowing, but to be used for animal feed, food processing, etc. Monsanto, somehow, got a whiff of what Bowman was doing and sued him for violation of contract and patent rights. Bowman argued that whatever he did was protected under the patent exhaustion doctrine. The doctrine has been earlier explained by the US Supreme Court in a couple of judgement as '...the initial authorized sale of a patented article terminates all patent rights to that item ... and confers on the purchaser, or any subsequent owner ... the right to use or sell the thing as he sees fit ...'.

The US Supreme Court, however, did not agree that patent exhaustion doctrine would apply in this particular case also, and to the extent as had been argued by Bowman. The court held that making additional copies—growing seeds—of the patented invention could not be granted protection under the patent exhaustion doctrine, and had that been the case, Monsanto would not have benefited from its patent, and it would have been too simple for competing seed companies and farmers to grow seeds on their own after buying them once from Monsanto. The very purpose of getting the invention patented would have been defeated. For advocates of a strong patent regime, it may be an extremely interesting and bold judgement, but the moment it has to be balanced with public interest and for a large population depending on agriculture, it would be extremely difficult to go along with the companies holding the patent.

It is impossible for farmers in India to accept the position of companies like Monsanto holding patents for a variety of seeds—mostly hybrid, disease resistant and, at times, resistant to certain herbicides and pesticides—that the farmers can sow those seeds, but at the time of the reaping the crops they cannot keep any of those harvested seeds for further sowing. It has been a highly contentious issue in India, and, as India still has a large number of farmers who may be far below the poverty line—even by the low standards set by the Planning Commission of India—political masters, cutting across party lines, did not muster enough courage to force down such a patent regime, and even if it is done, it would be next to impossible to enforce it, knowing fully well that we are talking about farmers, who typically are in every nook and corner of the country where the reach of the law enforcement agencies is abysmally low.

Even in the United States, this decision created waves as it had reaffirmed the position of the courts in favour of strong patents and big companies holding the patents. In an extremely fast changing technological world, things are becoming much more complex and at times, some of these may be self-replicating, including software, living cells, etc. It would be difficult to enforce the patent law and protect the rights of the patent holder in a jurisdiction with a legal environment which may be even slightly weaker than what it is in the United States. Toeing the line of such patent protection may not be possible in India due to a different legal environment. Till the time it happens, we, in India, can safely say, 'as you sow, so shall you reap', literally.

Companies use contracts not only to have binding terms and conditions with consumers, but also with suppliers and vendors. An interesting case involved Coca-Cola and aluminium can makers and raw material suppliers.

Coca-Cola, Novelis and Hindalco

Novelis is a well-known aluminium company headquartered in Atlanta, with Coca-Cola, as one of its major clients. It supplies aluminium cans for soft drinks and other beverages. The American company was acquired by Hindalco, the Aditya Birla group aluminium company, based in India. This acquisition was made in 2007 for $6 billion. At that time, Novelis had a long-term contract with Coca-Cola for supply of aluminium cans at certain terms and conditions, which were not favourable to Novelis in 2007, but it had already entered into a contract. Such is the sanctity of contract, and particularly in the legal environment of the United States, that Novelis was compelled by contract conditions to sell aluminium cans to Coca-Cola at a loss for almost two years. Disputes arose and the matter was taken up for legal remedial action in the US. The company suffered huge losses and the acquirer, Hindalco, had to take the rough with the smooth. It had no option as it had stepped into the shoes of Novelis.

The strategic purpose of Hindalco in acquiring Novelis was to get the benefit of technology used in making aluminium cans for supply to soft drink and beverages companies, which is considered to be a high premium segment, and somehow get this manufacturing done in India, which provides tremendous advantage of low cost of labour and undoubtedly for Hindalco better understanding of legal and business conditions on the domestic turf. At the time of acquisition, Hindalco might have thought that the contract with Coca-Cola would not be such a major problem, and might be dealt with in a satisfactory manner within a short period of time, however, this expectation was far away from reality. Hindalco did not anticipate that the contract would prove to be such a big irritant, particularly for the reason that dealing with a contract in India and dealing with a contact in the United States are two different things, primarily due to different legal environments.

Immediately after 2007, the world faced economic downturn and Hindalco was stuck with Novelis and the loss-making long-term contract entered into by the acquired company with Coca-Cola. Much later in 2011 and 2012, as the global economy improved and Hindalco took better control of the situation, it was able to negotiate with Coca-Cola to get another contract on mutually agreed terms and conditions that litigation in the US would be dropped. This provides the necessary breather to Hindalco and Novelis, as it is difficult, if not impossible, to financially survive without Coca-Cola as its client.

There is an important learning for the acquiring company as far as contracts are concerned. It is not prudent to take the contracts for granted while acquiring any company, or for that matter, even in routine course of business. It is understandable that implementation of contracts depends a lot on the legal environment and the prevalent norms in any jurisdiction regarding contract adherence, however, even in jurisdictions where contract adherence is not high, it is much more prudent and advisable to read the contracts carefully, understand their implications, and make decisions based on the conditions mentioned in the contract. Otherwise, any company can do business by keeping aside any contract, but, it surely will be at a huge risk.

Salient features of a valid contract

Contracts are entered into by the parties on their own sweet will, that is to say, 'voluntarily'. The consent of the party should be absolutely free—free from any coalition, undue influence, misrepresentation, mistake of fact and law, threat of any kind or any such element which may possibly have a negative impact on the free consent of the party. There are a certain number of factors which have been well defined in the Indian Contract Act, 1872 and these factors may convert a valid contract into a "voidable" contract. These are more or less the same in all the evolved jurisdictions.

A good contract must reflect the intention of the parties in unambiguous terms. It must be realistic. A contract is entered into by the parties to be performed and thereafter discharged. Parties do not enter into a contract just for the heck of it. Thus, it is important that the contract includes only those terms which are realistic and which can be performed by the parties, either without any difficulty or with some difficulty, but it should not be in such a manner that from the very beginning any reasonable and prudent person can make it out that the terms of the contract are so onerous that both the parties or either one of the parties will not be able to perform it.

In case the parties enter into an unrealistic contract, and later on it is found that one of the parties is not able to perform. Such a situation gives a very bad impression of that party's reputation. Credibility of that party goes down in the market and thereafter other companies may not willing to do business with that party on those terms, which are entered into the earlier contract. Thus, it is essential for each contracting party to understand that it is not going to serve any purpose by biting more than it can chew. It is fine to have great expectations from each other but those great expectations should not cross the line and transgress into unrealistic expectations. At times, the unrealistic expectations may also not be legitimate expectations.

Ultimately the test of a contract is 'whether it works?' Any contract which works for both the parties and helps them in achieving their goal—the goal which they had envisaged at the time of entering the contract. A contract which serves the needs of the parties to the contract can always be said to be a good contract.

A contract must be a 'concluded contract'. By concluded contract we mean that there has been an 'offer' and that there has been 'acceptance' along with all the essential conditions which are necessary for a valid contract. You can enter into a contract with the other parties for anything and everything for which they have a right to choose, but for anything which is imposed by law on each and every person in the country, there is no choice and everyone has to abide by it. For instance, if people in India are supposed to drive on the left side of the road, by no stretch of imagination a contract can be entered into by which a party is supposed to drive on the right side of the road: for the simple reason that driving on the right side of the road is illegal and the contract itself will become void.

It is important for business leaders to pay attention to the formation of a concluded contract, which does not mean performance of a contract to the satisfaction of the parties, but entails the formation of a valid contract with all the necessary ingredients so that it can be enforced in the desired jurisdiction. The following case highlights the issue well.

Concluded Contract: Pennzoil, Texaco and Getty Oil

Pennzoil, a Delaware corporation with its principal place of business in Texas, had a handshake deal with Getty Oil. In late 1983, dissension between the Board of Directors of Getty Oil Company and Gordon Getty, who owned about 40 % of the outstanding shares, was well known, and equally well known was the fact that Pennzoil wished to take over Getty Oil. Being proactive, Pennzoil announced an unsolicited public offer for 16 million shares of Getty Oil at $100 each. Meetings were held between the representatives of Pennzoil and Getty in the first week of January 1984. A memorandum of agreement was drafted to reflect on the issues discussed and decided during the conversation. A press release to the same effect was also made, however, it was made absolutely clear in the press release that both the companies had agreed only in principle to merge and the deal would be closed after the approval of the shareholders of Getty Oil and completion of all legal, regulatory and administrative requirements.

Thus, there was no doubt that both the companies had not entered into a formal written agreement and did not close the deal, but, in principle, had agreed and made up their mind to merge and to complete the formalities in due course of time. Not fully satisfied, the top management of Getty Oil and its bankers were still looking for a better deal and just to take a chance, one of the bankers for Getty Oil, the same day, called Texaco, a Delaware corporation with its principal place of business in New York, and sought a higher bid. Seeing it as a great opportunity and something offered on a platter, Texaco agreed to buy hundred percent of Getty Oil at a price of $125 per share. Without losing precious time, Getty Oil board accepted this offer. What confirms the eagerness of Texaco to seal the deal is the fact that it agreed to indemnify Getty for any claims arising out of this contract.

Feeling aggrieved by Texaco's actions, Pennzoil, under the impression of having concluded a contract with Getty Oil, and rightly so, moved the court to enforce its contract with Getty Oil and claimed a large amount as damages from Texaco for tortious interference with contract. The matter was heard by the jury, which decided it in favour of Pennzoil and awarded more than US $10 billion in damages—about $7.5 billion in compensatory damages and $3 billion in punitive damages. It was and is still a huge sum of money. Texaco appealed in the Court of Appeals in Texas, which upheld the decision, however, punitive damages were reduced to $1 billion.

As enormous money was involved, the losing party—Texaco—would have liked to play the legal gamble and appeal in the US Supreme Court. But, as one can understand, both the winning party and the losing party live in uncertainty whenever a matter goes in appeal to a higher court, as one can never be sure how the court would look at the matter and decide it. Thus, Pennzoil was too happy at that point of time to be awarded almost $10 billion as damages, and as later was evident would have been satisfied even with a much smaller amount, whereas Texaco was not sure whether the amount would be reduced in the final decision by the US Supreme Court, what to talk of setting aside the verdict in favour of Pennzoil. So, it made sense for the parties to settle and they did settle. Texaco paid $3 billion in cash to Pennzoil, which forced Texaco to file for bankruptcy.

It is a different story that later on the matter finally reached the US Supreme Court, but only for ticklish legal, rather technically legal, issues to be decided. While discussing this case, the story will not be complete without talking about the corruption charges in the Texas Court of Appeals. There was a widespread belief that money had transferred hands during the decision made by the bench in the Court of Appeals, primarily due to the reason that judges in the court were elected and one of the lawyers, who had aspirations of becoming a judge, had accepted a contribution of about $10,000 for his election campaign fund from Pennzoil.

Even if we assume that the judges were honest, it would be extremely difficult to understand the position taken by Texaco while agreeing to indemnify Getty Oil for any losses suffered due to the contract entered into between Texaco and Getty Oil. There was no need for Texaco to walk the extra mile. It could have easily asked Getty Oil to give it in writing that there was no contract between Getty Oil and Pennzoil, or for that matter with anyone, and Getty Oil promised, on the contrary, to indemnify Texaco for any losses suffered due to the contract entered into between Texaco and Getty Oil.

What is extremely important is to understand that even an understanding between two parties, which may be called a simple handshake agreement, is as good as a concluded contract, provided both the parties had an intention to create a contractual relationship, and, putting that understanding down on a piece of paper and signing it will not make it a better legal document and will not give the parties any better rights. That piece of paper may, simply, be a better piece of evidence, and would satisfy the requirements of procedural law, however, it would make no difference as far as substantive law of contract is concerned.

The moral of the story is that before entering into a contract with any party, each party must ensure that there is no existing concluded contract regarding the same subject matter for which it is interested to enter into a contract.

E.U. Consumer Rights Directive, 2011

Consumer rights emanate from contracts and enforcement of different contracts depends on the legal environment. The more fragmented the legal boundaries, the more difficult it becomes to form, enforce and rely on contracts. To get the maximum benefits of a well-drafted contract, it is important to have a uniform law and thus similar legal environment. The European Union did not have a single and uniform law to protect consumers. There had been a proposal to create a single European Union contract law which can be used by buyers and sellers without confusion. In 2011 it was a combination of laws of 27 member states. Different laws in different countries used to give rise to confusion, uncertainty and disputes.

This was a very common problem which was faced by different countries when the law on any particular subject in these countries was not the same. For instance, country A and country B may have variation in their laws regarding capital punishment. But as the law relates to death penalty, it may not have that much impact on commercial transactions and day-to-day living of people in these countries. The impact will only be seen when any citizen of country A visits B and vice versa. But, for commercial transactions, it is important to have a uniform law so that the consumers as well as the merchants conduct business with confidence. For the past so many decades there has been an effort in the world to create free movement of goods and services. However, it is often hindered by the legal regime in different countries, rather than geographical barriers.

It was very often felt that European countries—particularly members of the European Union—were not able to make the best despite being politically and economically a union. The reason being different laws regarding protection of consumers, withdrawal of goods, delay in delivery, right to cancel a purchase in case of inordinate delay, etc. Theoretically speaking, it had been an economic union providing a lot of opportunities to companies to sell their products in different countries. With the advent of Internet and electronic transactions becoming very frequent in our daily lives, consumers demanded better protection for purchases made on the Internet. But for a consumer in Austria, for example, ordering goods from France might pose a problem as the legal protection was different in both the countries. Thus, the idea of EU as a single market made sense only for very large companies with deep pockets. Only they had the means to hire legal staff and find their way through the legal maze. Small-sized companies simply did not have this option. Moreover, individual consumers also found it difficult to rely on the law applicable to their purchase, as there were doubts in their minds: whether country A's law would apply or country B's law would apply. Most of the individual prospective buyers were put off by this uncertainty and therefore usually abandoned the thought of buying it online from a foreign company. Instead, they used to prefer to buy from a seller in their own country and thus, defeated the very purpose of integration of different nations.

In the Indian context, with the federal structure of the nations, different provinces exist with the centre. Just imagine, an Indian consumer in Gujarat wishes to buy a product online from a company in Karnataka. In case the applicable law is different in Gujarat and Karnataka, there will be confusion in the mind of the buyer and he may avoid inter-state purchase. Luckily, most of the laws of national importance in India are the same throughout the country as they are made according to the Union List mentioned in the Constitution of India. It is the central law in this regard—the Contract Act, 1872; the Sale of Goods Act, 1930 and the Consumer Protection Act, 1986. It is important to add that along with these laws, certain local laws of that particular state may apply. However, those will not be the primary law. Their affect would be minimal in the transaction. But if the law of contract in two states is different as well as the consumer law is different, there will be a lot of problem. The same was the position till 2011 in the European Union.

In 2011, the European Union passed the E.U. Consumer Rights Directive. It was expected at that time that it would become a law shortly and shall be implemented fully by December 2013. It mainly applied to contracts between traders and consumers and later to all contracts from June 2014. Some of the features of this directive are a 14-day E.U. wide withdrawal period for distance and off-premises sales during which consumers may return the goods they have purchased. It is to be followed very strictly and if the seller fails to inform the withdrawal rights to the consumers, this period of 14 days may be extended to 1 year. Needless to say, the price paid has to be refunded within a reasonable period of time which has been determined to be 14 days. It is also mentioned that the goods purchased online or by telephone or by post should be delivered within 30 days. Otherwise, the consumer can cancel the purchase. The consumer may be anxious to know his position regarding the costs of returning any unwanted goods. These should be very clearly informed by the seller to the consumers at the time the purchase is made. The purpose is to provide all the information to the consumer so that he is able to compare different products and make a conscious decision which is based on complete information. This law also aimed to put an end to all hidden charges. The identity of the seller must be fully disclosed to the consumer particularly while shopping online. The law also aimed to make provisions regarding repairs, after-sales servicing, replacements and guarantees to be really effective.

Did this new law benefit only the consumers? No. The law was primarily meant to safeguard the interests of the consumers while entering into contracts. However, it intended indirectly to have a very good impact on all the companies. The law made it difficult for unscrupulous companies and sellers to transact business and dupe customers by coming out in open fully while the contract was being formed. Thus it encouraged honest businesses. It therefore made the business environment friendly and conducive for growth. Contracts ideally should be formed with complete information about the parties and the entire context in which the transaction takes place. To that extent, the law made it mandatory for the sellers to be forthright and reveal everything.

Is there anything in this law for the Indian consumers and Indian sellers? There is certainly a lot of scope for Indian buyers and sellers to make good use of this law. It is well known that a good number of European companies source their products from India and Indian companies often face the problem of different laws regarding consumer protection and contracts in so many European countries. A uniform law which harmonizes the commercial transactions in all these countries has surely been much more predictable and certain. This new level of certainty has brought definite clarity for Indian manufacturers who do not have to grapple with many different norms and at times contradictory conditions. It is helping the Indian manufacturers in bringing down the cost as the same product with same specifications can now be sold all over the European Union. Further it is expected that it will help in manufacturing large volumes which in turn will help in further lowering the cost of production. Similarly, the new law will boost the confidence of Indian tourists visiting EU. They will buy goods with greater certainty. Indian manufacturers, in particular, should not miss this opportunity to make the best of the changing legal environment for business. It is a very good move and a move towards creating a real and practical united Europe, which may prove to be the step towards the idea of a true global village.

But, of late the issues arising due to Brexit in 2016 and rise of nationalism and protectionism may not be in tune with the effort of harmonisation and unification. There is a possibility that individual members may not adhere to the stringent conditions of a unified law and prefer to go on their own, according to their convenience and contingency. Nonetheless, one can hope that better sense will prevail leading to giving more meaning to contracts and consumer protection.

Google, Paypal and Trade Secrets, 2011

Trade secrets are often crucial to the success of a business, and are protected with the help of contracts. Future business strategy is known to the top management of a company and competitors try their best to get at least a whiff of it. Higher the stakes in a business, higher the risk of the strategy or trade secrets or confidential information being leaked out. It demands higher protective measures being put in place. Despite all the precautions being taken, competitors may find a way to know the trade secrets.

In 2011, PayPal—eBay's online payment unit—had sued Google for stealing its trade secrets related to mobile payment systems. The technology for online payment had developed with time and PayPal was a highly regarded company in this field. PayPal and similar other companies had been working on it to make it function with mobiles. The idea was to make payment as simple as possible. With mobile phones becoming more and more powerful, almost everything which can be done with the help of a computer was becoming possible to be done with a mobile phone. A mobile phone with a fast Internet connection, with 2G or 3G at that time, was as good as a computer with Internet connectivity. Thus, a mobile could have been easily used to make purchases. The only problem was that of keying in the long credit card number and other details. The benefit of a mobile phone vis-à-vis the computer was that the mobile number is unique and any transaction made from that number could have been identified easily, making the credit card details superfluous. Thus, companies like PayPal had been working on the technology to make the transactions simple so that the user needed to press very few buttons. Such a technology was already being used in day-to-day transactions in Japan at that time.

With the launch of newer and better mobile phones, smart phones, etc., Google was in negotiations with PayPal to share its mobile payment technology with Google. The law recognizes a company as a distinct legal entity. Any company, however, cannot transact on its own as it is inanimate, and, hence, needs human beings to transact business. These human beings, representing different companies, have a mind and heart of their own. They have likes, dislikes, fears, apprehensions, greed and emotions. Law casts upon them a fiduciary duty—the duty of loyalty and duty of care. But, the law also sets them free. They are free to work for any company, keeping in mind the contractual obligations of the former employer, which, in most of the cases, include a non-compete clause and a non-disclosure clause. Thus, it is for the former employer to invoke these clauses and take legal action in case of violation. Any employer will take legal action only if the contract clauses have been drafted very well in its favour and, moreover, there is presence of a very strong legal environment for protection of contractual obligations.

In the instant case, the legal environment was very strong in the United States and non-disclosure agreements had been upheld in several cases. However, this had been the case vis-à-vis former employees, but the position vis-à-vis competitors who hire the employee were different. One, the competitor did not sign a contract. Two, the competitor was free to hire any employee. And, three, the competitor hired an employee for his qualifications and experience. Absence of any contract between the competitors typically makes it difficult to take any legal action even if the legal environment is very strong. The only thing which is required by law is fair play and total compliance.

In this background, it was extremely difficult to prove the allegations of stealing trade secrets. By the very nature of trade secrets, they cannot be registered. They are best protected within the company, e.g. Coca-Cola formula, and it is best done by a contract. The question of a top executive of a company, in the know-how of the trade secret, being hired by any other company is a difficult one. How can the employer ensure that the person does not carry any trade secrets with him? It can be prevented by not allowing him to carry any papers or electronic data. But what about the secrets and information he carries with him in the head? What about the experience and understanding of the work? It is extremely difficult, or rather impossible, to be prevented from being used.

For the purposes of producing evidence of theft, it is again impossible to do that in the absence of any concrete material, which is highly improbable for a person of above average intellect to leave. It is mostly based on circumstantial evidence, which was also true in the PayPal–Google case. Osama Bedier was negotiating with Google on behalf of PayPal. While the negotiations were on, Osama left PayPal and joined Google. There were chances that such a move might have given Google access to PayPal's strategy through Osama. For a moment, let us say that Osama had been truly loyal to his former employer and did not share any details to the new employer. In such a scenario, the new employer was not getting the full benefit of experience of an employee, which in turn meant that the employee was not giving his best and that can also be interpreted as not being loyal, which is essential as fiduciary duty. The fact of the matter is that any such employee is hired primarily for the knowledge and experience of his previous job. But, it is very difficult to prove it in a court of law and more so for a competitor.

It is no secret that trade secret cases are often lost due to lack of evidence. Usually, such matters are settled between the parties and suing the competitor is a tactical move to bring the competitor to the negotiating table. This case was no different and gave a loud and clear message that trade secrets are fragile. One crack and they are gone forever. Businesses need to be extra cautious in retaining persons who are privy to such secrets. Contractual clauses help in compelling the parties to negotiate and not facilitate litigation. Making best efforts to retain key employees is better than relying on enforcement of contractual obligations.

Business Contracts and Bribery

In February 2012, KBR and its parent company Halliburton had agreed to pay $579 million as fine in the United States. KBR chief was found to be in violation of the Foreign Corrupt Practices Act. The company agreed to have paid bribes to Nigerian officials to win construction contracts between 1995 and 2004. The company won contracts worth more than $6 billion. The former Chief of the company KBR, Albert Stanley, had been sentenced to 30 months in prison.

The role of government in a welfare state is tremendous. In emerging economies as a lot of infrastructure has to be built, there are numerous opportunities for construction companies. With the advent of the idea of the public–private part-nership–PPP–it has become almost the norm all over the world, particularly backed by global funding agencies like World Bank, that the work should be allotted after global tendering and it should go to the best company. It is interesting to note that finally the decisions are made by individuals, even if the decision is in the name of either a company or a government or any other institution. Hence any individual exercising his or her discretionary power—within a band of discretion to be exercised—can be swayed by a number of ways to make a decision either this way or that way. Money often plays a role in such decision-making process. In one of the landmark judgments—R.D. Shetty's case, the Supreme Court of India in 1979 observed:

> Today the Government, in a welfare State is the regulator and dispenser of special services and provider of a large number of benefits, including jobs contracts, licences, quotas, mineral rights etc. The Government pours forth wealth, money, benefits, services, contracts, quotas and licences. The valuables dispensed by Government take many forms, but they all share one characteristic. They are steadily taking the place of traditional forms of wealth.

The things have not changed. The governments, whether in India or Nigeria or anywhere else, surely control the award of contracts. It is not possible to imagine that a business company can get a government contract without the blessings of the ruling party and particularly the person making a decision regarding the contract. I am reminded that about 25 years ago in late 1980s or early 1990s the popular magazine India today had commented about the symbols of the Indian political parties Congress and the palm; and Janata Dal and the wheel. It wrote that both had something in common—they needed to be greased to work properly. Very true! Often we read and hear about corrupt practices in award of business contracts.

In the instant case of KBR and Halliburton, it is interesting to note that the legal proceedings had not been started in the country where the act of bribery was performed, that is Nigeria. The legal proceedings had been started in the United States and under the American law. This is a very good illustration of the legal principle of conflict of laws in different jurisdictions and how business leaders should keep in mind the different legal environments in which they are doing business. So, it is not always advisable to follow, 'when in Rome do as the Romans do'. If a person does like that without application of mind, he may be penalised for his activities in Rome when he comes back home. Thus, one needs to take the common points of both the places and follow them. That will, hopefully, keep him and his company in good stead.

The basic purpose of the American law seems to be that no bribery would be accepted even if that has been done in a foreign land to get a business contract. In case one of the parties is American, the matter has to be subjected to the American law and the erring parties have to be penalised for that.

There have been earlier a couple of other cases decided in English courts and American courts also which have dealt with the issue of corruption and bribery in a foreign land either to get contracts or to make movement of goods possible from one country to another. In an interesting case, government officials in one country were bribed by a company making defence equipment from another country. I am not talking about the Bofors case. Bofors, the Swedish gun company became synonymous with bribery in India during late 1980s for alleged kickbacks in defence contracts. It is about a Yugoslavian company and the Kuwaiti government, which had clearly mentioned that in case of any bribery by a company the government would not go ahead with the contract. Later, arbitration was invoked and finally the arbitration award was challenged in a British court, which held in unequivocal terms that to enforce any judgment vitiated by acts of bribery would undermine the dignity of the British courts and Her Majesty. The courts refused to do so.

It is heartening to note that the American courts had taken the Halliburton matter so seriously and had sent the former head to prison. In a globalised world, where transparency is the norm and people of the world need to be informed of how business is being done in different countries, it is imperative that the courts in evolved jurisdictions take a strict view, even at the cost of creating chaos and confusion for business players. Such turbulence is needed to set the things right and make the flow of money and award of contracts laminar. Of late, the Supreme Court in India has also pronounced judgments on the same line and it is only a matter of time when the dust shall settle and a clear signal will go to the business companies as to how much grease is too much grease.

Man Proposes, God Disposes: *Force Majeure* in Business Contracts

Most of the contracts often contain a *force majeure* clause—a clause which frees a party from performing the contractual obligation in certain instances which are beyond his control. Over a long period of time, the understanding of the law of *force majeure* has evolved by legislative developments and mostly by judicial interpretations. In October 2012, storm Sandy in the United States had caused unprecedented damage—several lives had been lost, there had been widespread damage to buildings and other infrastructure, besides damage due to closure of the stock exchange, markets, offices, schools, etc. It took a fairly long time for the people of the United States to recover from such a huge tragedy.

During that time period, a good number of people had started reading very carefully the contracts they had signed either with their employers or employees, suppliers or distributors or buyers, government—local, state and federal—and other government-controlled bodies, insurance companies, etc. Most of these contracts, without fail, had incorporated the *force majeure* clause. In evolved jurisdictions like the United States, these clauses are typically detailed and cover most of the situations which could be anticipated and foreseen. Still, there are limits to human mind and it is not possible to include each and every situation, as it is not possible to foresee everything. One has to be a clairvoyant to include every possible event, and that is not what law expects of a reasonable and prudent person. Business leaders and consumers are expected to *anticipate* as to what may happen, and the anticipation becomes better and accurate with more information and proper analysis of that information.

In business contracts, most of the situations which are covered under the *force majeure* clause are situations of war, law and order problems, natural calamities such as unprecedented rains, floods, drought, earthquake, volcano, cyclone, storm, etc. Some of the contracts even include political developments such as change in government, strike, and similar other activities under the *force majeure* clause. However, the clause needs to be read very carefully as even a single word may make or mar the entire contract. Some of the obvious things cannot be brought under the ambit of *force majeure* clause. For instance, anything which is beyond the control of a particular person is not per se to be read under *force majeure*. Heavy rains in Cherrapunji—for a long time it was the wettest place on the Earth, now replaced by a place called Mawsynram, and both in Northeast India—mild tremors in Japan, dry conditions in a desert, snowfall in Srinagar, etc., will surely not qualify for inclusion in *force majeure*. If a person does not do a thing, which he could have done with normal and reasonable effort, or even a little more effort, will also not fall under the ambit of force majeure. Thus, force majeure clauses are subjective and can be highly contentious.

So, what should a person do to protect himself in case of any of the above-mentioned situations? The answer is simple: buy insurance. But, insurance companies are out there to make money and not for charity. Their business is based on principles of probability and the total premium charged should be more than the amount they are liable to pay to remain profitable. Insurance, as it appears to the uninitiated, is the solution for all such problems. Unfortunately, this is not so. Every insurance policy contains several clauses which provide the insurance company a definite route to escape from the liability. In case it is not clearly mentioned in the policy, it is a matter of interpretation of whatever has been mentioned in the policy and it becomes extremely difficult to counter the well-oiled legal machinery of insurance companies, which are created and maintained to deny most of the claims.

During the unprecedented rains and floods in Mumbai on 26 July 2005, and earlier during the earthquake in Gujarat on 26 January 2001, there was huge loss of life and property. A large number of claims were rejected by insurance companies, which resulted in a lot of litigation. Later, to avoid any such litigation, insurance companies—gaining from the wisdom of earlier incidents—modified the clauses in the insurance policy to exclude most of such unprecedented situations. The same, to a large extent, had been the situation in the United States, post-Storm Sandy. As had been reported, the predictions made by experts regarding the storm were quite close to the real thing, and a lot of damage was avoided.

Despite such technological advancements, we will do well to remember, 'Man proposes, God disposes', and *force majeure* shall remain a vital clause in most of the business contracts.

Technology Transfer and Business Contracts

One of the most interesting issues in technology transfer is that of protection of intellectual property and the resolution of dispute if it arises. While it is important and necessary for businesses to innovate and protect any of those innovative steps through intellectual property protection, to commercially exploit that intellectual property protected by patents, it is incumbent for the patent holder to license the patented technology and allow the licensee to exercise rights over it. In this process it is also necessary to keep a control over the licensee so that the licensor does not lose the right to improper use or misuse of the license.

In doing so it is extremely important that the terms of the license are clearly written down in the intellectual property license agreement—commonly known as IPLA—and often is a matter of dispute whether the licensee has violated the terms or not, which many a time leads to disputes. It is interesting that it may even lead to a dispute regarding whether there was any intellectual property license agreement signed between the parties or not. The importance of a concluded contract—

performance of a contract or termination of contract are very different from a concluded contract—can never be over emphasised. In a multinational contract when both the parties are corresponding by modern means of communication like e-mail, it is quite possible that the parties do not meet for a formal signing of the contract, however, the contract is supposed to be concluded by the communication and the intention of the parties to get engaged into a contractual relationship can be inferred from the spirit of the communication between the two parties.

A dispute of this type had arisen between one of the pioneers of the windmill turbine companies—Enercon, in Germany, made popular by its founder and chairman, Dr. Alloys Wobben—and its India's licensee, Enercon (India). Technology transfer has one of the inherent risks and that is the licensee may continue using the licensed technology even after the termination of the contract, thereby clearly violating the terms of intellectual property licensing. In such a scenario, the only available option is to seek a legal remedy by asserting one's rights, seeking temporary injunction and compensation. As the use of intellectual property is non-rivalrous, there is hardly anything which the licensee has to return to the licensor after the license is terminated, and this particular feature of non-excludability of intellectual property makes its protection extremely difficult. And, the protection becomes even more difficult in jurisdictions where the perception regarding intellectual property is not too great. China is one such place, and India also, unfortunately, does not have a very high reputation in this regard, though steps have been taken to make the situation better in India and court decisions, of late, bear testimony to it.

It is commonly known that Chinese factories—China itself is known as the factory of the world—receive detailed procedure, methodology and design from some of the best-known companies in the world, a large number of them being American. It is the technology and intellectual property which are licensed to the Chinese companies, maybe for a particular period of time, but knowing fully well the abysmally low level of legal protection to intellectual property provided by the Chinese judicial system, it should not be shocking to know that in most of the cases there are flagrant intellectual property rights violations and though there are number of disputes between the licensor and licensee, however, due to hardly any realistic measures of intellectual property protection being taken in China, the licensor has no option but to turn a blind eye to such violations.

Such is the immense bargaining power of Chinese manufacturers that global companies are unable to resist from using their production facilities. It is simply too tempting to be resisted. But, India is a different place. Neither the manufacturing companies in India have that immense bargaining power nor is the judicial system so opaque that the licensors will not move the court. Despite the stories of corruption in judiciary doing the rounds sometime, still the image of Indian judiciary is that of impartial and fearless and fair, and that gives immense confidence to the foreign licensors to initiate a legal battle in India against the Indian licensees. Surely it is one of the benefits of an evolved judicial system in India and gives tremendous confidence to foreign patent holders while entering into agreements for technology transfer. Similarly, in other jurisdictions, while transferring technology, patent holders and protectors of confidential information should be vigilant and perform due diligence to understand the efficacy of the enforcement of contracts in that jurisdiction.

Takeaway for Business Leaders

1. Addressing Real Issues of Business
   As a business leader, your aim is to make profits while working within the legal framework. Contracts definitely help you to achieve your goal in a legal manner. You would be able to use contracts in a meaningful way only when you address real issues of business in a contract. It is important for you to anticipate as to what can happen in the future regarding different parties with whom you do business, your suppliers, your buyers, your employees, the government and at times your competitors also. If you are able to anticipate and foresee what can be the shape of the business in the times to come it will be easier for you to draft a contract and put all those conditions in writing which you would like the other parties to abide. Remember, you are there to make profits and not to prove a point. However, it is important that you make profits in a legal manner and at times if it becomes essential you would like to prove a point also by taking the other party to a court of law and insisting on the enforcement of a contract, which may cost you a lot of time, effort and money. Thus, do not underestimate any contract, and do not think that you will not be interested at any point of time in using the piece of paper—the contract—and taking the other party to the court of law. At times it is a question of survival and you would like to go back and read the fine print, which your lawyer might have drafted at some point of time. So, a contract may come handy if you want to win the war. For winning battles it will not be very important to go to the court of law; the existence of the contract itself may provide the requisite deterrent effect.
2. Insist for a Binding Contract
   A contract to be effective must be a binding contract. The contract should not have any such conditions which are not binding in nature and the courts in general would not permit the enforcement of such conditions in the contract. For instance a number of bonds between employer and employee have been held to be unenforceable by several courts. A contract, particularly a written contract, forces the parties to stick to the options they have chosen. As there is a predictability about the behaviour of the parties, there is much more certainty when parties enter into a contract and write their rights and obligations in a proper manner in the contract. Thus, it helps the parties to be open, and make their credibility and integrity reflect in the document they are signing. It also helps to avoid disputes in contracts have been drafted properly between the parties.
3. Finding the Right Balance
   By thinking about the future of your business, you would like to focus on what forces are going to be important for your business. It is purely a business

decision and has nothing to do with law. Thus your lawyer may not be able to help you in identifying the forces that are going to have the maximum impact on your business. It is your business acumen which is going to help you in identifying such forces. Your lawyer will help you in drafting the contract properly so that any adverse or favourable impact on your business by such forces is taken care of by different clauses in the contract. A contract, in a fantastic manner, creates restrictions. And, these restrictions are created for all the parties entering into a contract. That is, if you are in a commanding position, it would be advisable that you create restrictions for the other parties and never ever write any such conditions which are going to put restrictions on your business and you. It is for the other parties—to whom the draft contract is provided—to point out such clauses and not agree with them. However, if they feel that they are in a lesser bargaining position or they may be desperate to do business with you, they would like to go ahead and sign such a contract. But, it is important to note that any such condition should not be absolutely unreasonable or so onerous that any fair and independent court would strike it down. That would prove to be detrimental to your business. Thus, a fine balance has to be reached.

4. Wriggling out of a wrong contract

   The contracts are entered into by the parties in good faith. The first and primary assumption by the parties is that each of them is going to perform what has been mentioned in the contract as part of their obligations. Thus, it is the duty of the parties to write in the contract properly what they are willing to do and what they expect the other party to do. It is also important that the terms of the contract are unequivocal and unambiguous. It is not the job of the courts to correct mistakes in a contract. Hence, at any point of time if a party realises that it has entered into a contract, which it should not have entered into, it must at the earliest possible opportunity wriggle out of the contract and not perform what he is not willing to do or never had envisaged to do. It is fine that you are a gentleman and you would like to behave like a gentleman—that is you would like to keep the promises you had made. I am not saying that do not keep your promises; the only thing I would like to say is that, first, be very cautious and prudent at the time of signing a contract or entering into an oral contract so that you don't make promises which you never wanted to make. It is always a good idea to perform the contract not only in letter but in the spirit also—the spirit with which the parties had entered into the contract. But, remember the basic principle: it should be on your own sweet will and with your free consent. As any party enters into a contract voluntarily, it is not one of the wisest things to do to enter into a contract which is going to put many restrictions on yourself, or, something that you would have never thought and agreed to do; something for which you do not have the complete idea of what you are supposed to do and what repercussions it may have.

   It is advisable to insert an "exit clause" which possibly gives you the opportunity to wriggle out of a difficult situation. If you're able to identify a mistake in the contract, correct it as soon as possible. This mistake may be regarding the language used in the contract, which might give rise to misunderstanding between the parties or it may be regarding the facts which have been mentioned in the contract. Whatever the mistake is, it is best to bring it to the notice of the other party, correct it and act accordingly. If the other party does not agree, go ahead and rescind the contract.

5. Best Efforts, Certainty, Anticipate and Create Options

   Often a contract will contain 'best efforts' clauses, which makes it an obligation on the parties to do their best efforts to achieve the desired purpose of the contract. But, such best efforts could possibly be done only for something which is in your control and which can be done with reasonable efforts. Reasonableness is paramount in determining whether a party has done his best efforts or not. It is difficult to achieve certainty with best effort clauses as there is a lot of subjectivity in defining best efforts. It is desirable to have specific and measurable parameters in a contract to minimise subjectivity and move towards certainty. If it is possible to anticipate breach of a contract, a business leader must try to create options to tackle any such situation in the future. That prior planning helps in minimising the injury and getting the best possible solution in the worst case scenario.

Chapter 6
Will Intellectual Property Help My Business?

Businesses create, protect and commercially exploit intellectual property. Tangible properties, like buildings, machines, etc. are secondary in importance to patents, copyright, design, trade secrets and trademarks. These are all different branches of intellectual property rights (IPRs). It is said that the American economy gained its strength as the patent law that gave tremendous protection to inventions. The electric bulb, telephone and many other inventions became accessible to the masses due to protection given by the patent law. The inventor is sure that he would get his due during the term of the patent and, therefore, puts in a lot of effort to make it better and better. The same applies to copyright, trademarks and other form of intellectual property.

Some companies and individuals are very particular about protecting their intellectual property like Microsoft, Coke, Harvard Business School, etc. and exploit them commercially. It is a wrong notion that only high-tech companies have intellectual property. All the businesses, including the roadside vendors have certain knowledge and information if not strictly speaking, intellectual property, which needs protection for competitive success. A natural corollary is that intellectual property of others should be given due recognition and respect. Trade secrets like Coke formula deserve special protection as there is hardly any law to protect secrets besides the contract law. With global business becoming the norm, businesses have to ensure that global protection is accorded to the firm's intellectual property as it strategically helps in erecting entry barriers, reducing costs and much more.

One of the most important salient features of intellectual property, unlike tangible property, is non-excludability. The use of intellectual property is non-rivalrous. In simple words, if A has a pen and he lends it to B, then A does not possess the pen, but B possesses the pen. Now if B hands over the pen to C, B does not possess the pen but C possesses the pen. Thus, we can see that the pen physically transfers from A to B to C, however, ownership of the pen remains with A, assuming A owned it from the beginning.

In the case of intellectual property, the situation is very different. If A knows a formula, let us say, $X + Y = Z$, and he tells the formula to B, A is not deprived of

© The Author(s) 2017
A.K. Agarwal, *Business Leadership and Law*, DOI 10.1007/978-81-322-3682-5_6

that formula. Both A and B know the formula. Now if B tells the same formula to C, neither A nor B is deprived of that formula. And, if C shares that formula with a group through a social networking site, everyone in the group now knows the formula. Thus, A, B, C and all group members know the formula. So, we see that the use is non-rivalrous and any number of people can be in the know-how of the same formula, without depriving the other person.

This is one of the most important features of intellectual property, but this one feature makes the protection of intellectual property so very different and difficult as compared to that of tangible property. If a person possesses a diamond ring, she can really protect it in a manner she likes: wear it, keep it in a safe or a bank locker, etc. If any person snatches the ring from her, or she loses the ring somewhere, she will get to know of it. But in the case of intellectual property if a person knows a particular idea and owns it as the creator, and if that idea leaks out to any other person, the former may not even get to know that the latter knows it. And, this makes intellectual property so very precarious.

For instance, Britannia in India had developed the Tiger brand of biscuits. It had a long lasting intellectual property dispute with Danone of France regarding sharing of royalty. Such a case highlights the fact that companies must pay due attention to intellectual property.[1] Very recently in May 2016, the IPR tussle between Google and Oracle over copyright issues saw a new turn in the shape of jury decision.

Copyright: Google–Oracle API

In May 2016, Google had scored a historic legal victory against Oracle in a copyright dispute related to Application Program Interface (API), which was really good news for consumers. The jury rejected Oracle's claim of about $9 billion (almost Rs. 60,000 crores) and upheld Google's right of fair use of the copyrighted APIs. The case simply was as follows. Oracle got the ownership of copyright in the Java APIs, when it took control of Sun Microsystems. APIs, as the name suggests, are the interfaces which make it possible for software developers to use a common language to interact and give commands for performing certain functions. Android smartphones use Java APIs extensively and the sheer number of Android users in the world—more than 1.4 billion—makes the legal battle worth pursuing.

Google had used 37 out of 166 of Java APIs packages, and Oracle interestingly had won a case last year in the Federal Circuit court when the APIs were held to be copyrightable. Prior to that, a Federal District court had ruled that the APIs were not copyrightable. Google had moved the Supreme Court against the Circuit Court's

---

[1]DNA Money. 2006. September 1, 2006. Danone puts Tiger brand on a roll; http://www.dnaindia. com/money/report-danone-puts-tiger-brand-on-a-roll-1050586, last accessed September 14, 2016.

decision, but the SC had refused to hear the matter, considering it not to be important enough. Unlike the Supreme Court of India, which hears almost all the matters that are filed, the US Supreme Court is highly selective and does not hear all the filed matters. It exercises discretion at the first stage itself. Thus, the matter had gone to the jury for deciding the compensation.

With this chequered history, the matter seemed to be finally settled, but it may take another interesting turn when the jury verdict shall be appealed by Oracle. Fair use of APIs by Google appears to be quite simplistic as the company has made huge profit by using copyrighted APIs. It is not only Google, but there are so many companies like Samsung, Lenovo, etc. which use Android for their smartphones. In case Oracle finally wins, there may be a cascading effect with all the consumers using Android being liable for copyright violation. Had the courts finally held that there was no copyright in the APIs, it would have been a different scenario. Everyone, including Google, would have been free to use that material. But once the APIs were held to be protected by copyright, it became very difficult to imagine how pure commercial use can be termed to be fair use, a ground for using copyrighted material without paying a single penny as license fee to the owner and even without seeking the consent of the owner.

Undoubtedly, the jury's decision will be beneficial to the consumers worldwide, but it is not in the right spirit which has been the guiding light to the intellectual property legal protection and economic development in the United States for a few centuries. Often the economic development of the United States is said to be because of the patent protection given to inventions and so systematically guarded. Whether it is the electric bulb or telephone or the modern day microchips, patents have been at the frontier in making the technical ideas commercially successful. Similarly, the copyright protection to films, music, books, software, etc. created hugely successful: Walt Disney characters, Microsoft users' agreements, affordable legal downloading of music along with protection of performers' rights.

It will be a sad day for copyright protection advocates if Oracle finally loses this case, not because Oracle will not be able to get the billions of dollars of damages from Google, but because there will not be any commercial gain despite getting the APIs copyrighted. Jury trial is not the best way to decide intellectual property matters, as these are highly technical in nature and members of the jury, by its basic composition and concept, are individuals from different walks of life, and not necessarily trained either in law or technology. It is perplexing that the United States still uses the services of a jury to decide such complicated technical matters. Jury members are typically tilted towards benefit to the society at large, which may not always be the best criterion to decide matters based on hard facts and cold legal principles.

It is not only the copyright but the protection of design is also important in the commercial world as the following case about a kids' suitcase tells us.

Trunki Versus Kiddee Case: What is in a Design?
UK Supreme Court, 2016

In March 2016, the Supreme Court of the United Kingdom decided a case about the design of a suitcase used by kids. It was a landmark judgment and would possibly have serious implications globally. Design of products appeal solely to the eye and get protection by law in different jurisdictions for the aesthetic appeal. Law in most of the evolved jurisdictions provides protection by either a separate law meant for design, or by the patent law itself. In India, the design law is a separate law, however, in the United States it is a part of the patent law. In the United Kingdom, the protection is by the European Union law for Registered Community Design for a maximum period of 25 years. It is managed by the Office for Harmonization in the Internal Market.

'Trunki' branded suitcases were designed as small-sized ride on suitcases for kids with wheels at the bottom. The suitcase was decorated with eyes, nose, mouth of an animal with horns to hold on while sitting on it. This was a new concept and the designer, Robert Law, founder of the Magmatic company won a prize for the design in 1998. Thereafter, he had got the design registered in 2003 as Registered Community Design, which consisted of six images prepared by a 3-D Computer Aided Design (CAD). These suitcases gained popularity among kids and Trunki became a very successful brand and made huge profit from the sales. However, the products were sold at a premium and often the customers felt the pinch. Cashing in on this opportunity, Hong Kong-based PMS started selling lookalike children's suitcases with the brand name 'Kiddee case' in the United Kingdom, Germany and several other countries. By its own admission, the PMS' design was inspired by Trunki.

A few years back Magmatic sued PMS in the United Kingdom for wilfully ripping off Trunki as both the suitcases were designed to look like animals and can be ridden by children. Magmatic had argued that its registered community design had been infringed and hence, PMS must not be allowed to sell its products with confusingly and deceptively similar design. On the other hand, PMS had argued that fair competition required that such design rights should not stop competitors from using the idea as their suitcases were significantly different. Whereas Trunki's design was related to an impression of an animal with horns, Kiddee case's design gave the impression of an insect with antennae or an animal with ears.

These are interesting arguments and without going into too much detail, one can very well say, what the big deal is. Even if one can give the shape of a suitcase to look like an animal, should there be an intellectual property protection? What may happen if one protects a tiger, and the competitor makes an elephant like suitcase? Or a horse. A horse may be a bit too skinny to fit in things, so how about a hippopotamus or a rhinoceros or a whale? The number of fat bodied animals may not be too large and then the entire animal kingdom may be owned or rather 'protected' by enterprising businesspersons. It all depends on the legal environment in the local jurisdiction. One can possibly say with confidence that had such a protection been applied for in India, in all probability, it would have been denied. Such a thought appears to be a bit too impractical for protection in India.

The UK Supreme Court did not agree with Magmatic. It is a good signal that intellectual property protection for ideas, far-fetched thoughts, minute and minuscule changes is not a good idea and needs to be dumped. Discarding such protection will help in competition throwing equally good, or sometimes better products, which the people would have been deprived of had the protection been granted or extended. There is a very thin line to be followed.

Design protection by its very nature poses such difficult questions. For instance, Apple had sued Samsung and several other companies for what it called as the design patent for curved corners. An English judge had even commented that Apple products were cool. Millions or rather billions of dollars ride on unique design of products. But, in a world where copying any product has been made a child's play by technological advancements like 3-D printing, it is going to be a real tough time to protect such designs. Highly technical and strict legal environment may give strong protection, but that may be difficult to be enforced.

Protection of confidential information depends on the legal environment in which the contractual clauses have to be enforced. Many a time, these clauses compel the parties to negotiate and settle.

Confidential Information: Thompson, Abramson and Sloan-Kettering

There have been several instances for the last so many decades when employees have left their companies and joined new employers bringing with them experience and a lot of information from their earlier job. There can be two methods—particular clauses in the contract—to prevent the employee from sharing vital information gathered from the earlier job with the new employer. These clauses can be a Non-Disclosure Agreement (NDA), as a separate agreement or a clause in the employer–employee contract. Or, it can be a non-compete clause in the agreement, which restraints the employee to take up employment with the competitor of the earlier employer for a said period of time, typically 1 or 2 years, known as the cooling off period.

In February 2012, the president of the famous Memorial Sloan-Kettering Cancer Center in New York was charged with divulging ground-breaking research of the former employer to the new employer. Dr. Craig B Thompson was working with Abramson Cancer Institute at the University of Pennsylvania since 1999. In 2010 he moved to Sloan-Kettering as its president. He had been accused of using proprietary technology and research of Abramson Institute at his own company—Agios Pharmaceuticals, which he had started.

Abramson Institute held patents for its research. Agios wanted to get as many patents as possible but was not able to get them from Abramson. The concept of a patent is that the invention is known to the public with full details and hence, anyone who is skilled in that particular art known as PHOSITA; person having ordinary skills in the art will be able to enable that particular invention after going through the complete details of the patent. It is only after furnishing the entire details, a patent is granted to the inventor. This is the beauty of the patent law that the invention is not kept as a secret but is known to the world and is still protected by legal framework.

In this case, it was crucial to know whether Dr. Thompson had shared patented technology with Agios, or it was sharing only of knowledge related to that particular research. In February 2012, the matter was heard in the US District Court in Manhattan and it was for the court to decide, based on the facts of the case, as to who was on the right side of the law. However, as most of such matters result in bringing the accused party to the negotiating table, the case was finally mutually settled in September the same year. The terms of settlement were kept confidential, but interestingly, neither Agios nor Thompson had admitted to any wrongdoing. All the parties took the moral high ground of working for the benefit of cancer patients.

On the face of it, it might appear that litigation, which usually is lengthy and uncertain, could not have helped cancer patients and further research on the subject. However, on the contrary, a proper decision by the competent judicial forum could have put an end to the controversy and confusion regarding the ownership of any such research and also the transferability to any other person. That would have been better by clearly laying down the rights and obligations of the concerned parties.

Anyway, what we need to appreciate is the highly evolved legal environment for such patent disputes in the United States. As the second best option, the best would have been a conclusive court decision; it was in the interest of cancer patients that the dispute was settled at an early stage and facilitated the researchers to go ahead with their work. This is one of the greatest advantages of a proper legal framework which creates deterrence and thus allows the rightful owner of a research to reap the benefits—money and reputation—of research. It is essential that original research is recognised and rewarded, which encourages other researchers and scientists to work on the unsolved mysteries of human body.

It is imperative that such intricate issues regarding complex and advanced research are handled deftly by the courts. American courts have displayed tremendous maturity and competence in several patent cases earlier and this particular case would not have posed any foreseeable difficulty. Legal certainty is good for research. Court decision or settlement, the dust must settle. The show must go on.

According to intellectual property law all over the world, trademarks are forever, however, just like a driving license or passport, they need to be renewed whenever the term gets over. Because of this fantastic characteristic of trademarks, as contradistinguished with patents or copyrights, which have a definite term and after that term these rights fall into the public domain and anyone is free to use them, trademarks, if registered and renewed properly, can last forever. But, what is to be protected as a trademark is a question which does not have a clear and straight answer. Businesses have tried their best to include any and all features of their products—name, logo, graphic design, shape, packaging, colour, aroma, smell, sound, phrase, jingle—to be included in the definition of trademarks. There have been serious disputes between companies for protection of a particular colour. One interesting dispute was between the giants Cadbury and Nestlé.

Roses Are Red, Violets Are Blue... Is Cadbury Purple?

Are all roses red in colour? Are all violets blue in colour? Surely not. Mother Nature has created roses in so many different colours—red, white, pink, yellow, to name a few—and also violets in so many different shades of blue—and the fact of the matter is that violet and blue are two different colours—that it would not be completely true to say that roses are red and violets are blue. But, that is being a bit too technical, rather than romantic. Yes, love and romance are fine, and one would appear to be a big fool to ask the same question to love birds, but when it comes to law, there is a different connotation. What would a lawyer say when asked the same question?

In all probability, a trademark lawyer would never agree to this statement as he would demand specificity of the colour to hold the statement true. For instance, one of the biggest chocolate makers in the world—Cadbury—has used a definite shade of purple, defined in the experts' parlance as Pantone 2685C, for almost a century and in October 2013 lost the trademark legal battle in the British Court of Appeal to its arch rival Nestlé.

In evolved jurisdictions like the United States, the United Kingdom and other places where intellectual property law has evolved due to legislative development, and also due to newer interpretations by the judiciary, colour has been given protection as a trademark, which certainly makes sense as a number of consumers can directly connect the product with the colour; however, one of the most fundamental and basic questions which deserves to be answered is, does any company have the right to use any colour exclusively and call that particular colour as it is own? It appears to be a bit moving towards the extreme side of intellectual property protection as nature provides us innumerable colours, and it would be incredulous to side with the law which gives protection for a particular colour. Despite this basic difficulty, law has provided protection to the colour of certain products as trademark.

With this idea, Cadbury had applied for the protection of purple colour as its exclusive colour as a trademark. Nestlé had opposed it, but had lost the first round of legal battle last year in a British lower court. It appealed in the Court of Appeal, and the judges did not agree with Cadbury's reasoning and decided it against Cadbury. The purple colour was chosen by Cadbury in honour of Queen Victoria whose favourite colour was purple and Cadbury started using a very specific shade, but as the Court of Appeal reasoned, the company attempted to register multiple signs, with several uses of the shade in different permutations and combinations. The law, typically, protects the 'predominant colour' but as the company used multiple graphical presentations, instead of using a single and consistent block of colour, it could not get the protection.

It is easy to understand the view of the British Court. Had the company used only one single method of applying the colour to the wrappers, it could have been given the protection, but greater creativity and ingenuity in the used of the same colour in multiple ways did not translate into one simple recognisable manner of connecting with the product and the company. In the court, the company had argued that giving protection to Cadbury for the purple colour would not give it an unfair advantage as there were so many other shades available to be picked up and monopolised by other companies whether selling chocolates or other goods.

Tiffany, the famous jewellery company, already has a colour—Tiffany Blue—in its name and protected in several jurisdictions as colour trademark. It was first used by Tiffany in 1845 on the cover of its Blue Book and since then the company has used this colour extensively. The American courts allow colour trademark and in an interesting case—Qualitex versus Jacobson—regarding the colour of dry cleaning pads, the US Supreme Court in 1995 gave protection to the green gold colour.

In India, the courts have not favoured granting trademark protection to colours. Soap companies selling soaps of different colours—red, green, pink, brown, etc.— have tried their best to get protection for colour, but could not succeed. The conditions regarding lighting and availability of power are not conducive to give the consumer the opportunity to differentiate between two close shades. The poverty, illiteracy and lack of awareness make the ordinary consumers in India quite gullible to be easily befooled by unscrupulous businesspersons to pass off their products.

The Cadbury judgment should be welcomed as it is a step in the right direction— ending the unethical and unreasonable, though at times held to be legal, monopoly of a company over a colour. And, the best test for a chocolate should be its taste, not the colour of its wrapper.

European courts have been deciding interesting cases about trademarks, but there was a case when a French court changed the name of a young girl in January 2015.

What is in a Name? A Lot

Whatever the Bard of Avon might have thought about a name and said that a rose by any other name would smell as sweet, the French do not seem to agree with him. In January 2015, a French court refused to recognise the name of a girl who was named Nutella by her parents, as the court reasoned that Nutella—the trade name of a hazelnut spread—may cause the child to face embarrassing situations in life and she may be the target of derision. The Court went a step further and simply dropped 'Nut' from Nutella and named her Ella.

It seems to be a very simple manner of dealing with changing names. However, the incident forces us to ponder over this issue of naming of children, and for that matter naming anything else also. Talking about naming individuals, a few years back, a Chinese couple wanted to name their child with a word which would be so very common that almost everyone might have been using it. After a lot of research the couple zeroed in on '@', which is used in each and every e-mail address. But Chinese government authorities refused to register '@' as the name of an individual.

About the same time, the North Korean government had decided that no one in the country could be named Kim Jong-Un, which is the name of the North Korean leader. And interestingly, all those who have already been named so by their parents have to mandatorily change their names. If they refuse to change their names they have to jolly well face the wrath of the North Korean leader.

In late 1970s and early 1980s, Indian space programme was experimenting with the Skylab. To commemorate that a couple at that time had named their son as 'Skylab Singh', who surely has grown up and today even has a Facebook account. It is very common to find people naming their children according to their aspirations and often one will find boys named as Jarnail Singh, Karnail Singh, etc. to match the inner desire of the parents that one day their child would be the General and Colonel in the army, respectively, and pronounced in the local language as *Jarnail* and *Karnail* respectively. The law in India does not prohibit naming the child anyway the parents like that to do. Or, for that matter, once the child is grown up, if he does not like the name, he can very well go and change the name to his own liking.

Individual names may be a very personal choice and there may be very few jurisdictions in the world which would like to interfere in the exercise of such choice, however, there are trade names—trademarks and service marks—which are very well regimented and controlled by the legal environment in different countries. Trademarks and logos are some of the most important intellectual property rights of businesses all over the world and most of the businesses would like to protect them to the best of their ability and would oppose any action by any other business entity, particularly any competitor, to use either the name or the logo which may be deceptively or confusingly similar to theirs.

Bala shoes for Bata shoes, Likeboy and Lifeboy for Lifebuoy soaps, and similar other deceptively and confusingly similar trade names can easily be found in the market. There are also a lot of confusingly similar logos used by unscrupulous traders in the market often by either changing the colour scheme or slightly changing the pattern. Though imitation may be the best form of flattery, the original users are not amused by such imitation and often resort to restrict legal remedies. In all such matters pertaining to trade and business, it is understandable that the statutory legal remedy of trademark action or the common law remedy of passing off may be pressed into action, however, it is a bit difficult for us to appreciate the fact that the law and the government—as we have discussed—can really have a say in the matter and that too with authority of law.

We can very well imagine what would have happened to a country of 1.25 billion people. The courts are already loaded heavily with unresolved matters, and it would surely be prudent to leave the naming exercise to the parents and the individual. Businesses can not have a proprietary protection for individuals' names. The issue of names may appear a bit trivial, however, issues related with pharmaceuticals, biotechnology and patents have often been taken to the highest courts in different jurisdictions. One such case was about gene patenting in the United States.

Myriad Case: Biotechnology Business and Gene Patents

In June 2013, the US Supreme Court decided a case about gene patenting and held that 'a naturally occurring DNA segment is a product of nature and not patent eligible merely because it has been isolated, but cDNA is patent eligible because it is not naturally occurring'. Earlier in 2011 August, the United States Court of Appeals for the Federal Circuit had upheld a gene patent which is used in cancer test. This patent was for a test to predict breast and ovarian cancer in women and is owned by Myriad Genetics. The patent was challenged and the lower court had decided that human genes could not be patented. It was appealed and in the last week of July 2011, the appellate court overturned the lower court's decision.

Granting a patent is an act of fine balance. On the one hand, there is the inventor who has made a new invention and hence he needs to be encouraged and provided with sufficient incentive to continue his research. Other scientists and researchers also conduct research for new and useful things for the society and it is the duty of the society to encourage them. On the other hand, it is also important that the society benefits from the inventions. For this purpose, the inventors are supposed to disclose their work in totality and enable a'person having ordinary skill in the art' (PHOSITA) to make it.

The patent laws in different countries aim to achieve this purpose—a win–win situation for both, the inventor and the society. In most of the countries, the inventors can apply to the patent office for grant of a patent, as per the law in that country. A patent is usually granted to a new, useful and nonobvious product or process for a term of twenty years. In case there is no such provision of a patent law in a country, the inventor may choose not to disclose it to anyone and keep the invention a closely guarded secret. That would result in a big loss to the society.

The United States has a developed and highly evolved patent law, which has surely contributed in its economic development, though there have been long legal battles. For the last more than hundred years, inventors of bulb, telephone, car, colour TV etc. have fought such battles to get patent protection.

In an interesting case, *Diamond versus Chakrabarty*, the US Supreme Court in 1980 decided that genetically modified organisms can be patented. Chakrabarty was working for General Electric and had developed a genetically modified micro-organism which was capable of breaking down crude oil. It had great industrial usage in the cases of oil spills. He filed for a patent and the matter finally reached the US Supreme Court. By a razor-thin majority (5–4) the court ruled in favour of Chakrabarty and upheld the patent and observed, 'a live, human-made micro-organism is patentable subject matter'. The court held that patent laws in the

United States have to be given wide scope and thus the interpretation should be wide and not narrow.

Since 1980s—and Chakrabarty's case was, of course, an important decision—the biotech industry took birth. Since then tremendous amount of research has been conducted in this field and one of the inspiring and guiding aspects has been the fact that path breaking research will be rewarded with the patent. Gene patents are one of the most important and valuable assets of the biotech industry. That has continued to provide an environment of certainty to researchers and businesses. A sudden change in the environment, which makes it uncertain, will surely lead to confusion and anxiety.

In the Myriad case, which had been decided by 2-1 majority in the Court of Appeals, the judge writing the dissenting opinion said that genes should not be patented just because they were isolated from the body. He wrote, 'extracting a gene is akin to snapping a leaf from a tree'. However, the majority did not agree with this idea and said that isolating DNA created a new chemical entity and was not like snapping a leaf from a tree.

The majority wrote in very strong words that enactment of new law is the job of the legislature and the judiciary must refrain from usurping this power. The judgment says, 'Judicial restraint is particularly important here because an entire industry developed in the decades since the Patent Office first granted patents to isolated DNA. Disturbing the biotechnology industry's settled expectations now risks impeding, not promoting, invention'.

There have, however, been strong voices of opposition regarding the award of such patents as the patent holders demand, at times, unreasonable sums for granting a license for the use of such patents. For instance, the charges for using Myriad's patented technology are more than $3000 for breast cancer risk test. Even by American standards, this is not a small amount and there is discontentment among patients, who are supposed to pay this amount. Though it is taken care of by the insurance companies, the patients indirectly have to pay this sum. This is, therefore, the heavy price which the society pays for getting the patented invention.

Whether this price is low or high is a matter to be decided according to the context—place, persons involved, circumstances, etc. In this case, when it appears to be on the higher side in a developed country like the United States, then the chances of this technology being available for developing and under-developed world are remote. The population in the world living in these countries is much more than that living in the developed world. Whether these people have a right to get access to the latest developments in the field of medical sciences? Should the governments in these countries try to make the latest technology, methods and drugs available to their people? These are the questions which are bothering the leaders of developing and underdeveloped world. Thus, the tension between patent rights on the one hand and the human rights on the other hand is quite palpable.

India, being a developing nation, cannot afford such expensive tests, but it is essential that for its more than a billion population, the latest in the field of medical science is made available. This is what our political and business leaders should try to achieve. However, our business leaders, particularly looking at the growth opportunities in the biotechnology sector, should also be aware of the developments taking place in the United States and the changing legal environment for research and business. It is of utmost importance that before venturing out to the United States and other developed countries; the legal regime for intellectual property is taken into consideration and decisions are made after anticipating the changes at least in the near future. The future of biotechnology industry in India seems to be bright if care is taken to factor in the uncertainties of the ever changing law regarding patents.

The Supreme Court's decision had given finality to the debate about gene patenting by holding, in simple words, that anything occurring in nature cannot be patented. A business leader has to act accordingly while formulating the business strategy.

Trademarks and the Madrid Protocol

It would not be wrong to say that trademarks are an integral part of any brand, and companies can go to any extent to protect the intellectual property in the form of trademarks. This is true even regarding the geographical territories a company can venture into for safeguarding its trademark. For a multinational company selling its products in a number of jurisdictions, it is necessary to protect its trademark in all those jurisdictions and according to the law of the land of each such jurisdiction. This, practically, means dealing with multiple legal systems, different laws—substantive and procedural, and keeping track of the trademark applications in different countries, even when, ironically, the trademark is the same and identical.

In case anyone of us wishes to send an e-mail to a number of recipients, it can be done in one go; by a simple click of the mouse. There is no need to send separate e-mails to each of the recipient. The same convenience was envisaged for the registration of trademarks, so that for a large number of companies, which prefer to do business in multiple countries, with one filing of application, the mark could be registered, or at least get protected, in most of the jurisdictions.

As each of the countries, typically, is a sovereign nation—barring a few—there had been no international mechanism to do the same, except some of the countries coming together and entering into a multilateral treaty for providing the same convenience and protection to applications filed in either of such countries. This system for the protection of trademarks is called as the Madrid system—the Agreement and the Protocol—and India deposited its instrument of accession to the Madrid protocol on 8 April 2013 in Geneva at World Intellectual Property Organisation (WIPO). The number of countries which have joined the international trademark system is now more than 90, which includes most of the major trading jurisdictions.

Besides the obvious advantages of following the common international system for protection of trademarks, India's accession to the Madrid system is an extremely positive signal to the global companies and investors, who were till the recent past, wary about the protection provided by the National trademark law in the country and also a long period of time is spent, coupled with uncertainty, after filing for registration of a trademark in India.

There have been very interesting cases when some of the international brands have found themselves to be at the receiving end while doing business in India, or surprisingly, even when they had not been doing any business in India. The well-known washing machine company—Whirlpool—at one point of time, found that its trademark was being used blatantly by an Indian company, which forced the American company to fight the legal battle right up to the Supreme Court, which in turn resulted in a landmark judgement pronounced in 1996 recognising the well-known trademarks having a spill-over effect, which later on became part and parcel of the new trademark law enacted in 1999.

Unlike patents and copyright, which have a time period after which the term ends, usually 20 years and 60 years, respectively; there is no term for the trademarks. Like diamonds, trademarks are for ever. The only condition is that just like the passport, it has to be renewed by filing an application and paying the renewal fee, and also satisfying the authorities that the trademark had been used for the particular purpose for which it has been registered, and that it had not been lying unused. It is something like a reserved berth in the train—one passenger cannot get two berths reserved, even if he is willing to pay for the second, which he wishes to use for keeping his luggage.

The simple principle is: you use it or you lose it. For a moment, let us say that trademarks also had a certain time period after which it would become free, like any patented product, to be used by anyone. In such a scenario today, every Tom, Dick and Harry would be making and selling Coca-Cola, Pepsi, Ford cars and Singer sewing machines. We all very well-known that it is not possible. However, it is possible for anyone to go ahead and make an electric bulb, as the patent held by Edison ended a long time ago. The same applies to automobiles, colour televisions, telephones, etc.

Despite the new law enacted in India in 1999, awareness regarding trademarks leaves a lot to be desired. A number of things are available in the market which blatantly violate the trademark law and the enforcement machinery has not been able to really stop the proliferation of such goods and traders. Besides the enforcement part, they had been repeated requests, particularly by international business companies to streamline the procedural aspects of trademark protection law in India, which included doing away with multiple filing of applications. At least India has taken this bold, but long overdue, step which will be beneficial both for the international companies, as well as the Indian companies which are doing business abroad.

There is, however, a word of caution. Integrating ourselves with the global system exposes us to all the issues and risks—which any network does—to which we were earlier insulated. For instance, the idea of central attack, which has been labelled as one of the major disadvantages of the Madrid system, is that if there is a certain problem or deficiency found in the application in one of the jurisdictions, the application cannot survive in any of the jurisdictions. This is one of the commonly used tactics by competitors. This may prove to be a small disadvantage as compared to the immense advantages in terms of cost, time, simplicity, which one gets by following the international system of trademarks.

It is only a matter of time which will tell us whether the system is going to really help the Indian businesses, but one thing is certain—simply agreeing to do what most of the business jurisdictions are doing, we convey that we are ready to integrate and we mean business.

Aereo Case: Technology Versus Law

Not very often judges at the highest court are seized of a matter which may change the shape of things in the future for the mankind. Last month, the US Supreme Court heard arguments in a case—American Broadcasting Companies versus Aereo—which has the potential of changing the manner in which people receive TV signals. The decision is expected in a few months' time.

It is very well-known that technology precedes and law follows. The simple reason is that in several cases with cutting-edge technology; it is impossible to anticipate how the new technology will develop and therefore, it is not at all possible for law-makers to make the law proactively. It is only when a technology is developed, and particularly when it is successfully commercialised, the parties suffering try to blend their business strategy with a little bit of legal aspects, and that too in a jurisdiction with clear, confident and speedy legal environment, to regain the losing business turf. In other jurisdictions, with the legal environment for business on the other extreme, it simply does not make sense to waste time, effort and money in any legal pursuit and the existing business players try to use every possible trick—howsoever illegal it may be, as the law in such jurisdictions in all probability will not be able to penalise them—to keep the new technology out of the reach of public.

The United States is indubitably in the first category and existing players need to be extremely careful about the legal issues lest; they should be caught on the wrong side of law and thereafter heavily penalised.

A new and small company, Aereo, founded by an Indian-American—Chet Kanojia—developed a tiny device which has the capability of catching signals broadcast by TV companies over-the-air free and then using them for online transmission to customers. Aereo charges a small monthly fee from its customers. So, Aereo gets free signals from broadcasters and charges a fee from customers, which means that the broadcasters do not get anything from the end-customers. Others, who use cable TV, pay to the cable operator, who in turn pays a 're-transmission fee' to broadcasting companies.

A little bit of understanding of over-the-air broadcast will be helpful. This is also called 'terrestrial' broadcast and is free, as compared to cable transmission. Any person can use a small antenna to pick up the signals, however, there may be issues of the quality of reception, and all broadcasting companies do not offer free terrestrial broadcast. The question is of 'retransmission' if someone picks up the free signals and distributes them. Kanojia's device, in that sense, does not retransmit as the device is given, for a fee, to individuals for personal use. Then, can it be called 'public performance'? According to copyright law in the United States, and also in most of the evolved jurisdictions including India, public performance of copyrighted material is not permitted without the consent of the copyright owner. These are the critical questions the US Supreme Court will answer shortly.

Let us consider the case of solar energy. In case, a person installs solar panels, converts solar energy to electricity and then transmits it to, say, ten users for a fee, is there a legal problem? There may be if there is any law against conversion or such transmission, or the Sun objects that it does not permit 'retransmission'.

In the Aereo case, the Sun—the group of broadcasting companies—has objected that the content is copyrighted and should not be made available so easily for free. But then, what about those individuals who pick up the over-the-air signals broadcast by the same companies for free? The companies are fine with that. From the business point of view, the companies do not bother much about them, as their number is small. However, if their cable customers will switch to Kanojia's device, primarily because of small monthly charges as compared to hefty cable bills, they do bother. And, this is the real fight. The broadcasters have even contemplated to end the over-the-air transmission and continue only with cable transmission.

In June 2014, the US Supreme Court ruled against Aereo on the ground that it had infringed upon the rights of the copyright holders. The court ruled that the way Aereo was broadcasting television programmes, it was quite clear that the business model was based according to the law on a public performance for which copyright permission from the owners was necessary. The decision was by 6-3 majority.

Another US Supreme Court decision made headlines about business method patents. It was in 2014 when the Alice Corp. case was decided.

Patenting Abstract Ideas: Alice Corp. Versus CLS Bank

The US Supreme Court on 19 June 2014 decided the patent dispute between Alice Corp.—an Australian company—and CLS Bank, an American bank, regarding patenting of software and business method patents, which typically are not patentable in India. The Supreme Court held that the patents which were granted to Alice Corp. by the US Patent Office were not justifiable as they were simply abstract ideas and did not deserve patenting according to the American patent law.

It is a good decision and has been hailed by many, however, the Supreme Court has not gone further in terms of clarity as to what sort of software and business methods can be patented. To a certain extent, this is fine as there is no need for the Court to lay down everything with great clarity and may be close the options for any further interpretation with change in time and needs. Law in its true dynamic nature has been witnessed with ample freedom to innovate and push the frontier and test it as per the legal periphery in the country.

While it may be a good decision for legal experts and innovators, it is surely a big blow to patent trolls—those patent holders who simply patent their inventions without any intention of manufacturing and making it available to the general masses, and thereafter suing everyone who uses their patent partially or even peripherally. All said and done, patent is a negative right granted by the law to the inventor for exclusive use of the right, to the exclusion of everyone else. The underlying unwritten understanding is that the patent holder will make the new and useful invention available to the public. Accessibility and affordability are the key issues in a patent. And, if the purpose is defeated by patent trolls, then it is undoubtedly desirable that the patent itself is revoked and everyone is allowed to use it legally.

The definition of what may be patented depends on intention of the legislature, as documented in the statute and interpreted by the judiciary. The subject matter is defined in the American patent law, however, it is subject to interpretation and the courts over several decades have held that abstract things cannot be patented, but a combination with machine or something resulting in transformation of the inputs—all are quite subjective and will face tremendous difficulty in an objective definition—can be patented, which resulted in the last 15 years or so in opening the floodgates for business and software patents.

There is a new thinking, as practised by Tesla, to open patents for use by everyone. This may result in a sea change and also requires change in fundamental thinking about patents. The exclusivity of patents may not help in furthering interests of mankind if the balance between interest of inventors and society are tilted in favour of inventors, always. The judiciary performs this difficult job of maintaining the right balance by keeping the pendulum of interest swinging only a little on either side. Dramatic changes with huge amplitude in swinging of the pendulum do not infuse confidence in the society.

The role of judiciary becomes even more important to correct the wrongs committed by the patent office officials. It is true, though may sound unbelievable, that the patent offices, including the US Patent Office, at times grant ridiculous patents. Just by doing a little bit of search on the internet, one can have a look—with amusement—the patents granted, which should never have been granted. One such patent granted by the US Patent Office is the motorised ice cream cone, which makes the cone rotate and saves the person from the trouble of rotating and just concentrating on licking the ice cream. Does it deserve patenting?

Similarly, abstract ideas—whether related to software or business—might be patented if the patent office is a bit too lenient in evaluating patent applications. Such leniency gives rise to patent trolls, flooding the business environment with avoidable and unnecessary patents and thereby giving rise to litigation. The patent office in India, to the chagrin of several multi-national companies, is much more circumspect. Long-term public interest is paramount in a democratic country and patent law interpretation has to be aligned to this fundamental policy.

Takeaway for Business Leaders

1. Acquire and Protect

   It is important for a business leader to understand the value of different branches of intellectual property in his business. There is a possibility that there may be more than one very valuable branches of IPR which need to be acquired and protected for commercial exploitation. Most of the branches of IPR—patents, designs, copyrights, trademarks, etc.—have to be registered and granted by the concerned offices in different jurisdictions. Some IPR can be used even without registration, but their protection may be a bit difficult. The business leader must proactively register all the possible IPR in different products and services of his business. Thereafter, every effort should be made for proper protection in case of violation of any such rights. Mostly, the remedy sought will be a legal remedy, however, before filing a case in any legal forum, smart business leaders would like to explore the possibility of negotiation and settling the matter with the other party. This is a good move to protect your IPR by sending the right signal that the company takes its IPRs very seriously. If it does not work, one should not shy away from the idea of taking the matter to the right judicial forum.

2. Challenge

   The age-old tactics in intellectual property disputes, especially patents and copyright, is to challenge the ownership. For the protection of the patent of electric bulb, the automobile, Happy birthday song, etc., the intellectual property rights have been challenged. It is often seen that IPR of competitor or any other party may be used without any qualms and then the ball is in the court of the owner of IPR to take legal steps. That gives the so-called infringer a golden opportunity to challenge the grant of the IPR to the owner in the very first place. In case, the legal proceedings are against the owner, he is stripped off from the ownership of that particular IPR and depending on the context, it becomes open for everyone to be used. The story of legendary Henry Ford and so many others is based on this style of business leadership. However, one has to have tremendous patience and the ability to withstand huge expenditure while taking this route of business.

3. Legal Environment

   Protection of IPR is not in vacuum. A proper legal environment is the sine qua non. A business leader must have the ability to understand the difference between a so-called good legal environment, which may exist on paper only, and an effective legal environment. In the former, he should be overenthusiastic about the protection being available to his IPRs. He can afford to have that luxury only in an effective legal environment, which also is quite expensive. In mature and evolved jurisdictions, protection of IPR can be assured but only through the route of legal proceedings. Proper evaluation of IPRs of the business and taking steps so that the valuation does not diminish is essential for a business leader. Any negative publicity may lower the value of any trademarks and the business leader should be careful to nip in the bud any such adverse comments. Copycats must be dealt with strongly to send the stern message and exhibit intentions of protecting IPR at every cost. But, all this can be done only in a proper legal environment. A business leader should never try to do any such thing in an extremely weak and ineffective legal environment.

4. Certainty, Anticipate, Create Options

To be certain about the IPRs is challenging. The way copying is becoming easier due to developments in technology, there is very little certainty about the benefits one can derive from IPRs. A business leader, hence, should not try for too much certainty for IPR protection. But, it does not mean that he should not take the logical and reasonable steps necessary for IPR protection. After doing all that a smart business leader is supposed to do and get done by lawyers, he should focus on anticipating about different scenarios in case of violation and infringement. He should keep the evidence ready in case there is a legal battle, and also try to create options if the legal battle does not provide answers to the problems, or the decision from the legal forum takes a long time to be pronounced. Creating options for doing business with the assumption that there are no IPRs can give the business leader tremendous confidence and insights in using other characteristics of his goods and services to earn profits. Thus, certainty of IPRs is only a mirage and a business leader must understand it clearly.

Chapter 7
I Love Peace. No Disputes Please

Business and disputes, usually, go hand-in-hand. In case a company is operating without disputes, it may be simply because of complacency or suffering at the hands of other parties, or it is plain lucky. P.B. Shelley wrote, 'If winter comes, can spring be far behind?' With respect to business, it can be said with a lot of certainty, 'If business comes, can disputes be far behind?' Disputes are inevitable for any business. What should a business leader do in case a dispute arises? Dispute avoid is considered to be better than dispute resolution. However, there are situations when avoidance is not possible and one has to fight.

If a business leader has made up his mind to fight and bring a dispute to its logical conclusion, it is essential to do it in a legal manner. There are several methods of resolving a dispute—litigation being the traditionally used method. But once a matter reaches a court of law, it is highly uncertain as to when the matter shall be decided finally, and how much money and effort needs to be invested in such litigation. Smart business leaders try to avoid taking their matters to a court of law; one reason being that there is no confidentiality when a matter is heard in a court as courts are public places. There are other methods which are called alternative dispute resolution methods—in short known as ADR methods—and the most common method which is used by businesses all over the world is arbitration.

There are other methods of ADR, which unlike arbitration, are non-binding. These methods are negotiation, mediation, conciliation and also a mix of two or more of such methods. Due to the non-binding nature of these methods, these are not so common in India, however, these are being followed in the west, particularly in the United States, with a great deal of success. With all its drawbacks, arbitration is still one of the most favoured methods for business dispute resolution, both for domestic disputes and for international disputes. In a landmark judgment in 1974, the US Supreme Court upheld arbitration in an international contract vis-à-vis

© The Author(s) 2017
A.K. Agarwal, *Business Leadership and Law*, DOI 10.1007/978-81-322-3682-5_7

litigation. It was held that when parties had decided to go for arbitration, courts cannot take up the matter.[1] Later in 1985, it was maintained in the case of Mitsubishi.[2]

In brief, arbitration is a private court by a private judge known as arbitrator. The parties to a dispute have a right to decide who the arbitrator shall be, where the arbitration proceedings are going to be heard, what shall be the law which will guide arbitration, and several other related issues. The decision of the arbitrator is called an award and it is a binding decision on the parties. The courts enforce the award of an arbitrator as a decree of the court. The losing party can challenge the award of an arbitrator in a court on certain specific grounds, which are determined according to the arbitration law enforced in that country and pray to the court to set the arbitration award aside. This process may take a very long time and it has been seen that a large number of cases, where matters are of very high stakes, do end up in a court of law. Willy-nilly, the matter finally reaches the court—a place the parties wished to avoid and for this very reason they agreed to go for arbitration. The purpose is, therefore, defeated in a good number of cases. However, a lot depends on the business and legal environment and culture in that jurisdiction.

There are interesting cases providing valuable experience to business leaders to avoid, resolve and handle the disputes, if any. Usually, these matters are business specific and also pertain to certain geography, but can be used to understand similarly positioned issues. Analogy and extrapolation often do provide practical tips to tackle the situation in an easy and effective manner.

Suzuki—Volkswagen Dispute, 2011

In 2011, Suzuki (Japan) initiated a dispute with Volkswagen (Germany) regarding their 2009 agreement.[3] Fiat (Italy) was also indirectly involved. Suzuki has been present in India since the early 1980s due to its relationship with Maruti, and is extremely well known to the Indian consumers. It also understands the changing aspirations of Indian consumers to a great extent. Volkswagen from Germany wished to expand its presence in India and thought that it would be a good idea to join hands with Suzuki, which was eager to get the cutting-edge technology for diesel engines—available with Volkswagen—for its small cars in India. Both the companies thought it to be a win-win situation, and in late 2009 they entered into an agreement for the same through cross-holding, Volkswagen taking 20 % in Suzuki, and the latter taking about 2 % in the former.

---

[1]Scherk v. Alberto-Culver Co., US Supreme Court, 17 Jun 1974, 417 US 506 (1974).

[2]Mitsubishi Motors v. Soler Chrysler-Plymouth, US Supreme Court, 2 Jul 1985, 473 US 614 (1985).

[3]Suzuki serves VW with legal notice, The Financial Times, 14 Oct 2011, http://www.ft.com/intl/cms/s/0/084dfeda-f60c-11e0-bcc2-00144feab49a.html#axzz1bP1EDx00, last accessed September 14, 2016.

Almost two years passed by and not even a single project was undertaken by the two parties to the contract. Due to different working styles, cultural differences, and primarily the availability of a substitute to Suzuki in the form of Fiat from Italy for supply of highly fuel efficient diesel engines, the alliance did not work. The relationship between Suzuki and Fiat was warming up, as Fiat also saw it as a good opportunity to sell its engines to a big customer–Suzuki—ready to buy them, much to the chagrin of Volkswagen. Hence, both Suzuki and Volkswagen were viewing the contract as a burden, and wanted to get rid of it. Commentators and automobile experts anticipated the same, and it was reported in the media

> The Volkswagen, Suzuki rift continues to make news so often that auto industry officials are convinced that it is only a matter of time before the two formally announce their divorce.[4]

And the two companies did break their ties. Suzuki on its own ended the alliance with Volkswagen, as it wanted to buy the stake Volkswagen owned in Suzuki, and at that time had enough cash to do so, but Volkswagen refused to oblige, and Suzuki made the final decision of breaking the ties. Chairman Suzuki said

> You can lead a horse to water but you can't make it drink … we need to mutually discuss and come to a conclusion.[5]

But the dispute could not be resolved amicably by discussion and the matter was taken to international arbitration in London. Business disputes, realistically speaking, do take time to get resolved, and the dispute between Suzuki and Volkswagen was no different. It was anticipated, and rightly so, that the dispute would not take less than two years to reach a logical conclusion, and it was not resolved by mid-2013. In November 2011, when the arbitration clause was invoked, the Wall Street Journal wrote

> Even though the Japanese car maker unilaterally declared an end to its partnership with Volkswagen, the dispute over the fate of the alliance looks poised to enter a protracted period of legal wrangling. Yasuhito Harayama, Suzuki's executive vice president, said at a news conference last Friday that it might take as long as two years to settle the dispute.[6]

Even in March 2013, Volkswagen in its Annual Report mentioned that the dispute might end by mid-2013.[7] About two years later by the end of August 2015,

---

[4]Fiat could step in if VW, Suzuki part ways, The Hindu Business Line, Sep 8, 2011, http://www. thehindubusinessline.com/companies/fiat-could-step-in-if-vw-suzuki-part-ways/article2436497. ece, last accessed September 14, 2016.

[5]Suzuki Motor cuts ties with Volkswagen over Fiat spat, The Economic Times, Sep 13, 2011, http://articles.economictimes.indiatimes.com/2011-09-13/news/30149608_1_executive-vice-president-yasuhito-harayama-germany-based-carmaker-suzuki-motor, last accessed September 14, 2016.

[6]Suzuki Takes Volkswagen Dispute to Arbitration, The Wall Street Journal, Nov 25, 2011, http://online.wsj.com/article/SB10001424052970204630904577057134044262976.html, last accessed September 14, 2016.

[7]VW Expects Suzuki Decision Mid-2013 at Earliest, The Wall Street Journal, March 14, 2013, http://online.wsj.com/article/BT-CO-20130314-703432.html, last accessed September 14, 2016.

Suzuki got the arbitration award in its favour which terminated the 2009 agreement with Volkswagen. At that time, Mr. O. Suzuki, Chairman of Suzuki commented that the last four years had been very valuable for the company. They got a new experience and understood that there are companies different from their own company. It was a tongue-in-cheek comment on the poor ethical and professional standards followed by VW—according to Suzuki—in an international symbiotic agreement which could have proved to be a win-win opportunity for both the parties. After that Suzuki decided to go alone.

ONGC—Sumitomo, 1991

Sumitomo (Japan) and ONGC (India) had agreed for arbitration as the dispute resolution method for a contract signed in 1983. Arbitration was initiated in 1991; final award given in 1995; award challenged in the Bombay High Court and finally the matter decided in 2010 in the Supreme Court of India.[8] There has been loss of so much time, money, effort, and opportunities.

Resolution of disputes by arbitration should ideally be speedy, however, in certain matters it is often seen that the dispute is resolved finally after a very long gap of time. ONGC, the Indian Oil and Gas Company, entered into a contract with Sumitomo, a Japanese company, in 1982. This was regarding the construction of a platform complex in Bombay High. Sumitomo appointed McDermott, an American Company, as the subcontractor for doing certain specific work. As per the contract, any dispute between ONGC and Sumitomo was to be resolved by arbitration.

At that time, whatever work was done by McDermott, it was falling outside the territorial water limits of India for income tax purposes. Later, the law was changed with retrospective effect and the territorial limit was enhanced. With the changed law, interestingly, the job done by McDermott had to be taxed. McDermott paid about Rs. 2 crores (less than half a million dollars) and claimed it from the main contractor, Sumitomo, who promptly made the payment. Thereafter, Sumitomo claimed it from ONGC citing clause 17.3 of the contract, which provided for compensating the contractor for all necessary and reasonable extra cost caused by any change in law. It made the provision in the event of a change in law and read as follows:

> Should there be, after the date of bid closing a change in any legal provision of the Republic of India or any political sub-division thereof or should there be a change in the interpretation of said legal provision by the Supreme Court of India and/or enforcement of any such legal provision by the Republic of India or any political subdivision thereof which affects economically the position of the Contractor; then the Company shall compensate Contractor for all necessary and reasonable extra cost caused by such a change.

---

[8]Sumitomo Heavy Industries Limited v. Oil and Natural Gas Commission of India, Supreme Court of India, 28 Jul 2010; AIR 2010 SC 3400, (2010) 11 SCC 296.

Shockingly, ONGC rejected the claim citing another clause 13.2.7 which provided that ONGC shall not be responsible for making any payment to contractor's subcontractor or vendor. The clause read as follows:

> The Company shall not be responsible/obliged for making any payments or any other related obligations under this Contract to the Contractor's Subcontractor/Vendors. The Contractor shall be fully liable and responsible for meeting all such obligations and all payments to be made to its Subcontractors/Vendors and any other third party engaged by the Contractor in any way connected with the discharge of the Contractor's obligation under the Contract and in any manner whatsoever.

A plain and simple reading of these clauses would tell us unmistakably that in this case ONGC was reasonably expected to make the payment. As ONGC refused to pay, a dispute arose and it was referred to arbitration in 1991 with two arbitrators. The arbitrators differed and the matter was referred to the Umpire in 1994. The Umpire gave his award in 1995 in favour of Sumitomo. Thereafter the long journey of challenging the award began from the Bombay High Court and finally ended in the Supreme Court of India in 2010. The Supreme Court finally decided that there was no error apparent on the face of the award and hence the decision made by the Umpire was correct. The Supreme Court categorically held that the payment was not made by Sumitomo voluntarily, but due to a change in law, hence Clause 17.3 would apply.

The Supreme Court also commented that the award was a plausible award and also a well-reasoned award. ONGC was, thus, bound to pay the amount to Sumitomo. After going through this case, the notable question arises regarding the ability of the top leadership—both at Sumitomo and ONGC—to anticipate the legal journey and time taken by the dispute, which as far as the amount is concerned, was pittance for each of these companies. They would have spent much more amount claimed in conducting arbitration and in pursuing the matter in various courts. A business leader, truly, should try to anticipate and avoid any such disputes. Such avoidance would save a lot of time, effort and money.

Rio 2016 Olympics, Disputes and Arbitration

Just a few days before the Rio Olympics were set to start in August 2016, a large number of Russian players were allowed to participate in the Olympic Games after an arbitral tribunal decided in favour of their participation. Earlier, these players were banned for using chemicals banned in the games. However, using the corollary of the principles of natural justice that anyone cannot and should not be punished for the same offence twice, they were allowed.

Interestingly, the Olympic Games have their own mechanism of dispute resolution—an arbitral tribunal—known as Court of Arbitration in Sport (CAS), headquartered in Lausanne, Switzerland. This is a very special arrangement which makes its decision binding on the competing countries and players. Its decision can be challenged in the Federal Supreme Court of Switzerland due to territorial jurisdiction. However, the Federal Court cannot go into the merits of the case, but can go through only to check whether procedure has been followed or not. The procedure incorporates the principles of natural justice, hence, 'due process' is an integral part of the procedure.

More than a century ago, when the Modern Olympic Games started in Athens in 1896, Pierre de Coubertin, the father of the Modern Olympic Games would not have dreamt even in the wildest of his dreams that there would be disputes related to the games requiring a tribunal for their resolution as his idea of the games emphasised more on participation than winning. Since then the international games have come a long way and often tested the fundamental principles of the international law. One of the renowned legal scholars, Holland, had said that 'international law is the vanishing point of jurisprudence'. Very true! International law is a very weak law and Olympic Games have often suffered because of politicisation of the games and lack of a global sovereign.

In 1936 Berlin Games, Hitler had played the racist card and never approved the highly acclaimed friendship between German Luz Long and the legendary American Jesse Owens, who had won four gold medals. Long's advice to Owens had gone a long way in making the latter win. The 1980 Moscow Olympics had seen the Americans not taking part and the reverse happening in 1984 Los Angeles Games when the Soviet Union was not present. The absence of such major teams, or for that matter even if a very small country goes unrepresented due to political reasons, the Olympic Games do not epitomise the best in the world of sports. Worse, with such powerful and large countries like the United States and the erstwhile Soviet Union, their allies also either did not participate on their own or were not allowed to participate on one or the other pretext. India had been a neutral country with a firm belief in non-alignment and hence participated in both the games. Internal politics in the country did not have any effect on our participation either. It all requires evolution and maturity on the part of individual sovereign member countries.

Till the time of decision by the tribunal, Russia had raised a very valid argument that a blanket ban on the players of a country was neither desirable nor tenable. However, there were serious allegations of state supported doping programme which covered almost all the players. With great alacrity, the arbitral tribunal had really done its job well and had decided the matter in the nick of time. Delay in decision-making or uncertainty in the decision-making process could be the worst thing for a player who might have gone through rigorous training for the momentous occasion which comes once in four years. For many, it might have been the only chance as by the next Olympic Games they may be well past their peak performance.

Seeing the speedy and timely resolution of these disputes, one cannot help from wishing the same speed, timing and efficacy of resolution of disputes by the regular courts. The business leaders of the world covet the spirit of the Modern Olympic

Games in their day-to-day business disputes as well. The world will become a much better place to live and do business. Along with speedy redressal system, business leaders also must think for business solutions to business problems.

Business Solution or Legal Solution

Business problems need a business solution. As a business leader one needs to find out business solution for such a problem. If one asks a lawyer, he, in all probability, will provide a legal solution. That legal solution may not be in tune with the overall picture of business which a business leader may have in his mind. That is why it is very important to remember as to whose business is it? Thus, the business leader must make the final decision and not his lawyer. If he allows the lawyer to make the final decision, it is not he who is managing the affairs of his company but it is the lawyer. And, that is a very unfortunate situation. Any business leader should not allow himself to get into such a situation.

The business leader needs to make a decision: whether he would like to be in a position which is a win-win situation or a win-lose situation? Does he want to use a method which is adversarial in nature or he would prefer a method which is non-adversarial? For example, Danone (France) and Britannia (India) were party to a long legal battle regarding 'Tiger' brand of biscuits. Their lawyers might have told them that their respective cases were very strong, but the business leaders decided to settle the dispute, end the uncertainty, move on and live in peace.[9] Danone had another dispute with Wahaha group in China. The Wahaha group bought Danone out of the joint venture in 2009, a deal which was brokered by the Chinese and French governments.[10]

Microsoft, Mits, Pertec and Basic

The importance of resolution of disputes by inserting proper contractual clauses was well understood by business leaders, Bill Gates and Paul Allen, founders of Microsoft. They had taken their rights seriously and fought for them in an arbitral tribunal. As is well known, Gates and Allen had written BASIC for the 8080 MITS (Micro Instrumentation and Telemetry Systems, located in Albuquerque, New Mexico) machine. Earlier, in late 1974, MITS had launched Altair 8800 computer, which used the Intel 8080 chip and had 256 bytes of RAM. Though this machine was a pioneer in itself, it did not have the provision of feeding input through keys

---

[9]Tiger issue tamed, Wadias get Britannia from Danone, The Business Standard, 15 Apr 2009, http://www.business-standard.com/india/news/tiger-issue-tamed-wadias-get-britanniadanone/355155/, last accessed September 14, 2016.

[10]China's Thirst Makes Wahaha's 'Poorest Boss' the Richest, The BusinessWeek, 9 Mar 2011, http://www.businessweek.com/news/2011-03-09/china-s-thirst-makes-wahaha-s-poorest-boss-the-richest.html, and Wahaha-haha! The Economist, 19 Apr 2007, http://www.economist.com/node/9040416, last accessed September 14, 2016.

and it also did not have a display terminal for output. Entries had to be made by flipping toggle switches, which was time-consuming and inconvenient. Gates and Allen saw this as an opportunity and made up their mind to write BASIC for this machine, and as they had rightly anticipated, to make a lot of money by selling it to Altair users and other 8080 based computers, competing with Altair 8800.

On January 2, 1975 they wrote and offered a BASIC Interpreter for the Altair computer. The next month they had to make a presentation to MITS in New Mexico and demonstrate the working of BASIC on the Altair. They were successfully able to do that despite the fact that Allen while flying to Albuquerque forgot to carry the loader—the software to make the Altair talk to the teletype, so the paper tape with the BASIC could be put into the computer—but managed to write down the loader in machine code on the flight. Allen—who had earlier scored a perfect 1600 on SAT—rose to the occasion and showed his genius.

It worked, and a few months later, in July 1975. Gates and Allen signed a contract with MITS. Gates had drafted the contract with the help of his father, who was a well-known corporate lawyer in Seattle. The contract had three interesting and important clauses

(a)   there was a cap of $180,000 on royalties. Both the parties believed it to be highly optimistic and unachievable.
(b)   MITS was supposed to make its 'best efforts' in marketing and selling BASIC. It typically goes without saying, and is usually not incorporated as a clause in the contract.
(c)   disputes, if any, had to be resolved through arbitration. This was the trend in most of the contracts in the US but was something novel, as the contract itself was, for a computer and software deal.

As luck would have it, there was a huge demand for BASIC, but Gates and Allen, through their company Microsoft, had entered into a 10-year deal with MITS for exclusive rights transferred to MITS. Like any young entrepreneur, Gates and Allen, after tasting success, wished to be out of the clutches of MITS and sell their product even to its competitors, however, contact conditions did not permit them to do so. It so happened that the customers were more interested in BASIC and demanded to buy it without being bundled with any product made by MITS, but this was not possible due to exclusivity clauses in the contract. Acting in a practical manner, a number of customers refused to buy MITS products and started passing around pirated copies of BASIC, and hurting Microsoft financially in a serious manner.

Ed Roberts, the head of MITS, did not understand the situation and was not able to anticipate that settling the matter with Gates and Allen could have given his company huge sums of profit. Roberts hardened his stand, did not settle with Gates and Allen, and thinking it to be a prudent move sold the company to Pertec, a Californian company, which believed that it had exclusive rights to Microsoft BASIC as part of the deal with MITS.

As the going was not smooth with MITS for Microsoft, it used this transition to Pertec as an opportunity and contested that Pertec had exclusive rights to BASIC. Microsoft alleged that MITS and Pertec did not make best efforts, as envisaged in the contract, to sell BASIC, and hence Pertec—which had stepped into the shoes of MITS—could not, legally, compel Microsoft not to sell BASIC to others.

As there was an arbitration clause regarding dispute resolution in the contract, the matter went to an arbitrator instead of a court of law. Those were nascent days for software litigation and dispute resolution, and the arbitrator had very little understanding of computers and software. But, one thing was sure: the arbitrator could easily understand that there was a big company, Pertec, which was fighting with two young entrepreneurs, Gates and Allen. Understanding it as a fight between David and Goliath, the arbitrator decided in favour of underdog Microsoft, maybe without fully comprehending the merits of the case. One of the websites about start-ups, writes about this incident

> ...the Pertec people and their three lawyers sitting across from Paul, Bill, and their single lawyer.[11]

And, to use the clichéd phrase, rest is history. Microsoft never looked back. Had the arbitrator that day decided in favour of Pertec, in all probability, there would not have been any Microsoft surviving Pertec's legal onslaught. A well-drafted contract saved Microsoft from extinction.

Also, an important learning is never to lose the sight of your goal. The other party might be trying to provoke you so that you get disturbed and annoyed and lose focus. Finally, that dispute may prove to be a small and insignificant issue in the long journey of your company towards its cherished goal to achieve more profits and make itself more meaningful to the society. Try to see the big picture so that you do not lose sight of the final goal and you do not fall into the trap of being penny wise and pound foolish. You must appreciate that even winners in litigation or in most of the dispute resolution methods also lose. The only point is that they may be losing lesser than the other party—the loss we are talking about is the loss of time, effort and money and also the opportunities which have been missed as you and your company were not ready to embrace them at the right moment. You and your company may be the ostensible winner at that point of time, but maybe in the long run you will feel that your company has wasted so many resources on one matter—either litigation or any other method of dispute resolution—for one or more avoidable disputes. In hindsight, you might think that it would have been a good idea just to avoid the dispute.

---

[11]*MITS versus Microsoft* is a story from the **It Happened in Albuquerque** section of the STARTUP Gallery. Available at http://startup.nmnaturalhistory.org/gallery/story.php?ii=59, last accessed September 14, 2016.

BG in Argentina: Catch-22 Situation

Businesses enter into a contract to eliminate, or at least, to reduce uncertainty. The same principle applies to dispute resolution clause, which in most of the domestic and international contracts is arbitration. In simple words, arbitration is a private forum for resolution of disputes, as the parties decide among themselves that they would not like to go to a regular court for resolution of any dispute. International disputes present an array of interesting issues, and one such dispute is currently ongoing between Argentina and BG, a British energy company. In early 1990s, BG invested in Argentina. It is interesting to note that there was a 1990-bilateral investment treaty (BIT) between Argentina and the UK. According to this treaty, any party could resort to arbitration, however, the party was supposed to first litigate in Argentine courts for 18 months.

At the turn of the century, Argentina faced an unprecedented economic crisis and the government took a number of emergency actions which in a real sense made BG's investment in the country meaningless. The company at that time wished to start arbitration proceedings, however, according to the treaty the company was supposed to litigate in Argentine courts for 18 months before invoking the arbitration clause. Due to the economic crisis and emergency actions, the government, in its wisdom, tried its best to make the judiciary ineffective, as far as matters related to heavy investment and international contracts were concerned. It was made clear by the government that any company moving the court to challenge the emergency measures would be dealt with severely and serious penalties would be imposed.

In such a scenario, BG understood, and rightly so, that its option of filing a petition in an Argentine court was closed as the fate of any such petition was well known even before filing. Thus, realistically speaking, the company had no option available at all—had it filed a petition in the court, the government would have taken serious action against it; and had it gone for arbitration, it would have been declared premature. The company, in such a situation, decided to go for the second option. It tried its luck with the arbitral tribunal, and as luck would have it, the tribunal—based in Washington DC—ruled in favour of the company with an award—an arbitral tribunal's decision is called an award—of $185 million.

Argentina challenged this award in the American courts—the district court decided in favour of the company, whereas the appellate court overruled it. Thereafter, BG had taken the matter to the US Supreme Court, which had asked the US government to give its view on the matter. Such is the strange nature of international law that a dispute between a British company and Argentina was being decided in the US, a country which has no role either in the contract or the dispute, but was the battleground for resolution of this dispute. Later the US Supreme Court decided in favour of BG in March 2014 and reinstated the $185 million arbitration award. The Supreme Court by a majority of 7-2 did not agree with Argentina's argument that the case should have been litigated first in the domestic courts before going for arbitration. Justice Stephen Breyer in the majority opinion said that in a contract with an arbitration clause, it was for the arbitrators to decide and not the courts. He wrote

> In our view, the matter is for the arbitrators, and courts must review their determinations with deference...[12]

There had been a possibility for Argentina not to pay despite the award. It would not have been surprising if Argentina had refused to honour the decision as in January 2012 Venezuela had refused to recognise the World Bank decision in a multibillion-dollar arbitration case with Exxon Mobil. Small wonder, the British jurist Thomas Holland called international law as the vanishing point of jurisprudence. BG was in a Catch-22 situation, but Argentina decided to honour the award and the US Supreme Court decision in May 2016. This is precisely due to the desire of the country to remain with the larger comity of nations to continue taking part in international trade and commerce. Though, if a country determines not to pay and be willing to be ostracised by the international community, there is hardly any force which may compel it to pay. Several nations and corporations do not snap relationships as they believe in keeping something alive in the relationships which can be rekindled if needed. Hence, it is advised not to burn the bridges.

Burning the bridges

And it is advisable not to strain relationships with the other parties. You never know when you might need to do business with a party with whom you are in dispute today. It is prudent to think in the long run and see the big picture. A term has been coined to depict such relationships—'frenemies', friends who may be enemies at times or enemies who may be friends at times. Do you want to forgive and forget and move on? Or do you want to harp on your legal rights and the legal rights of your company and keep on investing time, effort and money just to vindicate your position and the stand you have taken? It is a good idea to get your position on the stand vindicated, however, any business leader must also realise at what cost he is doing that. It is said, discretion is the better part of valour. It is a good idea not to put your company or yourself at risk, if it can safely be avoided. Your main purpose of trying to resolve a dispute is not to win the legal battle; your main purpose is to win the business war ultimately. And, law is simply to help you.

---

[12]United States Supreme Court, BG group PLC v. Republic of Argentina, (2014), No. 12-138, Argued: December 2, 2013; Decided: March 5, 2014.

Detroit's Revival and UAW, 2011

In early 2009, commentators were writing the obituary of the automobile industry in Detroit. The Time captioned its articles as 'Is this Detroit's last winter?' and 'Why Detroit is not too big to fail?' In June 2009, when General Motors filed for bankruptcy there was again a gloom in the automobile sector. Things, however, took a positive turn in about two years. There had been an unexpected expeditious revival of the automobile industry. This was the result of drastic measures which were taken at that time: government bailing out the companies, huge cuts in production and jobs, focus towards new technology, priority to smaller and fuel efficient vehicles, etc. Besides these steps taken by the three major automobile companies—General Motors, Ford and Chrysler—there was a very important legal aspect responsible for the fast revival. The companies entered into an agreement, as a part of the government bailout, that UAW (United Automobile workers) Union would not go on a strike. In case of any differences with the management, UAW had promised to resolve all the disputes in an amicable manner failing which the disputes had to be resolved by arbitration. This clause, however, did not apply to Ford, because Ford did not seek government bailout. It managed on its own.

Interestingly, it was Henry Ford, the legendary car maker, who introduced better conditions and higher wages for workers at his company. The idea which he propagated and practised was to keep the workers happy and satisfied, which in turn would mean better and more production. It was also vindicated by the research in management at that time and later. Other automobile companies were forced to follow Ford. This is how the workers in automobile companies started to get a taste of good life which included security in the future, particularly after retirement. The retirement benefits provided by these companies were immense which included huge medical benefits and to a certain extent contributed in the long run in making these companies bleed. This was also one of the major reasons for the automobile companies to almost fail in 2008 and 2009. Other reasons, of course, were poor design of vehicles, high costs, less of innovation and not adhering to the basic principles of management, whether financial or general management.

In this background the UAW, which was and is a very strong body, agreed to the clause of 'no strike and arbitration'. In the legal environment of the United States, a contract is supposed to be adhered to fully. On the contrary, in India, as several noted jurists have commented, contract adherence has a very low priority, even for the government. It is well evident in the cases of Enron and Dabhol Power Project and the cases of Cairn Energy, ONGC and Vedanta in the recent past. The government had resorted to arm twisting and left no option for the other parties. It is no wonder that very often international rating agencies rate India quite low in the list of countries which adhere to and enforce contracts. In other words, we can say that contracts in India do not have that great a meaning as they do have in the United States. And, that is why it is very important to appreciate that UAW accepted the clause.

UAW union knew very well that in case the matter went to an arbitral tribunal, in case of a dispute with the management, the award of the arbitrator would be binding and in all probability it will be a long legal battle to get that award set aside by a competent court. The opposite parties were the big automobile companies of Detroit and, hence, it was very well understood that these companies, with deep pockets, would have left no stone unturned to challenge the award, in case they would have lost out, to the highest judicial forum available, which is the United States Supreme Court. The UAW did not have that much bargaining power after entering into a contract with these two clauses. Hence, in a situation when luckily the companies had again seen profits, the UAW wished to get its pound of flesh. The union was going back to the management to get some changes made in the contract. The companies were also in a much better financial position and morally they needed to share the profits with the workers. However, legally speaking, the companies were not under any obligation to pay more and agree to favourable (to workers) conditions of work. It would have been very difficult to get even a single penny from the management. But, the companies needed the workers and with more demand for products, more workers were required by the companies. The bargaining power of workers was better a few years later.

Similar problems, though not of a contract, had been observed in India. In 2011, workers in Maruti's factory in Manesar had created a parallel union—parallel to their union in the Gurgaon factory. The management had not accepted and recognised that new development which had made the workers highly discontented and dissatisfied. There had been some local political intervention also, but the things were not sorted out timely. Even if the workers and the management had entered into a contract in India, it would have been only a matter of time when such a contract might have ended in breach and thereafter the matter would have either been resolved by certain politicians or through litigation. There had been problems also at the Hyundai factory in Chennai in June 2010. With inflation having taken its toll and the competition among automobile companies forcing them to cut down the cost of manufacturing, it was no wonder that the companies were under tremendous pressure to cut jobs, use the latest technology and somehow come up with an 'overall cost leadership' model. More and more companies were offering low cost models as they might have decided to put into practise management expert—unfortunately passed away a few years ago—C.K. Prahlad's idea of 'fortune at the bottom of the pyramid'.

Revival of the automobile industry was a good omen but the companies needed to keep their flock together. Contracts and dispute resolution clauses might not have helped in every jurisdiction as the ground realities usually differ significantly. However, resolving and avoiding disputes with the workers is one of the top priorities of the management and due care must be taken to have a cordial environment for working. In case companies are not able to do so, we typically see the headlines like what the Economist wrote in June 2009, 'The decline and fall of General Motors: Detroitosaurus Wrecks', by coining a new term using Detroit and the name of a dinosaur.

Lance Armstrong: Fame, Shame, Business, Charity and Law, 2013

Till the last few months of 2012, Lance Armstrong was considered to be the living legend as a cycling champion, who had won numerous races and awards, who had battled cancer and started a charity organisation for the benefit of cancer patients, and someone who was seen as made of steel and could have also been said, as grit and determination personified. His fall from the high pedestal in early 2013 was sudden, but was not unexpected. For a very long time, anti-doping agencies in the world had accused him of using drugs and substances which had been banned to be used by sportspersons. In January 2013, Armstrong confessed in a television show—hosted by Oprah Winfrey—that he had indeed used banned substances as he wanted to win at any cost. For him, clearly, means were not that important as the end, and as was evident, he would have gone to any extent to win, as he had simply got into the habit of winning.

It is very important for any sportsperson, as had been said by Pierre de Coubertin, father of modern Olympic Games, that participation was more important than winning. Armstrong thought in a different manner and he not only himself used banned substances, but forced the members of his team to follow suit. At every point of time whenever there had been an allegation of doping, he had left no stone unturned to deny that and even went to the extent of initiating legal proceedings against accusers.

It is really a matter of surprise and disbelief that he was able to continue doing this for such a long time without being caught. The global anti-doping agencies, including the United States Anti-Doping Agency, USADA, and the World Anti-Doping Agency, WADA, supposedly have the best of the professionals at their service and make use of the cutting-edge technology and expertise in conducting any tests. Despite all these resources, these two and other agencies were not able to catch hold of Armstrong and his other team members during the events. This is really unbelievable and speaks volumes about the sharp intelligence and genius of Armstrong, though used in the wrong direction, in getting away with any investigation.

In 2004, the United States Postal Service, one of Armstrong's sponsors, had promised him a bonus in case Armstrong was the 'official winner' of the Tour de France. An American company—SCA promotions—had insured the bonuses which the US Postal Service was supposed to pay to Armstrong. The amount was totalling almost $5 million. During that time, a French book had accused Armstrong of using banned substances and because of this doubt, Armstrong, not being the winner in a clean manner, of course without using any banned substances, SCA promotions refused to pay the amount. The contract, interestingly, contained an arbitration clause and Armstrong, without the slightest of hesitation, invoked arbitration and had the award in his favour as he was still the official winner of the Tour.

It was much later in 2013, after his confessional statement, official winner, at that point of time has no meaning at all and SCA promotions was contemplating recouping that amount, which had increased along with legal fees and interest to almost US $10 million.

There was a huge sum of money riding on Armstrong's name. Sponsors, which included footwear manufacturers and cycle companies, and so many other companies, ended their contract abruptly last year when Armstrong was stripped of his titles of Tour de France and other competitions and later was stripped of his Sydney Olympics bronze medal he had won in 2000. He faced legal action against him for perjury—making untrue statements on oath—on a number of occasions and his charity organisation, earlier called as Lance Armstrong Foundation, and later, renamed as Livestrong Foundation, had faced budget cuts and loss of credibility.

The long arm of law had surely got Armstrong in its hold, and he would find himself entangled in a lot of litigation. He, quite expectedly, was playing the emotional card by speaking in a rehearsed manner in the Oprah Winfrey show and also to the staff at his charity organisation. As is quite common in such instances, the guilty is portraying himself as a victim and trying to gain sympathy. It would be, indeed, improper to show any sympathy and mercy to a person who has been into the systematic operation of doping and putting not only the sport of cycling, but all sports to the risk of highly professional and technologically advanced doping methods.

What the world wants from him is that he should come out and tell the story in great detail so that the investigating agencies and anti-doping agencies are able to make the processes better and foolproof. Nothing less than this could have been accepted as confession and apology. The Lancestrong episode involving aspects of business and dispute resolution—though related to sports—highlights the importance of speedy dispute resolution methods and going to any of such forums with clean hands. It may be necessary for business leaders to fight for survival and existence, but should one fight when one is on the wrong side of the law? It is not advisable to do so.

Takeaway for Business Leaders

1. Business Leader, not a Lawyer

   Remember, you are a business leader, not a lawyer. As a business leader, your primary duty is to spend time thinking about your business—anything and everything which shall make your business more profitable and successful. Your job is not to think like a lawyer. You are concerned with law to the extent that it is helpful in your business and you can make your business thrive by being on the right side of law. To achieve your primary goal, you would like to channelise all your energy and time towards your business. You must not waste your time and effort in courts of law, lawyers' chambers and living in uncertainty as to what shall be the decision in a particular case being heard in a particular court. Like it or not, if you are a successful business leader, you may be handling a couple of disputes which need to be resolved. You may like to live in peace, however, your competitors, your suppliers, your customers, and the world at large may not like this idea of you living in peace and making clean profits. They would like to bother you: sometimes due to genuine reasons and at other times intentionally, with the purpose to trouble you. Disputes shall be thrust upon you. You have no choice but to take a stand and fight. It is up to the business leader as to what he should do: avoid such disputes or resolve them in a speedy manner. Many a time, avoiding a dispute is possible, but it is not always a possibility. Smart business leaders develop a knack for handling disputes and mental agony and stress associated with them. The best thing is to ignore them without being harmed. In case ignoring them may cause harm to your business, try to avoid them by anticipating them and changing the course of action. If this is not possible, try to nip it in the bud by taking reasonable and necessary actions. If nothing works, think about resolving it at the earliest.

2. Fight when it is necessary

   For business leaders, it is a good idea to avoid litigation and any other method of dispute resolution, however, there are certain disputes which you must fight as a business leader. What are those disputes? Disputes which are critical for the survival of your company; disputes which are going to position your company in the market with the least possibility of losing the matter; disputes which are necessary to clearly define your rights and other parties duties; disputes which are necessary to protect your property—both tangible and intellectual property; disputes regarding questions of law which need to be interpreted by a court to give a definitive meaning; disputes with the party which is so unreasonable that there is no hope and no possibility of any settlement, etc. are such disputes which cannot and should not be ignored or avoided. These categories are just by way of illustration and it depends on the business leader to think what other disputes he or she would like to get resolved in a proper judicial forum rather than settling them with the other party. In a case of arbitration the restaurant chain 'Hooters of America' drafted the terms so unreasonably and in its favour that the court held that there could not be any meaningful arbitration and the matter should be decided in the court. A waitress, Annette Phillips, had complained of sexual harassment and as per Hooters the matter should have been resolved in arbitration. Instead of letting it go, Phillips had decided to fight.

3. Doing the spadework

   When you have decided to fight a matter, it is essential that you do the spadework—prepare a case with proper documents, engage a good lawyer, understand the legal environment, evaluate your chances of success, try to anticipate the change in the legal, business and political environment in the near future and other important things as per the facts of the case. If after doing all this you think that it is prudent not to continue with fighting the matter, you still have a choice to settle the matter with the other party. It would be absolutely reasonable and prudent not to go ahead on a path on which you are not certain and feel that it is going to be very risky. But, after doing all this if you make up your mind and decide that you need to fight it out then do it in the best possible manner. Put your best foot forward. Do not go ahead half-heartedly. That may prove to be suicidal. Legal wars are like marathon. They are never a 100-metre dash. You must be confident that you will reach the finishing line. Simply not being able to even reach the finishing line will not do any good. Certain companies in India, particularly construction companies, are known to open a file for arbitration the day they decide to join the race for getting the contract for a project. Each and every bit of paper is filed meticulously. It all comes handy at the time of making a claim before the arbitrator.

4. It is never too early or too late to settle

If you have already initiated the process of dispute resolution after due consideration and due diligence with the anticipation that you shall be able to reach the finishing line, and later you feel that you may not be able to complete it due to whatsoever reason, it is not essential that you must complete it. Dispute resolution involves trade-offs. You must be ready to make sacrifices. So, the decision to fight can also be reviewed and corrective measures taken. Once you start the legal proceedings for the resolution of a dispute, have reached the midway, but now you feel that you do not have the energy to go ahead and complete, it is absolutely fine to review whatever has happened and make a decision that you do not want to go ahead with the dispute resolution process and it would be better for you to settle it. It is important to appreciate that it is never too late to settle. In the interesting case of Idea Cellular, three companies had joined initially—AT&T, Tata and Birla. AT&T decided to exit quite early. Later Tata also made an exit but the dispute with Birla continued and was being resolved in arbitration. In 2011, after pursuing arbitration for several years, both the parties decided to settle it. So, it is never too late to settle.

Also, it is also never too early to settle. The fact of the matter is that smart business leaders settle any dispute at the earliest and never allow the dispute to hang on their heads. If you are willing to swallow your pride, it is advisable to simply say 'I am sorry' and finish the matter. This should be done in those cases in which you agree that you and your company are on the wrong side and the other party is surely on the right side. In such cases it is always sensible for a business leader not to cling to the wrong thing and not to try to use all sorts of excuses, reasons, rules, laws—all the weapons in his arsenal—to somehow prove this point, which may be prima facie absolutely wrong. Avoid obstinacy, stubbornness and obduracy. It is neither going to help your business nor you. Mattel accused Chinese manufacturers for the problems in its toys, but shortly thereafter accepted that it was a design fault for which Mattel was responsible and apologised. Mattel safely avoided the dispute and the bitterness it might have resulted in. It has been discussed in the chapter on the role of government in business.

Chapter 8
I Must Make Profits. Do I Need to Be Ethical?

The movie 'Gone with the Wind' was released in 1939 and was based on the novel with the same name written by Margaret Mitchell, first published in 1936. The love affair of Rhett Butler, played by Clark Gable, and Scarlett O'Hara, played by Vivien Leigh, was described and portrayed with great finesse in the backdrop of the American Civil War. Scarlett, from the beginning, knew that Rhett was a smart guy, but still considered him to be a gentleman, someone who really believed in the cause. On the contrary, Rhett was roguish, to the extent that he considered profit-making as the sole motive of his life, and the dialogue between the two revealed his truth brusquely:

> Scarlett: *But you are a blockade runner.*
>
> Rhett Butler: *For profit, and profit only.*
>
> Scarlett: *Are you tryin' to tell me you don't believe in the cause?*
>
> Rhett Butler: *I believe in Rhett Butler, he's the only cause I know.*[1]

Ethics, morality, just and fair conduct may not be some of the first things which may come to trouble a business leader while making a deal. On most of the occasions, profit is the driving force and the most important criteria in making a business decision. Such a tendency on the part of a good number of corporates has given birth to the thought, which may not simply be a figment of the imagination, that 'profits without ethics' is their ultimate goal, and of late, there has been a lot of emphasis on ethics and ethical conduct while doing business, and companies are walking that extra mile to show to the world that they conduct their business in an ethical manner, even if, regrettably, that may not be the truth. A number of questions arise.

Should a business leader aim to earn profits and profits only? Should the words honesty, integrity, trust, faith, morality and ethics remain alien to him? Does it pay in the long run to care even a little bit about these words? Should he care only about law? These are some of the doubts which a business leader is often confronted with. These questions do not have easy answers.

---

[1]Dialogue from the movie 'Gone with the Wind', available at http://www.imdb.com/title/tt0031381/trivia?tab=qt&ref_=tt_trv_qu, last accessed September 14, 2016.

© The Author(s) 2017

A.K. Agarwal, *Business Leadership and Law*, DOI 10.1007/978-81-322-3682-5_8

129

Ethics and Law

I have often asked my students at the beginning of a course on Law and ethics what according to them do the terms 'law' and 'ethics' convey. Most of the responses distinguish between the two concepts by focusing on the enforceable nature of the former in the society. They describe the difference between the two as, 'one can be punished for not adhering to the law of the land but cannot be punished by the State for not following ethics'.

The relationship between law and ethics is very interesting. Ethics is the science of morals and is concerned with the principles of 'right and wrong'. Morality means the standards and principles of good behaviour. Laws are made by authority for the proper regulation of a community and there are provisions for punishment in case of noncompliance. You as a business leader would like to aim to make profits in a manner acceptable to the society. Profits can be made by being ethical; and being ethical helps. You, as a business leader have no choice but to be legally correct. In case you choose to be on the wrong side of law, the long arm of law may get you sooner or later. However, regarding ethics, you need to make a decision as the law shall not punish you for being unethical, provided you have not broken any law. Often it has been heard, earlier in whispers and now in loud voices, that ethical values need to be strengthened in businesspersons. Whereas one school of thought supports it, the other rubbishes it as another fad of popular management thinking. The latter school believes in strict laws and total compliance rather than preaching good conduct.

Are law and ethics different? Is law necessarily ethical? Are all ethical acts legal? The interaction between law and ethics gives rise to four possible categories: ethical and legal, unethical and illegal, unethical but legal, and ethical but illegal. Ethical norms in any society, typically, are never well defined, but there is a sense and there is an understanding among the people in the society as to what is acceptable and what is not acceptable as per the societal norms. The first category—ethical and legal—includes some of the most simple situations in which ethical actions, which are accepted by the society to be morally correct have been given the status of being legal by the competent lawmaking body. As an illustration in terms of business law, delivery of merchantable goods as promised by the seller to the buyer is both a moral and legal duty of the seller. There are several other laws which truly represent morality codified. There is generally no dispute about these provisions of law. The second category—unethical and illegal—is exactly the opposite of what we have discussed earlier. All those actions which are considered to be immoral by the society have been declared illegal by the competent lawmaking body. There is, thus, neither any confusion nor any tension between legality and morality. In almost all jurisdictions, killing a person is unethical as well as illegal. There are certain exceptions which do provide protection to the killer, for instance in self-defence, killing by the authority of law by soldiers and policemen, etc. Another example can be of a businessperson cheating a consumer by supplying defective goods. This is clearly illegal and unethical.

Unethical but legal

However, it is tricky for the third category—unethical but legal. If a monarch makes a law that no one in his kingdom shall either sneeze or cough, then howsoever impractical, unjust, unfair, and thereby unethical the law may be, it is a law nonetheless. And if the same monarch punishes anyone who sneezes or coughs by a simple punishment, 'Off with his head'! Then there is nothing which can stop this unethical but legal action, as it gets legal sanctity due to the lawmaking power of the monarch. In such a scenario, the goodness or badness of law is not to be considered. If a person is hungry for the several days and steals a loaf of bread from a bakery, the State does not give him something to eat but punishes him for stealing. Similarly, if a person doesn't have any money and he wishes to buy medicines for his ailing child, he cannot simply enter into a store and run away with a bottle of medicine. For that he is going to be penalised. The purpose of law is to make people morally correct but in these examples we do not see such a thing happening.

By the same token, the fourth category—ethical but illegal—is a little complex. For instance, if a person—who does not know swimming—has been tossed into a river by the soldiers of a dictator and there's an order that no one will save the drowning person, it may be undoubtedly ethical on the part of anyone to jump into the river and save a drowning person, howsoever, it will be illegal as per the definition of law. A perfect example can be of Mahatma Gandhi, who defied the British law of not making salt, which can be considered to be unjust, unfair, and therefore unethical, but it was a law in the British governed India. In India, child labour is illegal, however, certain families are dependant on the income of children. What about the employers? On one hand, they are giving employment and thus providing an opportunity to earn their livelihood. But, on the other hand, they are indulging in an illegal activity and are liable to be punished.

Grey areas

As we have discussed earlier that ethics or morality is all about the understanding of right and wrong. Thus, what is ethical or unethical depends on how the society understands certain actions. For instance gambling, prostitution, consumption of alcohol, abortion, euthanasia, woman driving a car, children working to earn their livelihood, dumping waste into rivers, living of a man with a woman without marriage, etc. may be considered to be ethical or unethical depending on the norms in a particular society. But if the lawmaking body in that society considers any or all of these activities as legal or illegal then these are surely legal or illegal, as the case may be. The tension is between such activities which the society at times considers to be unethical but the lawmaking body gives it a legal status.

Take the example of capital punishment. In some jurisdictions capital punishment is considered to be illegal. There are people who strongly oppose capital punishment as it is an irreversible and once a person has been awarded death sentence and that sentence has been executed, no matter what one does, the process can not be reversed. It is, therefore, considered to be unethical to punish a person by awarding him a death sentence. On the contrary, in a number of jurisdictions it is supposed to be legal as well as ethical to punish a person who has done something so blatantly wrong that he need not live in the society and he may prove to be a danger to the society. Thus, it is better to get rid of them. And, in such situations, death is the best punishment.

Same are the arguments regarding abortion. There are strong arguments that as human beings cannot give life, they have no right to take away the life of a foetus. There are, however, counterarguments which say that it is the right of a mother to decide whether she would like to have the child are not. This right should not be taken away from the mother and thus she ethically as well as legally is on the right side to abort the foetus if she decides so.

Corporate World

The world of business is full of dilemmas of law and ethics. It would be interesting to have a look at a couple of illustrations exhibiting how corporate honchos maintained the balance between law and ethics, or flouted it.

The doyen of Indian business JRD Tata was very well known for his extremely high ethical standards. It has been written by Mr. R.M. Lala—who has written a number of books about the working of Tatas, the humongous business house in India—that Mr. JRD Tata was not only concerned about complying with the law but would walk that extra mile to comply with the highest of the ethical standards.[2] Writing about an incident indelible in his memory, he had mentioned:

> The well-known tax consultant, Dinesh Vyas, says that JRD never entered into a debate over 'tax avoidance,' which was permissible, and 'tax evasion,' which was illegal; his sole motto was 'tax compliance.' On one occasion a senior executive of a Tata company tried to save on taxes. Before putting up that case, the chairman of the company took him to JRD. Mr. Vyas explained to JRD: "But sir, it is not illegal." JRD asked, softly: "Not illegal, yes. But is it right?" Mr. Vyas says that during his decades of professional work no one had ever asked him that question.

> Mr. Vyas later wrote in an article: "JRD would have been the most ardent supporter of the view expressed by Lord Denning: 'The avoidance of tax may be lawful, but it is not yet a virtue.'"

Another illustration, however poles apart, is from the autobiography of Lee Iacocca.[3] He had risen to become the President of the Ford Motor Co., and was later fired by Henry Ford II due to clash of personalities. Thereafter he brought back Chrysler from the brink of extinction. Iacocca wrote that the grandson of the illustrious Henry Ford, also named Henry Ford—Henry Ford II, or HF2—did not pay taxes and squandered company money by engaging in frivolous activities like

---

[2]The Business Ethics of JRD Tata, The Hindu, R.M. Lala, July 29, 2004, http://www.hinduonnet.com/2004/07/29/stories/2004072905951200.htm, last accessed September 14, 2016.
[3]Lee Iacocca: An Autobiography, Bantam Books, New York, 1984, pp. 110–111.

using company jets to fly his sister's pets for a trim or a shampoo. He had no qualms about that and was shameless to the extent that he would use each and every loophole in the law not to pay even a single penny as tax even when workers in his car factory where paying substantial amount of money as tax. There were allegations that he even charged the company for hotel accommodation on trips to London while he had his own house and used to live in that on his trips to London. Henry was not bothered whether it was 'right'. For him, 'the name of the game was: take the government for all you can'. He did not care a damn about the shareholders. Even after the company had been made public, Henry would manage it as if he was the proprietor.

In 2008, Siemens, which is one of Europe's biggest engineering companies, pleaded guilty to charges of bribery and corruption.[4] It had agreed to pay fines in the United States and in Germany to the tune of $800 million and €395, respectively. Interestingly, Siemens had devised unique methods to bribe corrupt officials and politicians all over the world. Believe it or not, it had even set up 'cash desks' in its offices. Employees were given cash in suit cases and they could have withdrawn up to a million euros at a time. Many a time, the business leaders indulge in unethical and illegal activities to get favourable decisions made by political masters and bureaucrats. Cash often is the king. It reminds us of that rather infamous allegation that the 'big bull' Harshad Mehta paid the then Prime Minister of India, P.V. Narasimha Rao, Rs. 1 crore (ten million rupees) in a suit case. Some people raised the doubt that at that time—early 1990s, when the 1000-rupee note was not in circulation—how could anyone fill a crore in a suit case. To prove the point, noted Indian lawyer Ram Jethmalani had called a press conference at the Hotel Taj Colaba—owned by the Tatas—in Mumbai and had shown how Rs. 1 crore can be fitted in a suit case.

Coming back to the Siemens case, the *modus operandi* was simple; not at all complex, which is common in the underworld and is strictly followed. Siemens unabashedly was claiming tax deductions for the bribes paid and these amounts were listed as 'useful expenditure' in its account books. The employees never had any doubt that they were doing anything wrong and illegal. Thus, there was not even an iota of suspicion about the whole operation. Siemens was indulging in this activity mostly for its telecom related business and the sums involved were huge. It continued without any check for some time. But, when Siemens listed its shares on the New York Stock Exchange in 2001, trouble began. American prosecutors were quite strict regarding bribery and Siemens was subjected to the American law, which was much more stringent as compared to the German law. The act was declared illegal, which was passing off almost as routine, and hence thought by many as 'it must be OK'.

It surely raises certain questions: why did Siemens employees not bother to ask themselves the question about the legality or at least propriety of what they were

---

[4]The Siemens scandal: Bavarian baksheesh, The Economist, 17 Dec 2008, http://www.economist.com/node/12800474, last accessed September 14, 2016.

doing. Any 'reasonable and prudent person' may get suspicious if being handed over huge sums of money in cash rather than a negotiable instrument like cheque, demand draft, etc. Highly reputed companies typically do not require their personnel to deal with too much cash. It is very risky and thus the employees must have known that there was something fishy about the entire exercise. They were, therefore, jointly liable as individuals along with the company.

In another case, Columbia Healthcare[5] had agreed to pay the United States in 2006 a huge sum of 631 million dollars in civil penalties and damages which arose from false claims. It was alleged that the company had submitted large number of false claims under federal health programmes. These claims had resulted from unlawful practices like cost report fraud and payment of kickbacks to physicians. It had violated the public trust and accepted it. The fraud had come to light due to certain whistle blowers. The American law protects the whistle blowers and they also receive a certain percentage of the amount paid as damages and penalties. No doubt, litigation is expensive in the United States and Columbia Healthcare must have taken this fact into account while making a decision to plead guilty. Had it not done so, there might have been a lengthy and costly litigation and much severe penalties. Such penalties are often not seen in the rest of the world. In the US, the punishment acts as an effective deterrent and elsewhere with low penalties these are taken lightly by business leaders in most of the jurisdictions of the world.

Among others, this is a reason why Satyam's Raju decided to accept his wrong doing in India rather than in the United States.[6] Who was Raju and what had happened? Let's read.

India: Satyam, Raju and Pricewaterhousecoopers (PWC), 2009

Ramalingam Raju, the Chairman of Satyam Computer Services was highly regarded in the corporate world as his company was the fourth largest IT company in India. Despite these accomplishments, he took the risk of forging bank documents, fabricating interest income, overstating receivables, hiding debt, faking invoices and fictitious employees, and in general, overstating his company's assets by more than Rs. 7000 crores (about $1.4 billion at that time). This was done with express or implied consent of the auditing firm PricewaterhouseCoopers and the Board of Directors of his company.

According to his own confession, when he started cooking the books of the company, it was merely a marginal difference between the real state of affairs and as

---

[5]Largest Health Care Fraud Case in U.S. History Settled, Department of Justice, http://www.justice.gov/opa/pr/2003/June/03_civ_386.htm, last accessed September 14, 2016.

[6]Raju confesses to fraud, quits; The Business Standard, 8 Jan 2009, http://www.business-standard.com/india/news/raju-confesses-to-fraud-quits/345600/, last accessed September 14, 2016.

was stated in the account books, however, this gap grew bigger and bigger, as his success in manipulating and managing emboldened him. With the passage of time and by the year 2009 the gap was so much that even Raju, with all his experience of faking the numbers and brazenness to do that, did not have the confidence and courage to continue doing it. It was simply a bit too much and he yielded. On 7th January, 2009, he wrote a letter to the Board of Directors of the company which included the statement that he felt as if he was riding a tiger and did not know how to get off without being eaten.

The Hindu reported:

> Chairman of Satyam Computer Services B. Ramalinga Raju described his situation as: "It was like riding a tiger, not knowing how to get off without being eaten," while referring to the widening gap between the real and artificial numbers in the company's books. In his resignation letter to the board of directors of the company, Mr. Raju rued: "I am now prepared to subject myself to the laws of land and face consequences thereof." What started as a marginal gap between actual operating profit and the one reflected in the books of accounts continued to grow over the years....[7]

It was widely reported in the media and all hell broke loose. The Securities and Exchange Board of India (SEBI) directed an investigation in the entire matter. A day later, the government of India directed an inspection of the financial statements of the company and its subsidiaries. A few days later, PricewaterhouseCoopers, which was the statutory auditor of the company, wrote to the Board of Directors that the financial statements of the company for a substantial period of time—June 2000 to September 2008—could not be considered reliable as Raju had confessed exaggerating and overstating. The Serious Fraud Investigation Office (SFIO), a multi-functional investigating agency working under the Ministry of Home Affairs, was directed by the government of India to investigate into the matter.

On 21 January 2009, Raju admitted diversion of funds from the company to two real estate firms held by his family and others. Later, he admitted using company's money for buying prime land in and around Hyderabad and also admitted that the funds of the company were being diverted for the last 4 to 5 years. Talluri Srinivas and S. Gopalakrishnan, associated with PwC, were arrested for their alleged role in the misstatement of accounts of the company and they later confessed that Raju had planned elaborately with them to exaggerate the accounts of the company and they had attended several meetings with Raju with the motive of falsifying accounts. Unhesitatingly and with great candour, Raju himself used to chair those meetings. Almost a month later, the Central Bureau of Investigation (CBI) started the probe.

In April that year, the Enforcement Directorate initiated an investigation into the matter for alleged money-laundering. It was also brought to the notice after serious investigation that huge sums of money, particularly foreign earnings by the company, were diverted to tax havens like Mauritius before routing it back to a

---

[7]Riding a tiger without knowing to get off: Raju; The Hindu, January 8, 2009; http://www.hindu.com/2009/01/08/stories/2009010859911500.htm, last accessed September 14, 2016.

company Maytas Infrastructure (Maytas is mirror image of Satyam, that is Satyam spelled backwards) and other companies owned by Raju and his relatives.

Raju was arrested and was granted bail in November 2011 as the prosecution could not file the charge sheet even after 33 months of his arrest. The judicial process in India, at times, can be excruciatingly slow. The matter is still pending in the courts in India. In the United States, a class-action suit was filed against Satyam and some of its independent directors with allegations that they had recklessly disregarded their responsibilities and had been grossly negligent in preventing the fraud committed by Raju and team.

In January 2013, the court dismissed the class-action claims, primarily on the grounds of lack of jurisdiction. In Satyam's case securities were traded on the New York Stock Exchange, National Stock Exchange of India and the Bombay Stock Exchange. Clearly, the judge in the US saw the latter two beyond the jurisdiction of the American courts, and, hence, dismissed the suit on the basis of jurisdictional issues.

Regarding the role of independent directors, called outside directors in the US, the American court said that they did not intentionally do anything wrong and they had even asked pointed questions during board meetings, and if they were not able to prevent the fraud, they could be negligent, but could not be held liable for gross negligence. And, if they were not grossly negligent, there was no case against the directors.

It can be understood and accepted that the independent directors and other directors on the board who were not privy to the information Raju and other members of his team committing the fraud had, could not rightly so be held liable, however, Raju and other members of team committing fraud were intentionally doing something wrong, and they had complete information about it. They were not in the dark and are accountable without any doubt. Certain members of the audit team of PricewaterhouseCoopers could also be held liable if they did not ask relevant questions and did not do their job diligently so as to uncover the mysteries of the fabricated accounts. If it was possible for Raju to fudge accounts so easily, professional team members of a well-known audit firm PricewaterhouseCoopers are expected to catch hold of such misstatements in a jiffy. And, if they were not able to do so, they should be held liable for not doing their duty with due diligence, sincerity and the level of expertise expected from professionals working in a well-known international firm of global repute.

The Satyam saga brings to the fore questions about ethical standards to be followed and the tussle between those ethical standards and legal standards as countered by business leaders, including the Chairman, Board of Directors and also the professionals conducting the audit. Each of these persons, at some point of time, compromised with ethical norms he or she was expected to follow.

View of Courts in India

In several matters, courts have to draw the fine line between the acceptable and unacceptable norms of conduct. Sometimes, it is a lethal mix of business, politics and law. This tension between law and ethics might have guided the Bharatiya Janata Party (BJP)—the right wing political party in India—leader Mr. Nitin Gadkari to comment in December 2010 about the land deals of Karnataka Chief Minister Mr. Yeddyurappa as being 'immoral but not illegal'.[8] Later, he was arrested as the court considered whatever activities he had done regarding land deals to be both immoral and illegal. That is the beauty of law. At times immoral things can be codified to be illegal or the courts can give an interpretation to the existing law to cover under its ambit several immoral activities. According to the general principles of interpretation, tax statutes have to be interpreted literally and strictly. Emotions and sentiments have no place in taxation law. What about common sense? In *Gwalior Rayon* case,[9] it was held by the Supreme Court of India in 1992,

> ...common sense is stranger and incompatible partner to the Income-tax Act. It is not concerned itself with the principles of morality or ethics. It is concerned with the very limited question as to whether the amount brought to tax constitutes the income of the assessee.

Earlier, it was held by the Supreme Court of India in *D. S. Nakara's* case[10] in 1982 that law followed the social ethical norms. It observed,

> The rules of natural justice owed their origin to ethical and moral code. Is there any doubt that they have become the integral and inseparable parts of rule of law of which any civilised society is proud? Can anyone be bold enough to assert that ethics and morality are outside the field of legal formulations? Socio-economic justice stems from the concept of social morality coupled with abhorrence for economic exploitation. And the advancing society converts in course of time moral or ethical code into enforceable legal formulations.

The courts in India have often expressed their discomfort in deciding what is right and what is wrong for the society, as it is considered the domain of the legislature. In *Bachan Singh's* case in 1980,[11] the Supreme Court had observed,

> When Judges, acting individually or collectively, in their benign anxiety to do what they think is morally good for the people, take upon themselves the responsibility of setting down social norms of conduct, there is every danger, despite their effort to make a rational guess of the notions of right and wrong prevailing in the community at large and despite their intention to abide by the dictates of mere reason, that they might write their own peculiar view or personal predilection into the law, sincerely mistaking that changeling for what they perceive to be the Community ethic.... the role which properly belongs to the chosen representatives of the people in Parliament.

---

[8]The Hindustan Times, 30 December 2010, "Karnataka CM's act immoral not illegal: Gadkari", http://www.hindustantimes.com/Karnataka-CM-s-act-immoral-not-illegal-Gadkari/Article1-644 366.aspx and, BBC News, 30 December 2010, "Karnataka land deal immoral but not illegal— BJP", http://www.bbc.co.uk/news/world-south-asia-12093771, last accessed September 14, 2016.

[9]Commissioner of Income-tax, Bombay v. Gwalior Rayon Silk Manufacturing Co. Ltd.; Supreme Court of India, AIR 1992 SC 1782, paragraph 9.

[10]D.S. Nakara v. Union of India, Supreme Court of India, AIR 1983 SC 130, paragraph 41.

[11]Bachan Singh v. State of Punjab, Supreme Court of India, AIR 1980 SC 898.

The same problem is seen in most of the evolved jurisdictions with democratic form of government. The power of judicial review gives immense power to the courts and *ipso facto* makes the judiciary the institution where the buck stops. The interpretation has to be done by the courts. In an interesting case in 1998, the House of Lords, the highest judicial court in the UK at that time—now the UK has a Supreme Court since 2009—clarified the murky situation leading to conflict of interest.

House of Lords 1998: KPMG, Sultan of Brunei and Prince Jefri Bolkiah

KPMG, one of the 'Big Four' auditing firms in the world—the other being Deloitte, Ernst & Young, and PricewaterhouseCoopers—found itself at the receiving end in 1998 in the House of Lords, in the UK.

Brunei—officially known as the Nation of Brunei, the Abode of Peace—established the Brunei Investment Agency (BIA) in 1983 to hold and manage the General Reserve Fund of the government of Brunei and its external assets and to provide the government with money management services. It was never disclosed, but was believed by many that the fund was worth several billions of dollars. Since the BIA's establishment, KPMG had undertaken the annual audit of its core funds.

Prince Jefri, the third and the youngest brother of the Sultan of Brunei, had a close relationship with his elder brother, and hence was earlier made the Minister of Finance and later made the chairman of the BIA for many years. According to the governing act of the BIA, its affairs where secretive in nature, and unauthorised disclosure was a criminal offence according to the law in Brunei. The governing act made it possible to transfer large sums of money from the core funds, which were known as the special transfers, and the destination and use of these funds were not disclosed. Even the auditors—KPMG—had no knowledge of these transfers and there was only an annual representation from the Board of the BIA, with Jefri as the chairman, which included a declaration that whatever transfers were made as a special transfers were on behalf of or for the benefit of the Brunei government, and, hence, they did not require any investigation or audit.

Thus, it can be easily understood that Prince Jefri as the chairman had utmost discretion, along with the members of the board of the BIA, to manage these special transfers. With the passage of time, the Sulatan got suspicious that Jefri was using the modus operandi of the special transfers, permitted by the governing Act of the BIA, to feather his own nest, and from whatever information the Sultan gathered, he made up his mind not to allow Jefri to continue as the chairman of the BIA. The Sultan took the entire matter in his own hands and with almost unbridled powers as the Sultan of Brunei, he took control over all the companies of Jefri and transferred the control of these companies to Arthur Andersen, another well-known accounting firm in the world and at that time one of the 'Big Five', which later collapsed in 2002 after the Enron debacle in 2001, reducing the Big Five to Big Four.

It is interesting to note that during the tenure of Jefri as the chairman of the BIA, KPMG had undertaken over 6000 h per year of chargeable time for the audit and also about 4000 h a year of chargeable time for advisory and consultancy work for the BIA. KPMG must have grossed millions and millions by the BIA account, and as is quite obvious, the BIA, and, therefore, the Sultan of Brunei would have been a very special client. Or, it would not be wrong to say that it was because of the Sultan of Brunei, primarily due to immense wealth and therefore power, and not only because of the millions made, that KPMG must have held the BIA in one of the most important client/account categories. So, it can be easily assumed that it would have been difficult for KPMG to say no to the Sultan.

On the other hand, KPMG had a warm relationship with Prince Jefri as an individual, and Jefri retained KPMG, for one of his companies, to undertake a substantial investigation in connection with a major litigation. Jefri was directly and personally involved in that litigation, and hence, it was a matter of great prestige for Jefri. To facilitate the conduct of investigation properly, Jefri made available to KPMG all his personal records and documents and furnished extensive confidential information regarding his assets and other financial affairs. This entire project was known as 'Project Lucy' and over a period of 18 months during which KPMG worked for Jefri, KPMG were paid approximately £46 million by Jefri's company. That litigation was settled in March 1998. Thereafter, KPMG was working only on two minor assignments for Jefri and within a period of two months, by May 1998, the work on these minor assignments also finished.

Immediately, thereafter in June 1998 the government of Brunei, obviously under the directions of the Sultan of Brunei, started financial investigation into Jefri's activities while he was the chairman of the BIA. The government of Brunei approached KPMG to investigate the working of the BIA, which was not wrongly seen as simply an extension of the audit function earlier done for the BIA. KPMG accepted it. Sometime later, KPMG was approached by the government of Brunei to conduct further investigation into the special transfers made by Jefri as the chairman of the BIA. This was, obviously, a situation which created conflict of interest as KPMG had in its fiduciary position with Jefri, though the matter had ended, gone through minutely a lot of documents regarding Jefri's companies, and were also privy to almost all confidential and personal information about Jefri's financial dealings.

Common sense, prudence and propriety tell us that KPMG should have said no to the government of Brunei, or if the pots of gold to be offered by the Sultan of Brunei attracted them so much that they found it impossible to say no, then they should at least have taken Jefri's consent before agreeing to take up the new assignment, which, undoubtedly, would have exposed Jefri to avoidable risk. Surprisingly, KPMG took the stand that there was no conflict of interest as it had ceased to act for Prince Jefri for more than two months and it would create Chinese walls to handle the two matters separately. The new project—investigating special transfers—was named as 'Project Gemma' and a large number of professionals were assigned to conduct the investigation.

Jefri, obviously, was not amused. He moved the court and the lower court granted an injunction in his favour. KPMG filed an appeal and the Court of Appeal reversed the decision primarily on the ground that it was not satisfied that Jefri would have suffered any real prejudice if the injunction were discharged. The court further noted that the continuation of the injunction would have set an unrealistic standard for the protection of confidential information which would create unjustified impediments in the way large international firms conduct their business.

Jefri appealed in the House of Lords, which, after due deliberation, reversed the decision of the Court of Appeal and reaffirmed the decision of the lower court. The House of Lords framed the question to be decided as follows:

> ...the question in this appeal is whether, and if so in what circumstances, a firm of accountants which has provided litigation support services to a former client and in consequence has in its possession information which is confidential to him can undertake work for another client with an adverse interest. The question has become of increased importance with the emergence of huge international firms with enormous resources that operate on a global scale and offer a comprehensive range of services to clients.[12]

While deciding the case, the House of Lords discussed the basic principles applicable in a relationship between a firm of accountants and its clients. The relationship is almost the same as that of a solicitor and his client, which lays utmost emphasis on the duty of the solicitor not to communicate to anyone any information in his possession, which is confidential about an existing client, or even a former client. Interestingly, this duty extends well beyond that of refraining from deliberate disclosure; it also involves any careless, inadvertent or negligent disclosure. The duty further involves not putting any of the existing clients, or even the former clients, to avoidable risk, howsoever slight, without the consent of the client. Whenever any information is shared with the firm of accountants or solicitors, it is not only confidential, but also privileged; and the courts must follow the strict approach while exercising discretion to decide the possibility of conflict of interest.

The House of Lords observed:

> The former client cannot be protected completely from accidental or inadvertent disclosure. But he is entitled to prevent his former solicitor from exposing him to any avoidable risk; and this includes the increased risk of the use of the information to his prejudice arising from the acceptance of instructions to act for another client with an adverse interest in a matter to which the information is or may be relevant.[13]

The House of Lords did not agree with the Court of Appeal and commented that it would have been possible to prevent the flow of information by creating Chinese walls between separate departments, but it would not have possibly worked within a single department for the simple reason that if each project had a rotating membership and involved more number of people than working on the project at any

---

[12]Prince Jefri Bolkiah versus KPMG; House of Lords; 1998 Indlaw HL 24: 1999 (1) All ER 517; December 18, 1998; as per Lord Millett.

[13]Prince Jefri Bolkiah versus KPMG; House of Lords; 1998 Indlaw HL 24: 1999 (1) All ER 517; December 18, 1998; observation made under the head, 'The extent of the solicitor's duty'.

point of time, as in the instant matter, then some people would have joined the project and others would be sitting idle, making it far more difficult to ensure confidentiality and preventing unwitting or inadvertent disclosure.

Creation of information barrier between members in the same department who are accustomed to work with each other is next to impossible. The court further observed that in the branch of forensic accountancy, which faces rise of sudden problems requiring immediate attention and solutions, partners and managers in any accounting firm are trained and get accustomed to share information and expertise, and in most of the cases work as a team, making it impractical not to share information. In such a scenario, it would not have been possible for KPMG to create realistic Chinese walls so that information was not shared between personnel working on the two different projects—Project Lucy and Project Gemma. The court found that it was not necessary for KPMG to accept the investigation of special transfers as it was a clearcut and obvious matter of conflict of interest with the work done earlier for Prince Jefri, and the work could have easily been done by any of the top accounting firms which were also well equipped to do the job.

Thus, KPMG, by accepting the government of Brunei's offer for investigation of special transfers done during Prince Jefri's tenure, acted both in an unprofessional and unethical manner. While deciding such cases, the judges have to take into consideration the true and practical nature of the law of the land. It becomes important at that time to distinguish law as it is and as it ought to be.

Law 'As It Is' and 'As It Ought to Be'

The relationship between law and morality has been examined by H.L.A. Hart[14] in his famous 1958 Harvard Law Review article. He has discussed law as defined by the positive school of law. Law has been defined to be the command of sovereign which people follow as there is the threat of punishment in case of noncompliance. Law is the trilogy between sovereign, command and sanction. There is an understanding that law can be of two types: 'Law as it is' and 'Law as it ought to be'. The latter has to be just, equitable and fair. The former, on the other hand, can be any law which is neither concerned with the past stages of evolution of a law; nor is it concerned with the moral or ethical nature. It does not bother about the goodness or badness of law. It is the law as it exists. However, there can be two kinds of interpretation of law: strict or liberal; narrow or broad; literal or purposive. Hart also discusses the 'morally evil laws' which were enforced during Hitler's time in Germany. Such laws are not uncommon even in today's dictatorships.

Law provides excellent opportunities to regret, though there may be issues about righteousness and the normative position. In 2011, Hyundai's boss Chung Mong-koo

---

[14]H.L.A. Hart, Positivism and the Separation of Law and Morals, Harvard Law Review, February 1958, Volume 71, Number 4, pp. 593–629.

had donated 462 million dollars to charity in Seoul. He had paid this amount to Hyundai's Glovis, a foundation set up in 2007 by Hyundai automotive group.[15] The amount was the biggest ever charitable contribution made by an individual in South Korea and the money was supposed to be used for poor children's education. Chung Mong-koo had not donated the money because of certain philanthropic reasons but due to a pledge he made in 2006 while being investigated for corruption and for breach of trust. He was given a 3-year jail term after he was convicted of breach of trust and embezzlement of more than 100 million dollars in company funds. This may be his method of repentance, which may not be laudable by all.

There was another interesting person by the name Viktor Bout in Russia.[16] Presently, he is cooling his heels in an American prison, after he was arrested in Thailand and extradited to the U.S. He was an arms dealer and notorious for supplying anything to anyone for a price. He was known to supply weapons to Taliban, dictators in Africa and South America, Chechen Rebels and even, American forces in Iraq. He used the services of ex-Soviet pilots and used to send his aircraft anywhere for money. At times he was even supplying to U.N. peace keepers in Somalia or delivering aid to the British Government. His business has been detailed in the book 'Merchant of Death' by Douglas Farah and Stephen Braun. There has been even a Hollywood movie 'Lord of War' produced on the stories of Viktor Bout, played by Nicolas Cage.

What about sellers of tobacco or liquor? If mature adults consume them, on their own sweet will, should the seller be liable? The answer appears to be 'no'. Law allows it and if consumed in small quantity may not be harmful. Thus, it may be ethical also. But if someone follows Oscar Wilde's 'moderation is a fatal thing. Nothing succeeds like excess', should the seller be liable—ethically and legally? The 2005 movie 'Thank you for Smoking', directed by Jason Reitman, depicted this thought and emphasised on the power of articulation and lobbying. The choice is, therefore, to be made by the business leader and there are often no right or wrong choices. There is no lily white way forward. While exercising discretion, intentional wrong doing is the worst thing a business leader can do. It is aptly highlighted by the Libor case.

Libor and Criminal Action, 2012

In July 2012, the United States Justice Department mulled over initiating criminal action against big banks and their employees. That followed the Libor—London Interbank Offered Rate—fixing scandal in which Barclays had paid more than $450

---

[15]Hyundai boss Chung Mong-koo gives $462 million to charity, The Economic Times, http://articles.economictimes.indiatimes.com/2011-08-29/news/29941234_1_hyundai-motor-chairman-chung-kia-motors-corp, last accessed September 14, 2016.

[16]International man of mystery: Flying anything to anybody, The Economist, 18 Dec 2008, http://www.economist.com/node/12795502, last accessed September 14, 2016.

million to British and American authorities. Libor is a measure of how much a loan will cost to a bank when it borrows from another bank. It is one of the most important international reference points for interest rates. Action had been taken mostly by regulators, which was civil in nature and typically resulted in fines and settlements. Criminal proceedings take the form of fraud cases against the banks and their employees and result possibly in both jail and fines, as the settlements with the regulatory bodies do not shield the banks' employees.

Regulators had evidence that proved that bank employees and traders were colluding and rigged the interest rates intentionally. It was done to understate the bank's borrowing costs which would have resulted in false sense of security and wrong figures regarding the financial health of the bank. To regain investor confidence it was important that transparency was restored in the system and manipulators were punished. Criminal prosecution of the concerned employees of Barclays and other banks involved in trading had sent the right signals in the market.

For any criminal action it is essential that 'intention' is proved. According to the basic principles of criminal law, a crime is not committed if the mind of the person doing the act in question is innocent. The maxim says: *actus non facit reum, nisi mens sit rea*, which means the intent and act must both concur to constitute the crime.

As a general rule the mind must be at fault before there can be a crime, however statutory law may say otherwise. It is assumed that while enacting the law, the legislative body must have thought about the intention and incorporated it in the language of the law itself. Hence, the maxim has no application to the offences which are under the penal code or other statues in India or in other countries, until and unless it is mentioned specifically. If in a particular provision of law, the penal provisions have omitted to prescribe any particular mental condition, the presumption is that the omission by legislature is intentional and, therefore, *mens rea* cannot be applied in such instances.

Another general rule says that every sane person is presumed to intend the necessary or the natural and probable consequences of his acts. There are certain laws in the United States which surely found application in the case of the Libor rigging. Sarbanes Oxley Act of 2002 was one of them. It said, '…whoever knowingly executes, attempts to execute a scheme or artifice to… to defraud any person….' Any bank that had intentionally fixed interest rates was easily brought in the ambit of this provision.

Even the age-old antitrust law—the Sherman act—was used to catch hold of a manipulator as price-fixing was illegal under the act. Interestingly, it is not necessary that the accused had successfully manipulated the interest rates; just an attempt to do the same is enough in the eyes of law. The only important thing is: was there an intention to do the same? If it had been done by the person without his knowledge and without any intention—which is difficult to prove by direct evidence—then it is a weak case for the prosecution. Intention, in most of the cases, is proved by circumstantial evidence. It requires tremendous effort to complete the entire jigsaw puzzle using circumstantial evidence and convince the judge that the accused really intended to do something wrong. The law presumes innocence until the guilt is proved. And, the onus of proving everything lies upon the prosecution. In general, it is difficult to rely on oral evidence of witnesses as they may turn hostile at any point of time during the hearing of any case.

In the Libor matter, the Justice Department and the regulators had ample evidence—both hard copies and soft copies. They had the email exchanges and text messages which were used as electronic evidence in the court. The action by the regulators and the Department of Justice was a step towards cleaning the system and bringing in the much-needed transparency. Employees of banks and, for that matter any organisation, cannot simply use the excuse that it was the corporate entity for which and on whose directions they performed the task and not in their individual capacity.

Ultimately it is the individuals—human beings—who perform a task for and on behalf of a corporate entity and thus, it is the responsibility of these individuals to act in a responsible and reasonable manner. In the absence of due care and reasonable conduct, it would be impossible for them to argue that they had no intention of doing anything wrong. The doctrine of *mens rea* does not act as a shield to protect them.

Bankers deal with huge sums and must be very careful to be on the right side of the law and also on the right side of the ethical conduct. At times, it may mean to be a little more prudent to tilt towards idealism than pragmatism, even if that does not translate into a few dollars more. When banks lose money and bankers get pots of gold it is quite obvious for the masses to simmer in anger and resentment. Is it ethical for the bankers?

The Occupy Wall Street movement of 2011 was targeted towards bankers who made millions despite such acceptances of fraud, and had access to their golden parachutes. There was anger as people in general didn't have jobs and were also losing hope. A business leader must think about it. Raj Rajaratnam was sentenced to 11 years in prison for insider trading.[17] Rajat Gupta had been arrested for insider trading.[18] Both have been icons in business fraternity. The long arm of law with the help of the lethal mix of ethics and law may prove to be fatal for both. The fine distinction between legal and illegal depends on the interpretation and when ethics is codified effectively, it is really difficult for even the best of the brains to escape. Whether their actions were ethical or unethical; it cannot be said with certainty. However, legality of their actions had been questioned and the law had started taking its own course. Nick Leeson and the fall of Barings Bank in 1995 is another example of how one single person's unethical behaviour and audacity to circumvent the system can cause so much damage that the oldest merchant bank in London had collapsed.

---

[17]Rajaratnam sentenced to 11 years in jail, The Financial Times, 13 Oct 2011, http://www.ft.com/cms/s/0/19bf5730-f4eb-11e0-ba2d-00144feab49a.html#axzz1c9z0m060, last accessed September 14, 2016.

[18]With Gupta's Arrest, Insider Inquiry Goes Beyond Wall St., The New York Times, 26 Oct 2011, http://dealbook.nytimes.com/2011/10/26/gupta-surrenders-to-authorities-on-insider-trading/, last accessed September 14, 2016.

Takeaway for Business Leaders

1. Being the Role Model

   It is important for a business leader to keep in mind that the myopic vision of earning profits only does not pay in the long run. Shareholder value needs to be maximised and it is best to do it in an honest manner—both in letter and in spirit. The fountainhead of ethical conduct in a company is the top management. Other employees follow them. If rotting begins at the top, it may fast spread without any check in the entire company. In case it is somewhere at the bottom or elsewhere, it is the duty of the business leader to stem it. Business leaders can be the best role models for ethical conduct. And, undeniably, being ethical helps.

2. Intentional Wrong: Greed or need

   The worst thing a business leader can do is an 'intentional wrong'. It must be avoided at any cost. Often, it is because of greed, either for personal benefit or for the immediate gains for the company, that a business leader does something unethical and illegal with complete knowledge and understanding of both. This is unpardonable and the business leader has no right to even call himself a business leader. In such cases, there is hardly any difference between him and a mercenary. The first and primary purpose of any business recognised by the society and the law is to gel with the societal norms and work towards serving the society. Profit and loss are incidental and should be considered in the long run. Need and not greed should be the guiding force.

3. Certainty, Anticipate, Creating Options

   Being ethical in business tends to take a business leader and his business towards more and more certainty. Even if the law can be changed with a stroke of the pen, and things which were legal at one point of time may become illegal, the ethical norms and standards do not change radically and so fast. Equity—fairness—is an important criterion in delivery of justice. Any party who comes to the court with clean hands without doubt gets the benefit of doubt and usually the judges have a soft corner for it. In a situation of conflict between law and equity, the law ordinarily prevails, however, astute judges may use their intelligence and discretion to either distinguish the law from application in such cases or at least lessen the impact of their decision by making them milder. A well-informed business leader can very well anticipate the decision of a court in a particular jurisdiction and plan accordingly. He can create ethical and legal options to mitigate the damage if the decision is against his company.

Chapter 9
Please Get Me a Good Lawyer

Regarding lawyers, it is said in French, '*Bon avocat, mauvais voisin*', which means 'a good lawyer is a bad neighbour'. So, it is advisable not to live near a good lawyer, but how about having that same good lawyer on your side to tackle your problems, whether personal or professional. It is seldom a bad idea to befriend a good lawyer. Most of the business leaders would not take even a single step without consulting their lawyers. The same applies to a good number of politicians as well. Focusing on the business leaders, the role of lawyer is of paramount importance and can make or mar any business. Whether negotiating a contract, resolving a dispute, comprehending the complex laws, or in general, lawyers are of great value to any business.

What type of a lawyer is a good lawyer? The definition of a 'good' lawyer varies from person to person, time to time and place to place. A good lawyer maybe one with great knowledge of law, or may be highly successful, or commands great respect in the legal fraternity, or with all the three attributes. Typically, a good lawyer is one who can win cases. That depends on his capability to convince the judge. A judge shall be convinced according to the discretionary power enjoyed by him in that jurisdiction. Thus, simply getting a good lawyer is not enough. The legal environment should also be conducive. The judges, other lawyers, court staff, lawmakers, public opinion makers, etc., are a part of the legal environment.

For a business leader, a good lawyer helps him to remain on the right side of the law, counsels him to avoid disputes and guides him through the legal landscape. Let us go through some interesting cases which highlight the role of lawyers, judges and the legal environment in general.

Coca-Cola and Pepsi in India: Delhi High Court, 1999

The case witnessed leading senior lawyers bringing out the best legal arguments as P. Chidambaram, Arun Jaitely, Iqbal Chagla, Dushyant Dave and others appeared for the parties.

© The Author(s) 2017
A.K. Agarwal, *Business Leadership and Law*, DOI 10.1007/978-81-322-3682-5_9

Coca-Cola was doing good business in India till the time the Congress party lost power post-emergency in mid-1970s and the Janata Party came to power. The new government demanded from Coca-Cola in unequivocal terms that it should either tell the secret formula for the preparation of Coke or leave the country. Coca-Cola preferred the second option and decided not to waste even a single minute and left the country as it saw no future for its business with leaders like Morarji Desai and George Fernandes, who advocated simple living and high thinking, and also disseminated the message of nationalism, that it was not proper to buy goods from foreign companies, including the Coca-Cola Company. That happened in 1977. In such a scenario, who would have preferred in India to buy and consume a foreign drink? Coca-Cola, in its wisdom, made the right decision in quitting India.

With the exit of Coca-Cola from India, a number of Indian brands mushroomed, namely, Thums Up, Limca, Double Seven—77, Campa Cola, etc. As time passed by, with changing global economic scenario—dissolution of the USSR—Union of Soviet Socialist Republics, or the Soviet Union—led by Mikhail Gorbachev, who followed the policy of glasnost and perestroika—openness and restructuring, fall of the Berlin wall, German reunification—the world was moving towards paying more attention to economic prosperity and development, rather than communist politics and socialism. India could not remain insular and due to a number of weak governments at the Centre, and that too in quick succession, India had no option but to fall in line with the global trend. It also opened up its economy and decided to do away with the License-Permit Raj. It did not remain untouchable for multinational companies. On the contrary, MNCs, who typically found their domestic markets saturated, discovered India to their pleasant surprise as a new market with huge population and an insatiable appetite for foreign goods.

Coca-Cola did not miss this opportunity, and swallowing its pride re-entered the Indian market in 1993. Just about the same time, Pepsi, which was also eyeing the Indian market with great anxiety, also started its operations in India. As Pepsi was doing business in India for the very first time, it had to start everything from the scratch. It had no prior knowledge and experience of doing business in India, and, therefore, decided to go in a slow and steady manner. It started building a strong team of professionals who are well trained and motivated to work for the company. Coca-Cola, on the other hand, entered the Indian market with a different strategy— it acquired Parle trademarks—Thums Up, Limca, Goldspot, etc.—and, hence, got the entire infrastructure, including Parle's sales and distribution network.

As rivalry and competition heated up between Coca-Cola and Pepsi, demand of highly trained professionals in the business of soft drinks peaked. Often, they were trying to attract star performers of the other company with better emoluments, facilities and career prospects. Pepsi, according to its own submission, found itself on the receiving end, and, maybe after exhausting all the available options, filed a petition in the Delhi High Court alleging poaching by Coca-Cola.

Pepsi, *inter alia*, alleged that Coca-Cola had entered into a conspiracy to poach key personnel from Pepsi. It stated that at times Coca-Cola had made offers to the entire sales team of Pepsi in a particular territory to terminate their employment with Pepsi and to join Coke immediately. As Coke offers were highly lucrative, a number of these persons individually issued letters of termination of employment to Pepsi and joined Coke. Interestingly, each of the employees had signed earlier a contract of employment with Pepsi, including a confidentiality clause, another clause of giving reasonable notice of terminating the employment contract, and also another clause of not taking up employment with any of its competitor within 1 year of leaving Pepsi's employment.

Pepsi also alleged, in the petition, that one of the bottling companies in Goa, which was the franchise bottlers of Coke, had terminated its contract with Coke and commenced production and distribution of Pepsi products in 1997. At that time, the entire sales team of the bottling company had resigned and took up employment with Coca-Cola, jeopardising Pepsi's business and contract with the bottling company. Pepsi also stated that it was in negotiation with one of the leading Indian cricketers at that time—Javagal Srinath—who intended to sign an agreement with Pepsi for endorsing its products. Coke, however, was successful in convincing Srinath in endorsing Coke products instead. Hotel Hyatt Regency in New Delhi had an exclusive agreement with Pepsi, regarding use of Pepsi products only. But, as alleged by Pepsi, the hotel terminated the contract with Pepsi on Coke's behest.

Pepsi after providing details of all such incidents in its petition, tried to make out a case against Coca-Cola on the grounds that Coke's actions amounted to tortious interference in Pepsi's business.

Coca-Cola in its reply in the Delhi High Court denied all allegations and on the contrary, alleged that Pepsi was guilty of *suppressio-veri* and *suggestio-falsi*—the suppression of the truth is the suggestion of a falsehood.

Coca-Cola admitted offering higher and better emoluments and argued that it had not committed any actionable wrong, but acted only in furtherance of its legitimate business interests. The foundation of its argument was that in a free market competition was necessary and was in the interest of millions of consumers. Use of unlawful means in making any employee switch from one employer to another may attract legal action under the tort of conspiracy, however, offering better emoluments could not be termed to be unlawful means. Coke stated that all the employees who terminated the contract either with Pepsi or the bottling company or anyone else, before joining Coke, had done so on their own sweet will and Coke was not at all responsible for their actions vis-à-vis their former employer.

The Delhi High Court decided the matter in favour of Coca-Cola on the principal ground that the Indian contract law did not allow any clause restraining any employee from engaging or undertaking employment with the competent for a year after leaving the earlier employer service. Any such clauses would have made the contract unenforceable, void and against the public policy of India. The court observed that there cannot be any situation that 'once a Pepsi employee, always a Pepsi employee'. If that had been the case, it would be amounting to or a situation creating conditions of bonded labour. The court also observed that companies doing business in a market have to face the rough and tumble of the business including stiff competition, and courts were not the right place to decide what should be handled in the market place. It was also important for Pepsi to disclose the complete truth, and as is said in the courts, Pepsi should have gone to the court with 'clean hands'.

The Delhi High Court cited a passage from a 1998 judgement from the Supreme Court of North Carolina,[1] which in turn cited a passage from an 1895 judgment of Rhode Island court.[2] It primarily talks about competition and freedom to do business. It is as follows:

> Competition ... is the life of trade. Every act done by a trader for the purpose of diverting trade from a rival and attracting it to himself, is an act intentionally done, and, in so far as it is successful to the injury of the rival in his business ... to hold such an act wrongful and illegal would be to stifle competition. Trade should be free and unrestricted and hence every trader is left to conduct his business in his own way and cannot be held accountable to rival who suffers a loss or profits by anything he may do, so long as the methods he employs are not of a class of which fraud, misrepresentation, intimidation, coercion, obstruction or molestation of the rival or his servants ... are instances.

Concluding the judgement,[3] the Delhi High Court observed that it was difficult for it to hold that Coca-Cola resorted to business practices which were unethical, illegal, and which constituted tortious interference in Pepsi's business.

There can be no doubt that it was the professional expertise of the Coke lawyers that the company could save itself from the legal wrangle. It does matter how good the lawyers are. But, good lawyers do not come cheap.

Nani A. Palkhivala, the doyen of the Indian legal fraternity, noted lawyer, jurist, and above all, a kind-hearted human being, expressed in no uncertain terms, and also practiced to perfection, the finest qualities of a good lawyer, which, unsurprisingly, included being fair and reasonable in selecting the briefs and charging the fees. He, being the undisputed leader and the uncrowned king of the bar, along with several like-minded lawyers had started a movement in the Supreme Court of India of creating a ceiling for the lawyers' fees and he, without fail, never ever violated it. For most obvious reasons, he did not get the support from the entire bar in his endeavour, but that did not deter him from expressing his views, both in private and public, regarding the high commercialisation of the legal profession, which made it extremely difficult for anyone, without deep pockets, including businesspersons, to have access to expert legal advice and services. In the book, 'We, The Nation: The Lost Decades', which is a compilation of his writings over the years, he wrote unequivocally:

> Let me come to the United States. In that country legal profession is perhaps more commercialised than in any other country of the world, though India comes a close second. In America you can work on a contingency fee basis – i.e., fee depending upon the monetary redress awarded by the court to your client. You will recall how US lawyers rushed to Bhopal to make money out of the miseries of the poor victims of the Union Carbide tragedy. Ambulance-chasing and acting as scavengers is thought to be perfectly in order.

---

[1]People's Security Life Insurance Co. v. Milton S. Hooks, (1988) 322 N. C. 216; 367 S.E.2d 647.
[2]Macauley Bros. v. Tierney, 19 R.I. 255, 256, 33 A. 1, 2 (1895).
[3]Pepsi Foods Limited and Others v. Bharat Coca-Cola Holdings Private Limited, and Others, Delhi High Court, July 30, 1999; 1999 (2) LLJ 114, 1999 (4) CLJ 138, 1999 Indlaw DEL 178.

Small wonder that citizens of the State of Massachusetts and Pennsylvania demanded in the eighteenth century that the legal profession be abolished.[4]

Legal fees can be very high and there can be disputes even about the legal expenses. One such interesting case has been between Goldman Sachs and Rajat Gupta, who was arrested for insider trading.

Dispute About Lawyers' Fees for Resolving Dispute

There are two things certain in life: death and taxes. There is one more thing certain: lawyers' fees. In December 2012, Goldman Sachs and Rajat Gupta were disputing as to who should pay the lawyers' fees in the now well-known insider trading dispute in which Gupta had been held guilty. Quite amusing: dispute about dispute resolution.

I remember reading a law book with a very interesting cover page. It was, as a matter of fact, a very old painting, most probably of sixteenth or seventeenth century used as the cover page. It depicted a cow, with the plaintiff—the person who files the plaint, and initiates legal proceedings—holding the cow by the horns and pulling it towards him; the defendant—the person against whom legal proceedings are started and who defends himself—holding the tail of the cow and pulling the cow towards himself; the judge standing with due alertness to decide in which direction the cow has moved, so as to declare whether the plaintiff or the defendant has won. So, where is the lawyer? He is sitting on a stool next to the cow's udder and milking the cow. Lesson: the lawyer always gets the milk.

And, the dispute between Goldman Sachs and Rajat Gupta is no exception.

The fiduciary duty of any employee, more importantly of directors and others in the top management of a company, involves two important aspects—duty of care and duty of loyalty. The fundamental principle of a company being a distinct legal entity protects any of the employees, including directors, from any third party—the government and other regulatory bodies included—action, provided the employee and directors have acted within the framework of rights granted to them by the company, and in the regular and normal course of business of the company. And, it goes without saying that nothing must have been done in violation of any law, norm, or practise of trade.

Thus, for all the lawful acts, the company, typically, indemnifies to a great extent its directors. As the directors have tremendous powers of decision-making in a company, it becomes obvious that the company shall pay for legal expenses incurred in defending its directors regarding any disputes related to insider trading, breach of confidentiality, issues of trade secrets, shareholders' claims, etc.

---

[4]Palkhivala, Nani A., We, The Nation: The Lost Decades, UBS Publishers' Distributors Ltd., New Delhi, 1994, pp. 213–14.

The lawyers' fees incurred in the dispute related to insider trading by Rajat Gupta have been more than $30 million. Goldman Sachs paid the lion's share with an understanding with him that in case he was to be held guilty, he would reimburse the same. This is the general practise followed by companies regarding top management. In most of the cases, the companies are not able to recover anything, for the simple reason that these executives are, in most of the cases, left with nothing to reimburse the company. But Rajat Gupta's case is different. He can easily afford to reimburse from his personal assets.

As Gupta was also on the board of P&G, it also paid its part, but will not be able to recover it from him as Gupta had not been held guilty for the P&G insider trading. Regarding Goldman Sachs, the amount runs into almost $7 million, as claimed by the bank as 'direct and foreseeable' result of Gupta's offence. Gupta has denied. Companies usually buy insurance for such legal costs, but, in this case, insurance companies shall not pay as Gupta's conduct was beyond the scope of director's duties.

Lawyers, again, will benefit from this dispute between Gupta and Goldman Sachs, proving again that milk always goes to the lawyers. For businesses with deep pockets, it becomes possible to engage the most sought-after lawyers. And the games played by the rich and the powerful with the best legal brains on their side can be very entertaining for some at times and exasperating for others on most of the occasions.

Rich, Powerful, Courts and Law

In April 2016, the Supreme Court of India penalised two companies with Rs. 25 lakh (Rupees 2.5 million) each for resorting to delaying tactics and in the process wasting valuable time of the courts. This amount is unprecedented and is a definite positive signal towards ushering in of the new era of timely delivery of justice. However, it raises the fundamental question. Who is to be blamed for delaying the final decision—one of the parties, both the parties, lawyers, judges, the law or the entire system?

The Supreme Court observed that the matter had been pending for almost 20 years without much substance and real progress. Numerous appeals had been filed at different stages of the matter and access to the best of the counsel because of deep pockets, ironically, aggravated the problem of delay, rather than amicable settlement. Adjournments were sought and granted umpteen number of times.

Let us examine.

Usually in any matter, one of the parties is not interested in faster resolution, however, the other party looks forward to get it resolved at the earliest. It is very unusual for both the parties to delay the matter, and is typically experienced with the government being one of the parties, which may not at all be concerned even with resolution, forget about faster resolution for a variety of reasons.

Unfortunately, favouring the other party in consideration of certain monetary or non-monetary illegal and unethical benefits is one of the primary reasons for slowing the process by the government. Such matters are quite common and the court dockets are full of them.

If one of the parties is working towards fast disposal, in a fair litigation process, the courts do come forward and make all things possible for speedy decision-making, however, the law provides for a large number of appeals and special leave petitions for the intervention of the higher courts at various stages. Appeal, as a matter of procedure, is generally as a matter of right, but, special leave petitions and other writ petitions are considered to be a legal remedy which depends on the discretion of the judge. Thus, the role of the judge is extremely important. Exercise of discretion is not a mechanical process; it involves application of the law to the facts and making a decision supposed to be the most optimal and rational decision in those circumstances.

In Skipper Construction versus DDA case, decided by the SC about 20 years ago, the court had lamented that adjournments were granted mechanically and courts had often not exercised discretion judiciously. That case also had been languishing for a long time and several courts at all levels in Delhi. The lawyers in so many cases have been exploiting all the available appeals and truly speaking that is considered to be the job of a lawyer to find out all the possibilities in the substantive and procedure law and exhaust them before giving up. The deeper the pockets of the litigant, the higher are the chances of exhausting all the available options. It is akin to medical treatment. The more the resources available with the patient and his family, the more the efforts are to save him, even if he is a vegetative state.

In such a scenario, it is the duty and responsibility of the judicial officer to be firm and strict, but at the same time humane and flexible, to ensure that the matter is not delayed inordinately. One of the serious reasons as to why it becomes at time for the judicial officers to act speedily is the 'face value' of certain lawyers. Some lawyers, due to different reasons—seniority, popularity, nuisance creators, activists, political affiliations, etc.—have much higher perceived face value and they take undue advantage of their position. Often, many judges play to the galleries and do not wish to take the risk of making hard decisions lest they should become unpopular. This is absolutely undesirable.

The law must not provide for too many appeals as was advocated by the first Attorney General for India, M.C. Setalvad in 1952. Even Palkhivala, noted jurist and lawyer, had hinted for one and final decision to expedite the move towards certainty. The entire system needs overhauling, which can best be done by concerted efforts to the judges, lawyers and the legislature. Blaming and penalising only the parties for delay is not the right approach.

Lawyers, however, can give a new direction to any matter. In 2012, the Gujarat High Court passed an unprecedented and unexpected order in a Public Interest Litigation (PIL).

Natural Gas, Naturally: *Jus Dicere* and not *Jus Dare*

In July 2012, on the insistence of the lawyers arguing on the ground of public interest, the Gujarat High Court in India, in a landmark judgment directed the State government to pass necessary orders to make it compulsory for all the four wheelers registered in the State of Gujarat to convert to natural gas within a year as the natural gas was supposed to be, according to the understanding of judges as convinced by the arguing lawyers, the cleanest and the most logical energy source for automobiles. And, the judges were made to believe that the change could be easily made by a judicial fiat. Later, it was revealed that the entire exercise was done at the behest of a company dealing with natural gas, and obviously, the State government did not execute the court's order, which was stayed.

A lawyer is an 'officer of the court' and it is his bounden duty not to mislead the court. He must always follow the well-set constitutionally mandated path. Thus, the action of the judges was most surprising as such an order took away the discretionary power of the government and made it mandatory for the government to follow the orders of the court—on a subject which obviously fell in the purview of policy formulation. It is the prerogative of the Legislature or the Executive under the powers of delegated legislation to decide. Small wonder, noted lawyer and jurist Fali Nariman had written that we were living in a time when there was a 'Government of Judges'. One may like it or not, but the truth of the matter is that the latest orders—from the Supreme Court as well as the High Courts in India—are blurring the distinction between the three organs of the state—Legislature, Executive and Judiciary. And, many of these orders result from the devious ingenuity of some unscrupulous lawyers, who have no qualms in deviating from the straight and narrow path of equity and good conscience.

In a democracy, it is the elected representatives of the people who make the law and the role of the judiciary is to interpret the law made and also to uphold it. Judicial activism and the public interest litigation—PIL—have grown rapidly since 1980s in India. At times, after experiencing the undesired effects of this movement, noted lawyers and jurists have written that it cannot be termed as judicial activism; it is simply usurpation of powers and can be called judicial despotism or judicial anarchy.

It is interesting to note that Francis Bacon in his essay 'Of Judicature' had written, 'Judges ought to remember, that their office is *jus dicere*, and not *jus dare*; to interpret law, and not to make law, or give law'. That essay was written about four centuries ago.

In 1980, the Supreme Court observed in Bachan Singh's case, '*We must leave unto the legislature, the things that are Legislature's ...As Judges, we have to resist the temptation to substitute our own value choices for the will of the people*'.[5]

In July 2012, the then Chief Justice of India (CJI), Justice Kapadia, speaking at a conference had said, '*We can have facilitative mediation in disputes in pricing of*

---

[5]Bachan Singh v. State of Punjab, AIR 1980 SC 898.

natural resources like the pricing of gas and oil which are complicated matters. Judges do not have expertise to deal with those matters. The judgments delivered by judges sometimes can hit the economy of the country which is not good'.

The judges of the Supreme Court and the High Courts—excluding the Chief Justice—are called puisne (pronounced puny) judges who are in no way inferior or subordinate to the Chief Justice as far as judicial competence and power are considered. They are not bound by a non-judicial observation made by the Chief Justice, who including the CJI, is simply *primus inter peres*—first among equals. But still, even at that time, Justice Kapadia's words could be taken as wise counsel, though unsolicited.

In response to a PIL by a lawyer, in July 2005, the Gujarat High Court had ordered that all the cattle should be removed from the streets of Ahmedabad in 72 h. Forget about 72 h, even after a decade, it has not been done. Ab initio the order was unrealistic and the court should have refrained from passing such an order, which if not complied with, undermines the dignity of the court.

In 2005, the then Chief Justice of India, Justice R.C. Lahoti wrote about judicial activism and cautioned his brother and sister judges, *'To preserve the sanctity and credibility of the judicial process and to overcome the criticism of judicial activism, it is necessary to practice self-restraint while innovating new tools'*.[6]

Contrast the situation of openness and accessibility to courts in India to that of China. The legal system and the courts are not open in China will be an understatement. Despite engaging the best of the lawyers, foreign businesses are completely at a loss in understanding as to how the system works there. Some of the most misunderstood situations are of blatant copying with almost no redressal mechanism.

When Copycats Win in China

In May 2016, one of the Chinese courts held that a Chinese company making leather bags named iPhone can continue to do so despite the name being similar to the world famous iPhone made by Apple. This is not at all surprising as Chinese courts have been very often upholding violation of intellectual property rights of the well-known global companies.

It is a matter of serious concern that while courts in India had recognised globally well-known trademarks in the Whirlpool case even 20 years ago, when India had just signed the TRIPs (Trade Related Intellectual Property Rights) agreement under the umbrella of the World Trade Organisation, WTO, Chinese courts are reluctant to give due respect and honour the well-known trademarks whose reputation transcends geographical boundaries. The idea of well-known and globally recognised trademarks was incorporated in the Indian trademark law

---

[6]AIR 2005 Journal 177 at 186.

enacted in the year 2000. Since then a large number of matters have been decided in courts in India which have given protection to the well-known trademarks.

However, use of any well-known trademark prior to the enactment of any such law or which had not been challenged earlier cannot be stopped now. For instance, there are dozens of products in India which are sold under the brand of Maruti, Amul, Lux, VIP, Taj, etc. The manufacture and sale of any such products with these brand names cannot be stopped even by these well-known trademarks because of long usage either by copycats or sellers who genuinely believed that they had a right to use these names as some of them might be commonly used words, and it will be difficult to prove that these have been copied from another product. It may be another matter that a world like Maruti became famous as a car, however, a word like VIP is so very common in India, although for all wrong political reasons.

The iPhone bag case in China is very interesting because the iPhone had already been launched in the United States and other parts of world but it had not yet arrived in China, and before the iPhone as in the phone came to China, a copycat exploited it is a good commercial opportunity and branded its bags as iPhone. This is something very obvious as iPhone is not a common word—neither in English nor in Chinese—and there can hardly be any other source or reason, except Apple's iPhone, which inspired the Chinese company to brand its products as iPhone. Such copying is called deceptive similarity and there could not have been any other intention except to pass of its products as Apple's products. This should have been stopped by the Chinese courts at the earliest, however, mostly for the reasons of domestic protectionism and not caring at all about international obligations under intellectual property treaties, the Chinese court ruled against Apple. The matter is going to be escalated to the highest court in China, but the chances of a fair and reasoned decision are remote.

Small wonder that multinational companies and foreign governments find the intellectual property regime in India far better than that in China, though many a time India is branded as a country with extremely poor record of intellectual property protection. Things are changing, and changing fast towards better protection and enforcement of intellectual property rights in India. But blatant violation of intellectual property rights and upholding of such violations by Chinese courts will definitely send a wrong signal that universal protection and enforcement of intellectual property rights globally is simply a mirage and given the enormous clout China has as a manufacturer and consumer, it does not bother even to show a pretence of protecting such rights and being committed to the rule of law.

China with its humongous bargaining power is difficult to be tamed by international treaties. Till the time multinational companies and foreign governments kowtow to China and its policies, there is hardly any hope of getting true protection for intellectual property in the country. India, with all its efforts to provide a level-playing field to foreign companies desirous of doing business in India, wrongly gets branded as a country with poor enforcement of intellectual property rights. A little bit of proactive diplomacy on India's part may turn the tables.

The working of courts in any country is really speaking the working of the judges. The lawyers in any court try to convince the judges, and it depends on the experience, competence and integrity of the judges to understand the matter at hand and decide it in a proper and legal manner. Individual discretion does matter. And, judges of unimpeachable integrity and exceptional competence are needed.

Judges of Exceptional Integrity Needed

In the annual report on the state of the federal judiciary in 2011, Chief Justice Roberts of the US Supreme Court has strongly defended his colleagues on the bench and said, 'I have complete confidence in the capability of my colleagues to determine when recusal is warranted. They are jurists of exceptional integrity and experience whose character and fitness have been examined through a rigorous appointment and confirmation process'.

This statement is important as two of the nine judges in the US Supreme Court have some relationship, however indirect that may be, with a matter of national importance and President Barack Obama's dream project—the Healthcare Law, which makes it mandatory for almost everyone in the United States to buy health insurance or face penalty. The law has been challenged on the ground that the US legislature has gone beyond its power in making the law which is in conflict with the right of choice of the citizens of the United States of America. According to one view there is nothing wrong with the law as it is also mandatory to buy motor vehicle insurance, and that is true for India also, however there is another view which says that it should not be made mandatory and it should be left to an individual to make a decision whether he would like to buy health insurance or not.

It has been interpreted by the US Supreme Court long ago—1803 in Marbury versus Madison—that the judiciary has a right of judicial review over the laws made by the legislative bodies as well as the executive actions taken by the government and that is how this law has been challenged and is to be heard and decided by the United States Supreme Court sometime later this year, most probably by the end of June. To a certain extent this has been the situation in India also and it has been vindicated by the Coelho judgment—also known as Schedule IX judgment—in January 2007 by the Supreme Court of India.

According to critics, two judges of the US Supreme Court—Justice Clarence Thomas and Justice Elena Kagan—must not take part in the decision-making process of the Healthcare Law. They say that Justice Thomas should recuse himself as his wife works for certain groups opposed to the law and Justice Kagan was instrumental in the drafting of the law as she was the Solicitor general of the United States when the law was drafted.

In one of the landmark judgments of the United States Supreme Court, Caperton versus Massey, decided in June 2009 it was held that any judge must recuse himself in case there is a probability of bias. Actual bias need not be proved. Keeping this test in mind, it is quite clear that it is a fit case when both the judges must recuse themselves.

However, Justice Roberts has said that the constitutional mandate is for all the nine judges to sit together on the bench and there is no provision of a review by any other higher court because the Supreme Court is the highest court of the land. In such a scenario by application of doctrine of necessity there is no choice left and all nine judges must sit together to hear the matter. Chief Justice Roberts has also emphasised that he is no distrust about the integrity and competence of the judges sitting on the bench and that no one in the country should have even an iota of doubt about the outcome of the case because of any direct or indirect connection of any of the judges with the matter to be heard.

The same thoughts had earlier been written by the former Chief Justice of India, Justice J.S. Verma and noted jurist Mr. Fali Nariman. Justice Verma had written that 'dexterity of a skilled surgeon is necessary for use of the scalpel of new jurisprudence'. And, the idea of new jurisprudence translates to the fact that the gap between law and justice is to be bridged by the judges. There can be no justice if the litigants have a doubt about the integrity of the judge or do not have full confidence in the capability, competence and impartiality of the judge. It is not at all an easy task for any judge sitting on the bench to use the new tools which have been forged by the Supreme Court in India since late 1970s and early 1980s, like PIL and other different means of judicial activism.

Mr. Nariman has written that 'the people of India will have faith in the judicial process only so long as our judges are perceived to be persons of exceptional competence and of high moral integrity'. He further wrote that if that perception changed the constitutional system would break down. He wrote these words in the year 2007, the 60th year of independence of India. Due to several media reports and stories about corruption in judiciary, he was compelled to write the following words, 'Sixty years after Independence the people have come to trust the courts: but the people's trust rests in confidence—sometimes rudely shaken by gossip, rumour and a lack of transparency'.

Of late, the media reports have again highlighted numerous stories of corruption in the judiciary—in the lower judiciary as well as, unbelievably, in the higher judiciary also. The perception of the judiciary in India is presently now that of an institution which is mired in corruption, nepotism and at times incompetence. In his Law Day speech on 26 November 2011, Chief Justice Kapadia went defensive; accepted that there were certain black sheep in judiciary but requested his countrymen not to paint all the judges with the same brush. We hope that in the Law Day speeches the Chief Justice of India is able to share the confidence of the Chief Justice of the US Supreme Court in his colleagues on the Bench with conviction.

In June 2012, the US Supreme Court upheld the compulsory health insurance law, also known as Obamacare, and Chief Justice Roberts played an instrumental role.

Obamacare and Chief Justice Roberts

On 28 June 2012, the US Supreme Court upheld the Healthcare Law of 2010, also known as Obamacare. The law envisages that every person in the United States is bound by law to have a health insurance. There is no choice, and that was precisely the argument on which the law was challenged in a number of courts in the United States and finally the Supreme Court.

The decision was made five—four, with the Chief Justice Roberts being in the majority. The United States Supreme Court comprises nine justices and all of them sit together to hear all the matters. Thus, highly contentious issues are decided with razor-thin majority, five—four. This case regarding healthcare insurance had been a pet idea of President Obama. Had the Supreme Court struck it down, it would undoubtedly have been a huge embarrassment for the President. Hence, in a way Roberts saved Obama.

The four conservative judges gave a dissenting opinion and were not in favour of making healthcare law, compulsory. The other four judges were quite liberal and wished to uphold the law. Interestingly, the swinging vote came from the Chief Justice, who otherwise is supposed to be a conservative.

Roberts was confirmed as the 17th Chief Justice of the United States of America in 2005. He was only 50 then. The then President of the United States, George W. Bush, said at the swearing in ceremony—as reported in the Washington Post—'The Senate has confirmed a man with an astute mind and a kind heart'. He added that '(Roberts) will be prudent in exercising judicial power, firm in defending judicial independence and, above all, a faithful guardian of the Constitution'.

When his son Jack got the news, he asked his father, 'Daddy, do you get a sword?' as he had seen a statue of Lady Justice with her sword at the court. Roberts told the media that Jack was not very impressed as the Chief Justice did not get a sword.

Interestingly, Obama—as a senator—had opposed his confirmation. Both Obama and Roberts graduated from the Harvard Law School: Roberts in 1979 and Obama in 1991. Both have been associated with the prestigious Harvard Law Review—Obama as the president and Roberts as the managing editor. And, they were not contemporaries. Chief Justice Rehnquist—who preceded Roberts—held the position of the Chief Justice for almost two decades and as Roberts is too young—1995 born—he may remain the Chief Justice of the United States Supreme Court for another 25–30 years or even more, as there is no retirement age for US Supreme Court judges.

Roberts had the reputation of being a conservative, however, he played the key role in the health care case as it was his decision which became the final decision— the majority decision—of the Supreme Court. The judges, typically, do not have to be labelled and, more so, do not have to perform and make decisions as per the label. But, there are certain trends which are set in and the laypersons, and even legal experts, expect consistent decisions from individual judges, who, particularly in higher courts—which include the US Supreme Court, exercise 'wise and wide' discretion and are often said to be like proverbial camels. Just as the camels—until and unless a camel sits, no one can tell on which side the camel is going to sit—it is extremely difficult, rather impossible, to predict by the proceedings in the court, in whose favour the judge is finally going to decide the matter.

It is on record that during the hearings of this case, the perception in the mind of a general observer was that the Supreme Court would have held the law unconstitutional. The final decision was otherwise.

Roberts, immediately after taking over as the Chief Justice, tried to bring all the justices of the US Supreme Court together and experts were reminded of how the highly celebrated Judge, Chief Justice Marshall, had done the same 200 years ago. Roberts succeeded to a certain extent in the beginning, but later on he found it too difficult to get everyone together. Unanimity in decisions became rare, specially in cases involving contentious issues. Of late, it has been observed that a good number of very important decisions are generally decided five—four. In a few cases, Roberts has been in the minority also.

The manner in which the Chief Justice thinks and makes the decisions, and also the time for which he remains the Chief Justice of the United States Supreme Court, are all too important for the people in India. The judgments of the American court do not have a direct impact in India, but they do have a persuasive power and are often cited in Indian courts. Besides the legal and the business environment being impacted in India, the decisions of the American courts surely have an influence on the Indian businesses with interest in the United States. Indubitably, Roberts is the man to be watched.

When judges are to be appointed as arbitrators to decide disputes, they have the freedom to decide their own fees, until and unless they are a part of an institutional framework and have previously agreed to the fees structure of that institution. Even appointment of arbitrators through courts gives lawyers a good chance to appear in the case and try to convince the sitting judges about the advantages of getting a particular individual—whether a retired judge or subject matter expert—appointed as an arbitrator. The heavier the stakes, the higher are the chances of stiff opposition by the lawyers in acceptance of an individual as the arbitrator. An interesting case has been the appointment of the third arbitrator in the Reliance—KG Basin case in India.

India: Reliance–Government Dispute

The dispute between Reliance and the Government of India regarding oil exploration in KG basin, as per the contractual clauses, has to be resolved by way of arbitration, but both the parties were not able to agree on the appointment of a third arbitrator, and that is when the matter was referred to the Supreme Court. In 2014, interestingly the Supreme Court of India interpreted the arbitration clause to allow the appointment of a foreign national as the third arbitrator and a former Chief Justice of Australia was appointed as the third arbitrator, but immediately thereafter the Government of India pointed it out to the Supreme Court that the name of that Australian judge was at the top of the list submitted by Reliance and hence it would not be proper for the Supreme Court to appoint the Australian judge as the third arbitrator.

As we have discussed in a previous chapter, arbitration is currently the chosen method of resolving business disputes in India and elsewhere in the world. The most important difference between an arbitration and court proceedings is the person or persons making the decision: in arbitration, the arbitrator or arbitrators are appointed by the disputing parties, whereas in court proceedings, the decisions are made by a judge or judges, who are publicly appointed. Thus, in arbitration proceedings the disputing parties can freely decide who the arbitrator shall be and what procedure would be followed in resolution of the business dispute, and that is why one of the most important basic principles of arbitration is 'party autonomy'.

Parties in any dispute are expected to conduct themselves in an autonomous manner however they have to remain within the periphery of law. Recently there has been a problem faced by the government and one of the disputing parties— Reliance—regarding appointment of arbitrator. This is nothing new; neither happening for the first time nor for the last time. Disputing parties are often not able to see eye to eye as far as individuals appointed as arbitrators are concerned for the simple reason that one party may perceive the arbitrator appointed by the other party to be biased, and the same applies to the other party. In such a scenario, to a large extent, the purpose of giving this autonomy to parties by the law of arbitration in different countries is defeated as the entire dispute comes to a deadlock due to non-agreement on the name of an arbitrator.

To a large extent this problem has been resolved by the law itself by giving the power to the parties to appoint arbitrators in order numbers—the minimum being one and the next number being three, and so forth. In most of the cases where the stakes are low and the disputing parties wish to have the resolution as quickly as possible, they agree to appoint a sole arbitrator, but in matters where the stakes are high, and particularly when the government is also involved—whether a ministry, any department, public sector undertaking, or any other instrumentality of the state—it is generally observed that the number of arbitrators is three, with both the parties being given the freedom to appoint one each, and the third arbitrator who also acts as the presiding arbitrator appointed either by both the arbitrators, who earlier have been appointed by the parties, or by a neutral agency which has been given this power according to the arbitration clause in the contract between the two parties.

Often it is seen that the parties would have difficulty in accepting the third or presiding arbitrator and the problem comes back to the original issue of neutrality of the individual appointed as the third arbitrator. In case there is no agreement for third arbitrator, in case of three arbitrators, or the sole arbitrator in case of only one arbitrator, there would be a problem in proceeding further as the parties while entering into a contract have agreed that the dispute is to be resolved by way of arbitration and that is why they had included the arbitration clause in the contract. But without an arbitrator nothing can proceed further and that is why the arbitration law makes a provision for the appointment of arbitrator by the court in case an application is filed by one of the parties.

A day later the Supreme Court recalled its order of appointment of the Austrian judge as the third arbitrator. It simply does not make sense. There are two simple reasons: first, it is quite unlikely that the list of arbitrators suggested by Reliance was not perused by the Supreme Court while making a decision regarding the appointment of the third arbitrator; and second, is there anything wrong in appointing the person who is heading the top of the list of suggested names as an arbitrator?

The matter is back to square one, that is, a dispute which was to be decided by an arbitral tribunal cannot be resolved in an expeditious and efficacious manner due to absence of a tribunal. This defeats the very purpose of arbitration itself and reminds us of the very old saying in one of the Supreme Court judgements—Guru Nanak Foundation—where the court had observed that arbitration law in India had made legal philosophers weep and lawyers laugh. This is indeed a sorry state of affairs as main disputes cannot be resolved in this manner and even the dispute regarding the appointment of arbitrator is going to be fought in a bitter manner. One can very well imagine the acrimony and bitterness between the parties regarding the main dispute, and to what extent the parties—with one or both—can go to swing the decision in its favour.

Very heavy stakes in Reliance–Government dispute are creating serious problems, and it would be in the interest of the public at large that the Supreme Court itself decides the matter, of course, bypassing the legal technicality, taking into account the gravity of the situation and national interest. Arbitration may not truly work in the instant case.

Lawyers play an important role in getting matters settled. Dispute avoidance is better than resolution and settlement at any time is better than continuing with the dispute. One such matter was Lehman's settlement in 2012.

Lehman's 38 Billion Dispute Settlement: Better Late Than Never

October 2012 had been momentous for international business dispute resolution. It witnessed the settlement of a dispute worth $38 billion between Lehman Brothers Inc. and the bank's European arm, Lehman Brothers International Europe (LBIE). Lehman Brothers had been one of the four largest investment banks in the United States, but it filed for the largest bankruptcy in the American history in September 2008. Since then there has been a long-standing dispute over claims and counter-claims by the American arm and the European arm.

The European arm had claimed $24 billion from the US brokerage, whereas the latter had made a counterclaim of about $14 billion, thus creating the disputed claim of $38 billion. For almost 4 years, the parties had not been able to arrive at a settlement, and in the process must have spent considerable amount of time, effort and money in litigation, however, last week the European arm agreed to settle for $12 billion instead of $24 billion it had claimed. The US brokerage decided to be contended with not making any counterclaim against the European arm. Thus, the entire $38 billion claim and counterclaim was settled for a payment of $12 billion by the American arm to the European arm.

This settlement—which will be finalised by the two sides, hopefully before Christmas this year—has to be approved by two courts: the court supervising Lehman's bankruptcy matter in Manhattan and the High Court in England. There appears to be hardly any reason why these courts would not approve of this settlement, however, one cannot be so sure about it, as one of the courts last year headed by Judge Rakoff did not approve of a $285 million settlement between Securities and Exchange Commission (SEC) and the Citigroup.

The current Lehman Brothers settlement provides a practical learning. It is a matter of serious concern that unrealistic claims and counterclaims, which appear in hindsight to be highly inflated, were made in the beginning. Had it not been the case, neither of the parties would have agreed to settle for a much smaller sum. It is not so surprising that a number of people, including businesspersons, treat litigation as gamble—if you lose in a lower court, double the stakes and appeal in a higher court; if you still lose, treble or quadruple the stakes and appeal in a still higher court. And, this is precisely the reason why long ago when noted lawyer Nani A. Palkhivala asked Sir Noshirwan Engineer, the Advocate General of India in 1947, as to what would have been the best method of resolution of disputes, he replied that a *Kazi* system—a single and the final decision by a wise person—would be the best form of resolution of disputes.

About 60 years ago, the first Attorney General for India, Mr. Motilal C. Setalvad, had written that one of the banes of the litigation system in India was the provision of too many appeals. He at that time had written that it would have been in the interest of the People of India that the number of appeals available to the litigants was drastically reduced. Unfortunately, that has not been done and today we see so many matters, particularly matters with heavy stakes, reaching the doors of the Supreme Court invariably.

The two arms of Lehman Brothers—American and European—realised, though a bit late, that the litigation, including appeals in appellate courts and thereafter in the Supreme Court, would surely take a long time. It is good that they decided to settle, as it is never too late to settle.

Takeaway for Business Leaders

1. Societal Interest versus Client's Interest
   Gandhi, in the book 'The Law and The Lawyers', wrote in detail about the role of law and the lawyers in society and had been quite caustic about a large number of lawyers putting the interests of their client, even if they knew that he

was guilty, above the interests of the society and the country. He believed that the role of a lawyer was to unite the parties and get the matter resolved rather than let the dispute persist for a long time. He practised this belief. It is true that in today's world it is becoming increasingly difficult to find lawyers having these qualities, but there is surely a sizeable number of lawyers who still continue to believe that their primary duty as a lawyer is not to simply earn more and more, but to help the courts dispense justice, which can ideally be done only by bringing the truth and the relevant laws before the judge. Thereafter, it is for the judge to decide. Gandhi wrote:

Throughout my career at the bar I never once departed from the strictest truth and honesty. The first thing which you must always bear in mind, if you would spiritualize the practice of law, is not to make your profession subservient to the interests of your purse, as is unfortunately but too often the case at present, but to use your profession for the service of your country.[7]

A business leader needs to be careful of this fact and should look for a lawyer who can very well balance the societal good while safeguarding the interest of his business. Overzealousness can boomerang.

2. Legal Cost

A business leader should try his best to find an affordable lawyer. Many a time, the most expensive lawyer is not needed to be engaged. A reasonably good lawyer charging modest fee may serve the purpose. To get this understanding, information about different law firms is to be gathered, sifted and a conscious decision made to experiment with a particular law firm or an individual lawyer. If it clicks, well and good, otherwise, do the exercise again. There are no set rules for finding a lawyer who suits your purpose.

3. Wit and humour

The law is supposed to be a dry subject, full of legalese, sections, maxims and difficult words. A lawyer with wit and humour can be a great asset. Often there are interactions between lawyers and judges on different points of law tempered with jibes and retorts. A good lawyer must be capable of handling such a situation, and better to turn the tide in his favour.

I would like to cite from a conversation between Smith—the lawyer F.E. Smith, 1st Earl of Birkenhead—and the judge which is anecdotal, but there is no reason to disbelieve it:

Judge: Are you trying to show contempt for this court, Mr Smith?
Smith: No, My Lord. I am attempting to conceal it.
Judge: Have you ever heard of a saying by Bacon—the great Bacon—that youth and discretion are ill-wedded companions?
Smith: Yes, I have. And have you ever heard of a saying of Bacon—the great Bacon—that a much-talking judge is like an ill-tuned cymbal?

---

[7]Gandhi, M.K., The Law and The Lawyers, Navajivan Publishing House, Ahmedabad, 1962, p. 258; cited from *Young India*, December 22, 1927, pp. 427–28.

Smith (to witness): So, you were as drunk as a judge?
Judge (interjecting): You mean as drunk as a lord?
Smith: Yes, My Lord.
Master of the Rolls: Really, Mr Smith, do give this Court credit for some little intelligence.
Smith: That is the mistake I made in the Court below, My Lord.

4. Possibility Thinker

A lawyer can never assure certainty. The legal profession thrives on uncertainty. And, that is the hallmark of a good lawyer, usually a possibility thinker, to find the small island of certainty in the vast ocean of uncertainty. Whatever one may say, there can never be complete certainty about proceedings in a court of law, howsoever strong one's case may be. Hence, a business leader should be prepared for the unfavourable decision even if he was expecting—highly and with great optimism—the decision from the court shall be in his favour. One can only anticipate and that too to a certain extent regarding decisions in a court of law. These decisions depend on the discretion exercised by individual judges. Creating options for both the scenarios—winning or losing—is the wisest thing to do. Also, there can be a third scenario of partial winning or partial losing, which makes both the parties dissatisfied and typically both file appeals in the appellate court, resulting in cross-appeals. During the entire process and living with huge uncertainty, the business leader must remain a diehard possibility thinker so as to channelize all the resources—time, effort and money—in the positive direction. Only then a lawyer, with the best intentions and efforts, will be able to help.

Chapter 10
The Law Is My Friend, Philosopher and Guide

After going through different aspects of business law, we can say without doubt that the role of the law in business is immense. Some other thoughts which have crystallised in the previous chapters are summed up.

It is the law which decides whether the business is legal or illegal. The law of the land also determines how much tax needs to be paid by businesses. The law in many jurisdictions is the reflection of government policy, whereas in certain jurisdictions like India, the law is a mix of government policy as well as the interpretation given by courts. The 'will of the legislature' is not supreme and is subject to the constitution and principles of natural justice. The legal environment, in which the businesses function, is dynamic and changes with time. Even the businesses can have an impact on this environment and get it changed according to their convenience. This is not so easy, however, a number of firms have exhibited that it not impossible either. These firms use law as a tool and try to fine-tune it or get it changed altogether. In the international scenario, as there is no global sovereign, the dynamics of business law becomes much more interesting and interactive. There is no lawmaking body which makes the law for everyone. Each sovereign nation accepts the global rules in its sovereign capacity and out of its own sweet will. Smart firms use this grave lacuna in international business law to their advantage. Holland calls international law as the 'vanishing point of jurisprudence'.

Enforcement of law also varies from country to country. This gives rise to forum shopping in case of disputes and provides ample opportunity to sharp businesses to circumvent the law and law enforcement. On the other hand, globally respected firms take care to be on the right side of the law, irrespective of the jurisdictional issues. From the very beginning, these firms seek the advice of a lawyer and always try to make the law their 'friend, philosopher and guide'. On the other hand, certain firms never ever bother about law enforcement and they go ahead doing business in a reckless manner. Only when they are confronted by the law, they tend to either make excuses or blame the law, society and government for the problems faced by them.

A.K. Agarwal, *Business Leadership and Law*, DOI 10.1007/978-81-322-3682-5_10

Complying with the law is supposed to be the best policy, however, compliance or defiance or confrontation is the choice of business leaders. A few cases and business stories from different parts of the world will highlight it well.

Google, Competition Law and Compliance in Russia

In August 2016, Russia imposed a fine of about $7 million on Google for misusing its dominant position in the Russian market. This was a tiny dot for Google's annual revenue, however, a fine is a fine and always has a negative connotation. The important thing was that it was not for the first time that a fine had been imposed by any competition law authority in any country on Google. This had been observed quite frequently in a number of countries across the globe. The company in most of the countries had denied any wrongdoing.

The important question to be answered was: whether the competition authorities of all the countries in the world were against the technology giant Google, or Google really was on the wrong side of the law in most of the countries? Since the formation of the World Trade Organisation (WTO) in 1995, with the cherished goal of free movement of goods and services, there had been an effort to provide a level playing field to businesses—both domestic and foreign—in all the member countries. Russia became a member of the WTO in 2012. Though there have always been serious issues about the commitment of the country to rule of law, in the recent past, there had been instances which signalled Russia's better alignment to global practices—which might have been only a lot of eyewash—as far as competition law, intellectual property rights, and world trade laws were concerned.

There might have been a possibility that Google faced these problems of violation of competition law in some of the major jurisdictions of the world because of the fuzzy periphery dividing legal from illegal as the law was and is in its nascent stage in many jurisdictions, including India. The United States had been using this law—the Sherman Act—since 1890 and the application of this law has seen some major implications right from Standard Oil to AT&T to Microsoft. The story of the competition law in the United States is full of glories and tears for the last more than a century. The same, however, is not true for the rest of the world.

Because of the absence of such highly developed competition law in most of the developing and underdeveloped world, firms from the developed world, and Google was no exception, often take the situation a bit too lightly, forgetting for a moment the power of the sovereign in a nation. Google had been at the receiving end in China also for not complying with government's orders to share certain e-mail communication a few years back. Google had made a hasty exit from China, but such was the lure of a market of 1.5 billion people that it came back to China despite the existence of the omnipresent Chinese search engine Baidu. Of course, Chinese government does not come forward with clean hands in privacy and confidentiality matters, still Google had no qualms in doing business in the country.

The same is true about transgressing the boundary of law and pushing the frontier to try doing new things and keep testing the periphery. Law, usually, develops at the fringes. Imposition of fine on Google and its decision to challenge were positive signs of development of law. But, knowing the style of functioning of Russia—the knee-jerk decisions and irrational and unprecedented and many a time the absence of any judicial review process of executive and legislative decisions—posed a serious challenge for the evolution of law in a systematic and natural manner. Hence, the entire episode in Russia could simply be taken with a pinch of salt.

It is, nonetheless, also a fact that technology giants try to experiment with newer applications of existing technology, which hitherto might not be available in a particular jurisdiction, or they will create specific applications for different jurisdictions by pushing the productivity frontier and in the process may be getting entangled with the regulatory institutions. These issues, to a certain extent, are a good sign of the interaction of technology and law.

After all, technology precedes and law follows.

Thereafter, technology and business ought to comply with the law.

The taxation issue and use of certain tax havens have become critical in the debate on defiance versus compliance. Firms with deep pockets often do not pay the taxes the way they should be paying. Starbucks is one such example.

Starbucks and Tax Avoidance in the UK

It is often said that there are only two things certain in life: death and taxes. Starbucks, the famous coffee joint from the United States, started business in the UK just a couple of years before the turn of the century in 1998. In more than a decade of doing business in the UK, Starbucks was able to build inroads and develop a large body of loyal customers. One great advantage of loyal customers is that they are repeat customers for consumable goods like coffee, and it requires only a little consistent effort from the brand to protect loyalty, and prevent them from switching over to any of the competitors.

Starbucks had been successful, not only in maintaining the large number of loyal customers, but also attracting more and more customers to its well-established outlets, as well as a good number of outlets starting business now and then. It has grown to almost 800 outlets in the UK. Despite the fact that its business was thriving in the UK, Starbucks repeatedly showed losses from its business in Britain in its account books. And, obviously, it either did not pay any tax for a number of years, or, paid just a token sum as taxes to the UK tax authority, Her Majesty's Revenue and Customs (HMRC).

It is quite natural that one cannot blow hot and cold at the same time, however, Starbucks could not appreciate this idea, and, while on one hand it was making losses as per its account books, on the other hand, its top management was busy giving itself a part on the back in most of the meetings and media briefings. It made no bones that Starbucks was doing quite well in the UK, and that the business model followed in the UK should also have been followed in the US to make the company march on the path of growth and development at a much faster rate.

The British people, media and tax authorities, smelt a rat and started investigation, which revealed that Starbucks was taking the best advantage of loopholes in the British tax laws and was practising tax avoidance in the best possible manner by paying huge sums of money to a couple of its subsidiaries in Switzerland and the Netherlands. Starbucks denied the use of tax havens like Barbados, the Cayman Islands and Bermuda, et cetera, however, admitted to have been allowed a lower tax rate by the Dutch tax authorities. International tax consultants advocate the use of tax havens for incorporating different companies which own the intellectual property of a big multinational corporation. In this manner, the big companies pay a huge sum of profits made all over the world to the companies holding intellectual property rights, including patents, trademarks, copyright, designs, et cetera, as royalties for using the intellectual property rights. It should not be surprising that the large number of patents and other intellectual property rights are owned by small outfits in places mentioned above, which, otherwise, are not so well known for innovation and protection of intellectual property rights.

Starbucks, caught with its hand in the cookie jar, tried to placate the media and the British public by unilaterally announcing to pay £20 million—over and above its tax liability—over a period of two years to the British tax authorities. But, this has not been enough to pacify the public anger. On the contrary, this announcement attracted public protests outside Starbucks outlets. The protesters demanded that the British people in the country did not need any charity from Starbucks; what they wanted was that it should pay the taxes in a fair manner, without resorting to tax avoidance. And, that is all what the British people want from Starbucks, an American company.

History repeats itself. During the heydays of the British Raj in India, prominent Indian freedom fighter, Dadabhai Naoroji, talked about the drain of wealth theory, which made so many people understand how wealth was being sucked from India and dumped into England. Now, Starbucks is sucking British wealth and taking it to the US. It is up to the British government to frame laws in a manner which does not allow tax avoidance by any company, whether domestic or foreign. Once the rules have been set, it is naïve to expect any company not to look for loopholes to make the maximum profit and pay the least amount as tax. It is only the government, particularly the tax administration, to be blamed for indirectly giving this license to loot. Strong will at the top political leadership level is required to stop it.

Starbucks paid it in 2014 and further paid corporation tax. There is usually no escaping from the long arm of the law. Interesting issues can be raised regarding tax exemptions given to companies by different states and challenged by the people in courts of law. One such matter was decided by the US Supreme Court about the Willys Jeep.

Daimlerchrysler in Ohio

DaimlerChrysler—the company formed after the merger of German Daimler-Benz AG and American Chrysler Corporation, the so-called 'Merger of Equals' in 1998, which ended in 2007—was encouraged by the city of Toledo and the State of Ohio in the United States to expand its Jeep—the first off-road, four-wheel-drive vehicle— operation in Toledo. The city has a long history of Jeep manufacturing. In 1941, Jeeps were first mass produced for the US Army by the Willys-Overland Motor Company in Toledo, Ohio. About six decades later, to revive the tradition of Jeep manufacturing in the city, DaimlerChrysler, the manufacturer of Jeeps at that time, was offered local and state tax benefits for new investment.

DaimlerChrysler entered into a contract with the city of Toledo in 1998 and agreed to expand its Jeep assembly plant. The city, in exchange, agreed to waive the property tax for the plant. The company was also entitled to a credit against the state franchise tax.

Residents of Toledo and some other persons who paid the state and local taxes sued the state of Ohio, along with DaimlerChrysler in the court on the grounds that the tax benefits given to the company violated the Commerce Clause of the US Constitution—the clause states that the US Congress shall have power to regulate Commerce with foreign Nations, and among the several States, and with the Indian Tribes—and they also claimed that they were legally injured as the tax breaks for the company prevented the flow of a certain sum of money to the state coffers, and, had that sum of money been paid as tax by the company to the state, the same could have been used by the city and the state for development purposes. They, thus, argued that tax exemptions to the company resulted in an imposition of dispro-portionate burden on the residents of the city and state.

Interestingly, along with the residents of Toledo, a number of Michigan residents also sued the state of Ohio and DaimlerChrysler as they claimed that the company had earlier planned expansion in the State of Michigan and that it was only due to the exemptions offered by the State of Ohio and the city of Toledo that the company preferred Ohio to Michigan and decided to shift to expand its operations in Toledo, rather than in Michigan.

The company found itself embroiled in a very interesting case regarding issues of taxation and public policy. The matter proceeded from one court to another and the lower courts decided that the municipal tax exemption was fine, but, the state franchise tax credit was held to be in violation of the Commerce Clause. Both the parties—residents and the company—were dissatisfied with this decision, and hence, both appealed in the US Supreme Court.

Before going into the merits of the case—regarding the validity of the municipal and state tax exemption—the Supreme Court considered it proper to ponder upon the issue of 'standing' of the residents of Toledo in this particular matter and held that the residents did not have any standing to press their complaint and cited an earlier decision of the same court, in which it was held that allocation of state tax earnings was a matter of policy decision concerning the state spending. Such a decision was the very epitome of policy judgement committed to the 'broad and legitimate discretion' of lawmakers which 'the courts cannot presume either to control or to predict'.

A particular portion from the Supreme Court judgment is worth citing: "State policymakers, no less than their federal counterparts, retain broad discretion to make 'policy decisions' concerning state spending 'in different ways…depending on their perceptions of wise state fiscal policy and myriad other circumstances'".

The US Supreme Court, following the doctrine of separation of powers, rightly decided that imposition of any tax, including exemptions, was clearly a matter to be decided by the Legislature, and it would not have been prudent for the judiciary to interfere. The residents of any state, though taxpayers, do not have any legitimate right to connect each and every penny they have paid as tax and hold the Legislature accountable as to how each of those pennies have been spent. The idea advocated by the Supreme Court brings out the much larger issue of representative democracy where each and every individual has the right to vote under the scheme of universal adult franchise, however, each such individual has no right to question the prudence of decision-making, either of the legislature or of the executive on the mere ground that any of those decisions made hurt him or her directly.

But, as is clearly evident, in a fight between the residents of a state and the state government, any company may suffer. It is expected from the top leadership of the company that it is able to anticipate and factor in any such litigation as any company may be forced to get involved into it, and despite its best efforts cannot avoid it.

Similar is the case of Tata motors, which had planned and started work for manufacturing the cheapest car—Rs. 1 lakh car, equivalent to almost US$2000—in the State of West Bengal in India. Situation became turbulent due to alleged land acquisition done forcibly by the State government, and the landowners were up in arms against the state. Opposition political parties made the best of the situation and Tata motors was forced to exit. As luck would have it, the state of Gujarat offered the company huge tracts of land on a platter and within a short period of time, the company started operations in Gujarat, at a place near Ahmedabad called Sanand.

Later, in August 2016, the Supreme Court of India held the land acquisition in West Bengal illegal and ordered the land to be given back to the farmers. Compliance of this court order is going to be difficult and economists have criticised the decision as inconsistent with other land acquisition cases, usually when land had been acquired for private businesses.

Strange are the ways of not complying with the law, if not in letter, definitely not in spirit. The car and oil businesses in the US have been quite famous, or notorious, for not following the law in spirit, usually by getting the black letter law tweaked to favour their business interests.

Big Auto, Big Oil and the Law

Oil is a precious natural resource and it is impossible to imagine existence in today's world without using oil. Distribution of oil throughout the world is not controlled by any man and can be easily said to be nature's gift to any particular country controlling the oil beneath it. Countries in the Middle East have humongous reserves of oil and at the same time, do not consume much. So, their surplus oil and is exported. Oil prices globally depend on the simple principles of economics: demand and supply.

Developing economies like India, which need more oil for further development and growth, and developed nations like the United States, which often consume more than needed, and both the set of countries with huge demands for oil, typically, do not have sufficient oil reserves, depend heavily on oil-exporting countries.

It is no secret that Americans use huge amounts of energy, primarily produced by oil as the country did not pursue nuclear power vigorously after the accident at the Three Mile Island nuclear power station in 1979. Due to international geopolitical reasons the world witnessed Arab oil embargo in 1973–1974. Developing and developed countries, both without sufficient resources of oil for themselves, had to respond to non-availability of oil. Most of the European countries and Japan formulated their policies to encourage fuel-efficient vehicles, and also made a shift in policy to favour nuclear power and alternate sources of energy, including wind and solar power.

The United States also responded in an expected manner and the political leaders favoured the passage of a law in 1975, known as the Energy Policy and Conservation Act, which law made it essential for new cars to double their fuel efficiency to 27.5 miles per gallon within ten years by establishing tough corporate average fuel economy (CAFE) standards. It worked well. Within a period of ten years, by 1985, the mileage of passenger vehicles and even light trucks increased substantially and America's dependence on imported oil went down to such an extent that for the next five to ten years there was sluggish demand for oil in the world. Obviously, oil prices went down and the power and prestige of Organisation of the Petroleum Exporting Countries (OPEC) and other oil-producing nations eroded to a certain extent, thereby denting their bargaining power.

Had the United States continued with the tough policy for fuel efficiency, today, after almost two decades, it would have been leading the world with highly fuel-efficient cars. But, that did not happen. The reason is simple to understand: highly fuel-efficient cars would have needed less oil for covering the same distance, which would have meant lesser consumption of oil. And, this was unacceptable to Big Oil companies in the United States. At any cost, they wanted the American people to be addicted to consuming more and more oil so that they could sell more and make more profits.

The Big Oil, in conjunction with the Big Automobile companies in the United States, came up with a fantastic idea of offering the American people only huge cars—comfortable, luxurious, powerful, something which can be regarded as a status symbol—including sport utility vehicles (SUVs), with much more powerful engines than ordinarily required, and also making the vehicle strong, and thereby very heavy. Heavy vehicles burnt a lot of oil to get moving. It contributed in keeping demand for oil at a certain high level.

Additionally, these were the vehicles with extremely powerful engines with the capability to achieve such high speeds that when moving very fast they would have attained a very high momentum (product of mass and velocity, or simply speed as far as a number is concerned). It is a well-known scientific fact that it is difficult to make any vehicle with very high momentum stop rapidly. With extremely good controls and high manoeuvrability, there had been a tendency for anyone driving such vehicles to press the accelerator pedal a little bit more than necessary.

Thus, these vehicles turned out to be very safe and comfortable for the passengers, but, highly hazardous for the people on the road. If needed to be stopped all of a sudden, application of brakes would have dissipated large amounts of energy, which would have been simply wasted. The same principle of momentum would apply to other vehicles moving at a fast speed, but typically small and light cars move at a fast speed and heavy trucks generally do not move at such fast speeds. So, the possibility of other vehicles being as hazardous as SUVs on the roads is much less.

In such a scenario, it makes sense for the lawmakers to discourage the production and use of SUVs by formulating policies and enacting laws focusing at disincentivising the use of these vehicles. Due to intense lobbying by Big Auto and Big Oil, the U.S. Congress made no such effort. On the contrary, the SUVs were brought under the definition of light trucks and not cars, thereby giving them the advantage of lenient standards of 20.7 miles per gallon set for light trucks, rather than 27.5 miles per gallon, the standard set for cars.

The American car makers kept on defending themselves for producing such fuel guzzling and hazardous vehicles by saying that they were simply making what the market demanded. But that is not true. It can very well be argued with evidence that people, in the long run, demand what they are offered. And that is quite evident from the European experience.

The European countries, hit by the oil crisis in 1970s and even earlier, were trying their best to make each drop of oil cover more distance. Their policies and laws were very well directed towards very high taxes on higher consumptions of oil and also higher taxes for vehicles using bigger engines. Higher taxes worked as disincentive, or rather the car companies perceived higher taxes as a threat which could have resulted in lower demand for their vehicles if not by the higher sections but surely by the middle class of the society, and started putting all their time and effort in researching and developing highly fuel-efficient engines and smaller, and also lighter, vehicles. They have been quite successful in this endeavour, and in the process have rightly made the people aware of the advantages of using a smaller vehicle. Today, Europeans demand more and more fuel-efficient vehicles. Global oil prices play a critical role in determining the demand of the cars, and the type of cars.

Compliance or defiance depends to a large extent not only on the legal environment, but also the actors and players on the stage. In case of the actors and players being highly disciplined and working conscientiously to remain within the legal periphery by complying even a little more than fully—that is not only in letter but even in spirit to the best possible extent—it is surprising when scandals take place. Japanese businesses appear as a mystery to me in this regard.

Accounting Scandals in Japan: Difficult to Understand

In July 2015, one of the highly reputed Japanese companies, Toshiba, reported an accounting scandal which was systematically done for a number of years and its CEO and other top officials resigned. A few years back one of the famous camera companies, which also manufactures medical equipment, Olympus, had reported an accounting scandal. And these are not the only accounting scandals which have come to light in Japan. There have been very serious issues raised about corporate governance in Japan.

This is most surprising and unfathomable. The moment we think about a Japanese person, almost all the adjectives describing a good person and impeccable character come to mind—honest, sincere, hard-working, patriotic, scrupulous, meticulous, loyal, law-abiding, conscientious, reliable, trustworthy, etc. So, what happens when it comes to maintaining account books and reporting profits or loss? Toshiba and Olympus, both were incurring losses and it was on the directions of the top management that the account books were cooked not only by the internal accounting teams but audited by external auditors as well. Both are working in tandem and such conduct raises further questions about the credibility of external auditors.

It has been widely reported by experts doing studies about business in Japan that the majority of directors in any company are internally recruited and hence there is a deep sense of loyalty and obedience to the individuals managing the show in the company, and not the company itself. There is a lack of adequate number of external directors on the board of these companies which typically results in the formation of a caucus facilitating wrong doings like fudging the account books systematically over a period of time. The corporate governance norms in Japan rely more on self-discipline and self-regulation rather than external pressures and transparency. The western norms of accountability and transparency have been incorporated on paper in the recent past when Japan changed its corporate governance practices, however, it will undoubtedly take a lot of time to show results.

Issues of hierarchy are extremely important in Japan and it is unthinkable for subordinates to question the decision of their seniors, which often leads to following the orders blindly irrespective of their legal and ethical correctness. Even if the management has set unrealistic targets, the company executives will keep on trying to achieve them and even if they are not able to do so it is not considered improper to falsely report the achievement of unrealistic targets. Such reporting results in setting still higher targets in the next cycle triggering a vicious cycle. All this is allowed to continue in a planned manner till the time it becomes incumbent upon the company to spill the beans.

Another issue which is ailing the Japanese corporate governance system is what is known in Japanese as *amakudari*, literally meaning descent from heaven. It is the practice of retired bureaucrats and government officials taking up jobs in companies and industries—both private and public in nature. Thus they take jobs in businesses which were regulated by them prior to their retirement. The businesses get the double advantage of the huge network of individual connections and also customised guidance to manoeuvre the regulatory and legal landscape by the experts who were once manning the same.

It would be wrong to say that it is only restricted to Japan. Such a phenomenon can also be seen very easily in India, the United States and several other evolved jurisdictions, however, the distinction between them and the Japanese is the lack of independent questioning by the board members in a company. Such practices are bringing a bad name Japanese business, which otherwise has given tough competition worldwide by the use of cutting-edge technology and fantastic management principles put into action.

It is extremely important to instil professional understanding and confidence in the minds of management in Japan, particularly the top management, that loyalty and obedience do not mean compromising unbiased and professional thinking and action. For Indian businesses and government, Japan is an extremely important partner which brings in capital and technology, and, hence, we in India need to be a little more cautious while dealing with Japanese companies. It is in no way being suggested that we must shun them, however, reasonable due diligence will help us to steer away from avoidable complications and controversies.

It is not only compliance with accounting and financial laws, noncompliance with environmental laws can be very risky, expensive and affecting the reputation adversely, as BP experienced.

BP and Noncompliance with Environmental Laws

In November 2012, the American Environmental Protection Agency (EPA) banned BP temporarily from seeking any fresh contracts from the federal government. BP—a multinational company dealing in oil and gas, and headquartered in London—was earlier known as British Petroleum and long ago, started business in 1909 as the Anglo–Persian Oil Company. In the initial years, the company had business interests in Iran and later on started business in a number of countries. As depicted in a 1922 advertisement, the company called its motor spirit—commonly known as petrol or gasoline—as 'Best Possible' (BP). From those times of the 'best possible', the company has managed to deteriorate to be labelled as the worst possible as EPA has banned it, citing reasons, which primarily include 'lack of business integrity'.

The company has been responsible for one of the worst oil spills—Deepwater Horizon spill—in which about 5 million barrels of oil escaped in the Gulf of Mexico in 2010. The company failed to act with due alacrity and took 87 days to contain the leakage. During this time, there was tremendous irreparable damage to the environment, for which the company has been held to be solely responsible. The EPA has described this oil spill as the 'largest environmental disaster in the US history'.

The company had earlier settled private claims of about $8 billion, and claims worth $21 billion regarding environmental damage are pending. Environmental groups have said that the ban by EPA, which is temporary in nature, may not be enough deterrence for a company like BP, which has a proven track record of not following safety rules and regulations and being lackadaisical in its approach in following ethical norms in business. Often, the company has been caught on the wrong side of law.

For the last ten years or so, the company has been involved in getting itself a makeover to BP, from its earlier avatars, and is spreading the word that BP stands for 'beyond petroleum'—same as 'best possible' in 1922—so as to convey to the world that the company takes great care in nurturing alternate sources of energy. The company left no stone unturned, including a change in its logo to a vibrant green and yellow sunflower shaped logo Helios, which is the name of Greek Sun god.

But, as looks may be deceptive, logos may not truly reflect the real business of a company. BP has been responsible for a number of accidents in oil and gas sector, including explosion in a refinery in 2005, which killed 15 persons, leakage in the pipeline due to negligence which resulted in 200,000 gallons of crude polluting Alaska, and several others. Despite its track record, BP had the cheek to go for the image makeover exercise—which, according to global consultants, was imperative—and it bore fruit in the shape of several awards BP received all over the world for its 'Beyond Petroleum' campaign and also ironically, for being one of the most responsible companies.

It is heartening to see the American government being tough with BP, as it is widely known that companies like BP, with deep pockets, lobby the government in a manner which makes it extremely difficult for them to be penalised for anything. Experts, with long experience, are of the opinion that even in this case, BP will be able to manage the show—evidently, the company managed to get more than $1 billion contracts last year from the federal government—and emerge even stronger.

It would be most unfortunate, as even the well-known big banks like HSBC and Standard Chartered have been, of late, fined huge sums for their misdeeds, and the same story gets on repeating with so many other big companies, that the common man on the street is disillusioned with the system. BP had to shell out more $60 billion in civil and criminal settlements.

Compliance to any court order is subject to appealing to a higher court. Till that time, usually the previous order's enforcement is stayed automatically on appealing or the appellate courts grant a stay at the first instance of admitting an appeal. Parties willing to fight the long legal battle—for any reason whatsoever; availability of sufficient funds, appetite for taking risk, want to prove the principled stand taken, left with no option but to appeal for survival, etc.—appeal and delay the enforcement of the earlier order. The fight between Apple Computers and Samsung in numerous courts in different jurisdictions is a story of sometimes immediate compliance and sometimes using the appellate system as a dilatory strategic tool. In July 2016, the matter has been taken to the US Supreme Court.

Apple–Samsung Legal Fight: The Unending Saga

In July 2016, Apple requested the US Supreme Court to finally hear the matter and dispose it off regarding the allegations of infringement of design patents. Since 2007 when Apple's iPhone was launched in the market, and thereafter when Samsung and other companies introduced their smartphones on the market, Apple has been complaining in different legal forums all over the world that the iPhone's design had been copied by Samsung. Apple had continuously been demanding huge compensation.

The legal battle has seen many ups and downs in several courts around the globe, however, the conclusive decision—and maybe, to a large extent, which will put finality to the simmer between the competitors—has to come from the United States Supreme Court. Interestingly, before the matters reach the US Supreme Court, the matter has been heard by the Jury and thereafter other courts, which have awarded almost US$1 billion to Apple. For the last couple of years, Samsung had been fighting the legal battle in different forums to get this compensation reduced, which appears to be small change for both the companies. Though, it is not a matter of immediate victory for any of the companies because the larger question shall be the legal protection provided for the designs, and to what extent the protection can be granted.

It has often been experienced that the legal environment for protection of intellectual property in the United States is one of the strongest and provides speedy and effective remedies for infringement of intellectual property, however, the legal dispute between Apple and Samsung has seen both the parties swelling their coffers and also continuing the legal battle. One can easily imagine the fate of any such legal battle between two competitors with deep pockets in any other part of the world where the legal environment for protection of intelligent property may not be so strong.

There are strong reasons which have prevented a unanimous decision in favour of Apple in different legal forums. The fundamental issue is regarding what can be protected as a design? It all depends on the local law—the Law prevalent in the country—which to large extent has been harmonised after the formation of the World Trade Organisation (WTO) and the signing of the Treaty on Trade-Related Aspects of Intellectual Property Rights (TRIPs). Apple has claimed the curved corners of the smartphone, the arraignment of icons and a host of other design features. Samsung's argument has been that obvious things like curved corners cannot and should not be protected by design patents. Protection of designs in the United States is part of the patent law, whereas, it is protected by a separate law in India called as the Designs Act.

It is widely accepted by different companies that design is very important feature in the success of any product. According to the intellectual property law, design appeals solely to the eye. It is not supposed to have a very special, unique, functional aspect, as that would defeat the purpose of protection by design law; and in case there is a unique, functional aspect, it can be protected by the patent law, provided it crosses the high bar set for the grant of a patent. It is not that simple and that is why patents and designs are two separate branches of intellectual property protection.

One of the important features for design protection is novelty, which means that the design should be something new and it is very difficult to understand as to how curved corners can be said to be novel design. It was a possibility that curved corners in a smartphone may be supposed to be new, which of course would have been new as there were no smartphones. But thereafter, is it fair to provide protection to curved corners? Samsung has been challenging the curved corners protection as well as several other design features which may appear to be quite obvious and not novel. However, Apple's argument has been that putting together all these features in one single gadget has itself been a big achievement and that is why the product should be seen in its entirety and holistically. Thus, according to Apple, Samsung has violated the design aspects in totality, and therefore must be made to compensate, not only for those specific design features, but for the complete product.

This is truly going to be an interesting legal battle with gripping arguments and counter arguments. Business leaders and enthusiasts are watching with bated breath as the final decision is going to be an important guiding factor while aligning business and legal strategies of their own businesses. Full or partial compliance or defiance to any legal orders will be chosen carefully post this decision.

Using the law as a tool or weapon is possible only when the legal environment provides protection. Only then, a business leader can be assured of using the law to safeguard his business. Otherwise, the existence of any law and law-enforcing agencies does not matter, as is usually the case in China. In August 2015, a Goldman Sachs started operations in China, which had nothing to do with the global Goldman Sachs. Incredulous indeed!

Goldman Sachs and Landwind in China

In August 2015, the media reported the presence of Goldman Sachs in China which has no connection with the famous American investment bank. Earlier in the month, it was also reported that an exactly look alike of Jaguar Land Rover's Evoque was being sold in the Chinese market as Landwind X7 of act one-third the price of

Evoque. These developments are disturbing for the global business community sees China as a humongous manufacturing hub and also a tremendously large market.

But, whether it is manufacturing or selling, a proper legal environment providing protection to your rights is supposed to be the prerequisite for a business to flourish. To a large extent, intellectual property protection is a legal protection, however, its roots are somewhere in the ethical standards that one follows while conducting business. One is surely shaken by the audacity of copying the Western labels and even thereafter having the cheek to claim that China cares for intellectual property protection of foreign businesses.

India is often criticised for an extremely weak intellectual property regime, however, the legal environment in India, and particularly in the last 5–10 years, has demonstrated on several occasions that India as a nation is moving, slowly but surely, in the direction of strengthening the system of intellectual property protection, and undoubtedly is serious about it. We should not, by making this statement, be perturbed by the interpretations given to the black letter law regarding patents and pharmaceuticals in particular, by the courts in India. There has been a perceptible change towards greater protection of copyright, trademark, designs and geographical indications.

But, this is a matter of serious concern that China simply does not bother at all about the legal requirements or niceties of doing business globally. The CEO of Jaguar Land Rover has stated on record that it would not be possible for his company to litigate the matter in China as there was hardly any intellectual property protection given to the design of his automobiles despite blatant copying. Though he does not see much damage to his business as any of the customers eyeing an original vehicle from JLR would not be tempted to buy a copied version, yet his brand stands to be diluted. Brand dilution in the long run erodes market value, which takes years and decades to build.

Goldman Sachs, in all possibility, sails in the same boat with JLR. There is hardly any hope for the American Goldman Sachs to sue the Chinese company in China because of, first, pathetic black letter law, second, absolutely weak enforcement by the judiciary in China, which exists only for namesake, and third, a very strong idea of protectionism to domestic businesses vis-à-vis foreign businesses. All these factors acting together result in a dismal scenario for protection of intellectual property and other rights of foreign businesses in China.

This is nothing new. American companies getting products manufactured in China have to provide all details, including confidential information, to get them made. It is like providing family silver on a platter. Within a short period of time, smart Chinese businesses copy them and launch their own products in the market. To add insult to injury, they sell their products at a fraction of the prices at which original products are sold.

So, what brings the foreign companies to China? Precisely, the cheap labour and huge market are the main source of attraction. Any thoughts about the legal environment take a back seat. India is in a much better position with its commitment to the rule of law and respect for basic rights. India can potentially gain this advantage which often has been ignored by foreign investors and businesses.

Situation in a democratic country like India committed to the rule of law is different. The people of India have the reins in their hands which they can use during elections effectively. Thus, getting the VIP—very important person—status may be enticing for some, but heavy cost may have to be paid by the political masters in terms of being answerable to the people. One such matter which is sub-judice is about the purchase of helicopters from a foreign company. The ultimate test of law—public interest—has to be cleared which is proving onerous proving that the law can be the best friend of the people.

Choppers in Choppy Waters: *Suppressio Veri, Suggestio Falsi,* February 2013

Suppressio veri, suggestio falsi—the suppression of the truth is the suggestion of a falsehood—is adequate ground for rescinding a contract, or at least not executing it. By the very nature of the deal for the purchase of a dozen helicopters for VVIPs—Very, Very Important Persons—for Rs. 3600 crores (Rs. 36 billion), that is, Rs. 300 crores (Rs. 3 billion) for one helicopter, it was obvious that the deal was something special, and not routine. Such agreements, unlike purchase of tents and backpacks for soldiers, as must be quite obvious to any layman, are entered into rarely, and special permission ought to be taken at the topmost level.

In India, a democratic country, it is surprising and rather shocking to know that persons who consider themselves to be very, very important need helicopters for Rs. 300 crores a piece. The more scandalous fact is that the political masters, bureaucrats, and even topmost officials from the armed forces did not make any effort to tell the nation about the deal, and on the contrary, left no stone unturned to suppress the truth. As the saying goes, the suppression of the truth is the suggestion of a falsehood, and hence, all the persons involved in the deal could apparently be held liable for defrauding the nation.

It is amusing to note that now a special team of prosecutors has reached Italy to find out the truth. More public money shall be spent on this futile exercise, as the need is not to go to Rome but investigate it within the country and find out as to who made the final decision regarding placing the order, and who were the other persons and agencies involved in getting the deal finalised. Smart persons at that level seldom deal in hard cash as depicted in most of the old Bollywood movies, but transactions are more in the nature of *quid pro quo*, or through complex mechanisms, including, but not limited to, consultants, shell companies, banks, etc.

It is neither for the first time, nor the last time that allegations of bribery in such large deals have been made. India is no exception and the *modus operandi* adopted in the Italian chopper deal is also not new. I am reminded of a case which was decided by the Court of Appeal, England in 1999.

The matter pertained to the sale of military equipment by the Federal Directorate of Supply and Procurement of the Socialist Federal Republic of Yugoslavia—read Yugoslavia—to Kuwait in 1988. Yugoslavia appointed Westacre, a Panamanian company, its consultant, which was to receive a substantial percentage of the value of the contract entered into. Westacre entered into a contract with Yugoslavian bank Beogradska Banka, which guaranteed the payment of all fees due to Westacre under the agreement, which was expressly governed by the Swiss law and contained an arbitration clause for dispute resolution, to be held in Geneva.

Once Yugoslavia secured a sale contract, it alleged that Westacre was merely a vehicle, controlled by powerful Kuwaiti persons in the government, to influence the decision-making in the Kuwaiti Ministry of Defence to enter into a contract for purchase of military equipment. In other words, whatever consultancy charges were paid by Yugoslavia to Westacre, were in fact indirectly paid to certain powerful persons in the Kuwaiti government, which *ipso facto* would mean a bribe to persons in power to get the deal done. Yugoslavia repudiated the contract with Westacre, which meant the loss of consultancy fee. A dispute arose between the two parties and the matter was first decided in an arbitration in Geneva, then in Swiss Federal Court, and thereafter, for jurisdictional reasons, in English courts.

In all probability, similar is expected to be the fate of the Italian chopper deal, which undoubtedly is in choppy waters, and would surely see large sums of public money being spent on litigation, whether in Italy, India, or elsewhere. It is a sorry state of affairs. The country expects transparency and accountability from people holding positions of power. It has only been due to the media pressure and the power given to the people of India by the Right to Information Act that a number of such deals are coming out in the open, otherwise, confidentiality and secrecy of such high-level contracts prevented any revelation and thoughtful discussion.

For a vibrant democracy like India, nothing could be worse than suppression of the truth. We, the People of India, would like to say with pride and sense of belief, *satyamev jayate* (truth alone triumphs), the national motto. Law surely acts as the friend, philosopher and guide in this endeavour and pious duty. Business leaders need to be beware—unethical and illegal means do not give lasting value addition, and one always fears the long arm of the law coming and catching them.

Business Leaders and the Long Arm of the Law

The law is said to be the command of sovereign, which everyone follows as there is a threat of punishment. The law is applicable to individuals as well as corporate entities, which are given fictitious legal identity.

Two cases in 2012 have again highlighted the importance of individuals in running of corporate affairs and how law can catch hold of any individual who is acting not in his personal capacity, but as the agent of the corporate entity.

One of them is the highly celebrated case and currently ongoing litigation in the US in the arrest of Rajat Gupta. Last week there was a remark made by the judge that Rajat Gupta cannot take the defence that he has been so honest, so meticulous and such a great philanthropist that accusations of he being involved in insider-trading would be simply an act of imagination and a story put together by certain prosecutors who could see evil even in Mother Teresa.

Interestingly, the American court remarked that in the eyes of law everyone is equal and it is not the individual, but the act of an individual which may make an individual—who maybe honesty personified—liable for an indiscreet act. Rajat Gupta has often been talked about as a role model for young business leaders, however, if the allegations are true—of passing on confidential and privileged information to his friend Rajaratanam—it would surely be an illegal act and no amount of selfless philanthropy can protect Rajat Gupta.

Both Rajat Gupta and Rajaratanam were sent to jail.

Another case, if true, has all the potential of a record-selling mystery novel and a blockbuster movie. Reebok has alleged that its former Managing Director and Chief Operations Officer, COO, have been siphoning of company money for the last several years and that too not only in the account books but by physically setting up a couple of secret warehouses were Reebok products where stored.

It sounds like a fairy tale that the company had no knowledge of what its two top officers were doing and that too for the last several years. The fraud is worth more than $1.5 billion. It is a bit unconvincing that only two persons in the company could fudge the accounts and were able to run parallel business without the cooperation and support of other employees from the company.

Global norms in top-notch multinational corporations are so stringent that it is highly unlikely that any one individual or two or three individuals in a company can manage the entire show without the knowledge of others. There are generally a number of checks and balances and more so in a business environment today which is supported entirely by Internet and use of computers at each and every step.

It is quite unbelievable that only two persons in the company did everything in such a clandestine manner that neither the company people in India nor in the headquarters abroad were able to even get a whiff of what was going on in the company. For a moment, if we assume that it is true then this speaks volumes about the capability of the top management of the company at the headquarters.

After more than a decade of Enron, Arthur Andersen and similar other corporate wrongdoings, a number of steps have been taken by the law-enforcing authorities in different countries, including India, that individuals in any company are not able to make the company their fiefdom and operate without any sense of responsibility and duty.

The case highlights the importance of individuals manning a company and how ethical conduct is important in creating conducive business environment. Had they bothered to comply with the law, things would have been very different both for them and the company.

Takeaway for Business Leaders

1. Compliance is the best policy
   The law-abiding and absolutely law-fearing firms have no option but to totally abide by the law. It does not, however, mean that the business leaders should be docile and submissive. The idea is not to unnecessarily have skirmishes with the law. As far as possible, compliance is the best policy, just like honesty is supposed to be the best policy. There are not many problems for any business which is always fully compliant with the law of the land. Total and complete compliance may be a bit painful as it requires, in most of the jurisdictions, discipline, self-control and acceptance of an authority, howsoever, corrupt, unreasonable and impractical it may be.

2. Defiance and Confrontation
   In certain unacceptable situations, compliance emboldens the law-enforcing agencies and then it must not be complied. Bold and risk-bearing companies do not agree with the idea of absolute compliance and as Mahatma Gandhi broke the salt law in British India, these companies also go ahead and break the law in case they feel the law to be unreasonable. Thus, only reasonable laws should be followed. Unreasonable laws can be changed and firms should try to get them amended. This is only possible in jurisdictions where legal system is highly developed. Till that time, businesses have to play by the rules by developing skills that show the middle path of achieving their goal as well as not being labelled noncompliant. Complying with immoral, unreasonable and unconscionable laws itself is evil. But, a business leader needs to understand that fighting with Pope in Rome in not a wise choice.

3. Business of Business Leaders is Business
   A true business leader must always keep it in mind that his business is business. As Calvin Coolidge, the American President, had said that the 'business of America is business', similarly, a business leader needs to focus on the business and not make a prestige issue of certain situations or with certain individuals. It is important to win the war in business and not to win battles of egos at different stages of business. Sometimes, unfortunately, the power of position and money goes to the head of a business leader and he starts looking down upon others, including government functionaries and law-enforcing agencies. Nothing can be worse. A business leader will do well to remember that he is not there to settle any personal score, but to get the requisite licences, approvals, clearances, etc. from individuals who perform their roles as enforcers of the law and officers of the government.

4. Completing the paperwork
   I am reminded of a cartoon—Dennis the Menace—where Dennis is sitting on the toilet seat, the paper roll is hanging and the caption says 'nothing is complete till you complete the paperwork'. Paperwork is very important in business and is critically important when you are thinking of taking any matter to a court of law. Law demands evidence and a documentary proof makes your case stronger. It is

not only important to complete the paperwork, it is also important to save and restore those papers in a proper manner so that they are not destroyed; they are not damaged; and those papers can be retrieved at the right time with minimum effort and maximum certainty. Most of the work is now done on computers and hence a lot of documents are in electronic format. Law in most of the evolved jurisdictions accepts electronic evidence and electronic copies of documents. Evidence law in India has been amended to accept electronic copies and courts in India do accept them. As it is much easier to doctor up any electronic copy, it becomes more important for a business leader to take all the reasonable safeguards so that there is no possibility of electronic files being tampered with.

As a business leader you have to deal with so many people and communicate so many things. It is important to document most of these things. Best efforts must be made to either have a hard copy or an electronic version of the communication. At times, it is also important to understand that you would like to make a decision but do not want any record to be maintained for making such a decision. In such a scenario it is prudent not to write any such thing, either by e-mail or a as a note or memo. It is better to make such decisions in consultation with the other members either on telephone—but be sure that the telephone is not being tapped—or face-to-face. You need to be very cautious that such meetings are not being audio or video recorded. Nowadays, with so many small electronic gadgets available, one must be very cautious and discreet in conversation. The Niira Radia tapes in India which have haunted the mighty and powerful prove this.[1] We discussed these tapes in the chapter on lawmaking.

5. Certainty, Anticipate and Create Options

Compliance is a sure move towards certainty and, therefore, it is regarded as the safest and assured choice, if one considers compliance not to be mandatory. It is, though, prudent to anticipate the repercussions of noncompliance and act reasonably, if choosing not to comply. Not complying just for the heck of it is not a good choice; there must be compelling and cogent reasons. Also, it is expected of a business leader to anticipate the options created by complying fully or almost fully. One should not be caught on the wrong foot by acting—complying or not complying—too fast. That is a call a business leader has to take: when to act. There are no set rules. It all depends on the context. Thus, discretion needs to be exercised.

---

[1]CBI relies on Radia tapes in 2G investigation, The Times of India, 26 Apr 2011, http://articles. timesofindia.indiatimes.com/2011-04-26/india/29474650_1_kalaignar-tv-radia-tapes-niira-radia, last accessed September 14, 2016.

Lightning Source UK Ltd.
Milton Keynes UK
UKOW04n1438221217

314954UK00004B/90/P